Reading Nietzsche

Reading Nietzsche

An Analysis of *Beyond Good and Evil*

Douglas Burnham

ACUMEN

First published in 2007 by Acumen

Acumen Publishing Limited
Stocksfield Hall
Stocksfield
NE43 7TN
www.acumenpublishing.co.uk

ISBN-10: 1-84465-074-X (hardcover)
ISBN-13: 978-1-84465-074-3
ISBN-10: 1-84465-075-8 (paperback)
ISBN-13: 978-1-84465-075-0

British Library Cataloguing-in-Publication Data
A catalogue record for this book is available
from the British Library.

Typeset in Garamond by Graphicraft Limited, Hong Kong.
Printed and bound by Cromwell Press, Trowbridge.

In memory of my father, Hugh Danner Burnham

Contents

Preface

Beyond Good and Evil is among the most comprehensive of Nietzsche's works. No significant themes are missing, and the discussion of many topics is much more extensive (and often more "philosophical") than is found elsewhere. *Beyond Good and Evil* (let us just say *Beyond*) is thus an ideal setting off point for understanding Nietzsche's thought in general. Moreover, its structure demands that we attempt to understand connections that are not always apparent in other works, and thus are often overlooked even in the literature on Nietzsche. I refer to the hidden relationships that run between Nietzsche's treatment of metaphysics, psychology, philosophical methodology, style, the project of a history and physiology of value, and political and social analysis. However, that *Beyond* is an ideal starting point for studying Nietzsche does not necessarily mean that it is the easiest of Nietzsche's books to understand; indeed, Nietzsche represented his own next book, *Genealogy of Morality*, as a "clarification" of *Beyond*. *Beyond Good and Evil* thus contains in miniature the considerable problem of reading Nietzsche in general: namely, reading him as *at least akin* to a systematic philosopher.

This book has two main aims. First, to be a helpful guide and introduction to Nietzsche, and particularly helpful for someone attempting to read *Beyond Good and Evil*. With it, readers should be able to "raise their game" and thus be able to approach both *Beyond Good and Evil*, and other books by Nietzsche, with perception and well-informed judgement. Secondly, it aims to be a *contribution* to the contemporary philosophical study of Nietzsche. This contribution lies in part in several careful analyses of individual concepts but, more important, in laying out how, across and throughout the compositional strategies of a single text, ideas and inter-connections are elaborated. The result is not so much a commentary as the synthetic construction of Nietzsche's philosophical thought through a close reading of this great book.

This book aims to do just that: to provide a guide to the reading of a rich and complex text, while at the same time making the connections, and pulling out the key ideas and arguments, that will provide an excellent introduction to, as well as an analysis of, Nietzsche's thought as a philo-sophical whole. *Beyond Good and Evil* will serve as a pivot point, so to speak, around which we can usefully construct that bird's-eye picture of Nietzsche's work.

It should also be admitted that I am here completely indifferent to the *truth* or *validity* of Nietzsche's arguments or ideas. This is not because I think truth or validity are unimportant in philosophy; far from it. Nor is it because I simply agree with everything in Nietzsche. Rather, it is because of a preliminary task. Relatively few readers reach the point where such a judgement of truth or validity would be possible, for its precondition is that one understands the arguments and ideas, as well as the significance of how Nietzsche expresses them and what he might expect or hope that we *do* with them, in all their considerable richness and complexity. It is to this understanding that this book will be a contribution. Similarly, I have resisted the temptation as far as possible to update or rewrite Nietzsche's thought in a different philosophical language or system of thought, for example, the philosophical perspectives of anti-realism, moral naturalism, existentialism, "postmodernism", Bergsonism, and so on. Again, this is not because I am opposed to this kind of work; it is one of the key ways in which philosophy advances creatively. Rather, until one has reached the level of understanding described above, it seems essential to think using Nietzsche's own concepts and forms of expression.

Accordingly, this book has a straightforward structure. It proceeds through all the Parts and sections, in order. In order to ensure that the result is less Byzantine than Nietzsche's original, there are a number of additional elements. First, there is throughout considerable cross-referencing, which should help a synthetic image of the work to emerge. Secondly, a number of sections are picked out as appropriate places for a considerably more sustained and philosophically productive discussion of a particular theme; for example, near the beginning, the notions of perspective and inter-pretation. These sections are listed in the contents. Thirdly, I have introduced one piece of terminology – "realignment" – to stand for a notion that is present in Nietzsche but for which he does not have a con-sistent word. Fourthly, there are outside the main text items of textual apparatus (such as a short glossary) integral to the introductory side of this book's purpose.

Again, *Beyond* is very comprehensive, and I therefore wish to let it speak for itself, rather than provide here a large introduction or overview of Nietzsche's life and works. However, Nietzsche is a very easy philosopher to read poorly, and singularly difficult to read well. Because of the ease, his writings have been bestsellers for more than a century; but because of the difficulty, misconceptions or oversimplifications about Nietzsche have also been bestsellers. So, let us begin by rehearsing a few of these.

1. Without a doubt, decades after his death, Nietzsche was taken to heart by National Socialism. To do so, however, the Nazis had to edit out or simply ignore the many passages where Nietzsche pours scorn on both German nationalism and upon anti-Semites.

2. Again, Nietzsche is often considered an advocate of a radical individualism in the same mould as popular existentialism. To read him in this way, one has to ignore passages like §17 in the present book where Nietzsche argues that the "I" or the individual thinking and acting subject is not fundamental in his philosophy, but is rather a derivative effect.

3. Often, too, Nietzsche is identified as a relativist – that is, any belief in the sphere of morals (and perhaps even knowledge) has validity only for the individual or historical group that holds it. But then on what grounds could Nietzsche meaningfully espouse or repudiate aspects of ancient Greek society, or of contemporary society in Russia, France or England?

4. Nietzsche is widely thought to be thorough in his rejection of religion in general and Christianity in particular. There may be some truth to this, but it remains the case that the first two Parts of *Beyond Good and Evil* pass with hardly a mention of religion. The Part that follows is explicitly about religion, but is hardly "thorough" in its rejection. It includes extravagant praise of the Old Testament, at least (§52), and of the love of man (§60); moreover, it is only within this context of religion that Nietzsche is able to express the "new ideal" of the philosopher of the future (§56).

5. Often Nietzsche is identified as a nihilist, completely sceptical of all values, authorities, concepts or beliefs; and likewise sceptical about the effectiveness of existing institutions or efforts to change matters. Nihilism thus advocates the utter destruction of religions, states and ideologies. However, readers may have missed the fact that nihilism is generally the butt of Nietzsche's jokes, and in §10 we read that nihilists are "puritanical fanatics of conscience" and "nihilism . . . [is] the sign of a despairing and desperately weary soul".

6. Finally, there are two common and directly opposing characterizations of Nietzsche overall. First, Nietzsche is an unsystematic thinker who is (at best) "postmodern" or (at worst) careless, impressionistic, merely

"literary". Secondly, Nietzsche is actually a rigorous epistemologist and/or moral philosopher who, unfortunately and irritatingly, just happens to write in a literary style. Here, we shall not be arguing for a sitting-on-the-fence position between these two extremes. Rather, there is something about Nietzsche's philosophy which demands that rigour and seriousness be pursued, in part, by way of the "literary".

Each of these misconceptions contains at least an element of validity. To take two examples, Nietzsche does talk in some worrying ways about race. Also, he does speak of himself as a nihilist in a note from 1887, but much more consistently continues to critique it as, at best, a transitional pathology, which is parasitic upon previous beliefs rather than liberated from them. These elements of validity are why the misconceptions are so stubborn. This book, in carefully reading *Beyond* and thereby providing important critical tools, will help the reader to judge such misconceptions, in *Beyond* but also in the other works of Nietzsche.

We should also, for the reader entirely new to Nietzsche, locate him historically. Friedrich Nietzsche was born in Germany in 1844, and died there in 1900. Most of his work was written in just under two decades of the 1870s and 1880s, for Nietzsche had a mental collapse in Italy in January 1889 and spent the last decade of his life in care. The historical period is important because much of Nietzsche's work is a direct or indirect commentary on his time. So, the rise of German nationalism, which led to the unification of the German state, is discussed often. Similarly, Nietzsche turns frequently to the dominance in German music by Wagner, of whom Nietzsche was at first a devotee. Other contemporary ideas or movements that either influenced or informed Nietzsche's work include Darwinism, utilitarianism, Marxism, revolutionary nihilism in Russia, the introduction of Eastern thought (e.g. Buddhism) into Europe. We will remark on all of these as they appear in the text.

Nietzsche's father, who died when Nietzsche was young, was a Lutheran minister. Rather than entering the clergy, as his family expected and hoped, Nietzsche studied classics and in particular philology (comparative and historical study of language). His early promise in this field earned him an appointment to the University of Basel at the age of 24, and a professorship shortly thereafter. Nietzsche's ill-health, however, meant that he had increasingly frequent leaves of absence from the university and eventually left altogether in 1879. During this period he met and became, until the mid-1870s, a member of Wagner's circle of admirers. He also published his first and most consistently well-known work, *The Birth of Tragedy*, which used a highly speculative account of the growth and decay of classical Greek tragedy as a mirror to understand contemporary German problems and solutions. The book was heavily influenced by the ideas of Wagner and especially Schopenhauer, but in its synthesis original. It is written in an energetic and certainly not academic style, and its preoccupation with the relations between culture, metaphysics, art and mythology remains with Nietzsche throughout his more mature work. In this early book, the figure of the Greek god Dionysus is prominent, and significantly the god returns at the end of *Beyond Good and Evil*.

For the decade of his life before his collapse, Nietzsche travelled widely and continually, spending a few weeks or months in a variety of places, many in Southern Europe. From 1883 to 1885 he wrote *Thus Spoke Zarathustra*; in a mock biblical and prophetic style, the book narrates a period in the life of the prophet Zarathustra (who is reimagined as a Nietzschean). Nietzsche generally considered it his masterpiece, both in the sense of being an original and successful stylistic experiment in writing philosophy, and in the sense of being the definitive statement of most of his key ideas. Whether *Zarathustra* is quite this successful, in either sense, can be debated. Certainly, it contains some of his most brilliant writing, but also some of his most bombastic and cryptic. In any case, Nietzsche wrote *Beyond Good and Evil* shortly thereafter and, in a letter to his friend Burckhardt, suggested that *Beyond* was a stylistically different recapitulation of the philosophy contained in *Zarathustra*.

After *Beyond Good and Evil*, Nietzsche commenced three furious years of writing, producing among other things, *The Genealogy of Morality* and *Twilight of the Idols*. His work gradually became known in the years before his death, and by the first years of the twentieth century he was one of the most widely read and influential of recent thinkers. After his death, his notebooks were edited by his sister and selections from them are published as if they formed his last book, the systematic *The Will to Power*. In fact, the selections were chosen and organized so as to suggest a simplified and highly partisan version of Nietzsche's thoughts. For years, the English translation of *The Will to Power* was the only access a non-German reader had to Nietzsche's unpublished writing. So, despite its dangerous flaws, it was useful. Now, several other more scholarly collections of notebook entries have emerged, and *The Will to Power* has probably outlived its usefulness.

It remains to me to thank my family, students and colleagues both for the space and time to produce this book, and also for many helpful comments and suggestions in class or, indeed, in the pub: in particular, the participants on "Foundations of Modern European Philosophy" in the Autumn term of 2005, and Jon Egan, Catherine Burgass, Martin Jesinghausen and David Webb. Moreover, Staffordshire University funded a sabbatical at exactly the right time to make the underlying research possible.

DB

1 Nietzsche's Title and Preface

The title

The full title of Nietzsche's book is *Beyond Good and Evil: Prelude to a Philosophy of the Future*. As with most book titles, what is being referred to will not become clear until we are into the main text, but a few brief observations are in order.

First of all, the title is deliberately provocative. There is something sinister looking about going "beyond good", even if the title also says "beyond evil". Moreover, so much of philosophy, theology and political, social and psychological thought concerned itself with the nature of Good and Evil, that to sweep it all aside with this "beyond" must have seemed a staggeringly broad and high-handed gesture. It is as if Nietzsche is saying: you have all simply been asking the wrong question. In fact, this is *exactly* what Nietzsche is saying. Finally, the "beyond" and "future" introduces an element of *history* to subjects (good and evil) about which the reader might not be accustomed, or willing, to think in historical terms.

The first part of Nietzsche's book is on the "Prejudices of the Philosophers", and above all Nietzsche is criticizing the late-eighteenth-century German philosopher Immanuel Kant. Therefore, it is not surprising to find in Nietzsche's subtitle a subtle and joking reference to the title of a famous little book by Kant. Kant's title is *Prolegomena to Any Future Metaphysics That Will Be Able to Step Forward as a Science.* Just as Kant's book was an attempt to restate in a more accessible way what he had said in the huge *Critique of Pure Reason*, so Nietzsche evidently saw *Beyond Good and Evil* as a differently expressed version of his philosophy in *Thus Spoke Zarathustra*. Notice, though, that Kant's title seems to speak of a philosophy in the present that determines what can be "scientific" in the future, whereas Nietzsche's subtitle refers to a philosophy that is in the future, not here yet. We shall have much more to say later on the far from simply antithetical relation between Kant and Nietzsche.

Preface: the task of "we good Europeans"

Nietzsche's Preface begins with the famous sentence: "Presupposing that truth is a woman – what? Is the suspicion not without grounds that all philosophers, in so far as they were dogmatists, were amateurs about women?" We must start by considering a few things about this sentence.

First, let us think about what is often most difficult to ascertain: the tone. We need to get this problem right up front because it is so important for Nietzsche, while being so unimportant for most other philosophers. Nietzsche, here, is playful, almost vaudevillian: the "– what?" is the equivalent to a double take, or a sarcastic taunt. The author pretends to have just noticed (and perhaps to be shocked by), after a well-timed delay, the implications of what has just been said. In various ways, Nietzsche employs this little gimmick often; indeed, the "– what?" occurs often enough to be a catch-phrase (e.g. §15 or 56).

The tone is important because it is often one of our only clues as to how to "take" a certain statement: is it a joke, a seriously meant claim, gentle mockery or a vicious and spiteful provocation? Here, the playful tone is tinged with the faintest hint of venom. "*Das Weib*" [woman], for example, is not a perfectly neutral term but *can* have pejorative meanings. This hint of the pejorative introduces a misogynistic theme that becomes far from subtle, for example at the end of Part 7, although even there one must be constantly aware of Nietzsche's famous irony. There is a much more pronounced pejorative in the term "dogmatists" – one has the feeling, and quite rightly, that Nietzsche has in mind any number of philosophers who would not consider themselves dogmatists. The assumption is also that all these incompetent and unthinking dogmatists were and must be men – so in any case neither gender escapes Nietzsche's venom.

A second thing to notice about this sentence is that it involves a pun. The last phrase reads ". . . *sich schlecht auf Weiber verstanden?*" [which I have translated as "were amateurs about women?"]. The verb means "to be expert or proficient concerning" and this is not simply negated but modified by "*schlecht*" [bad]. The suggestion is of bumbling or cack-handed. However, the core of the verb is "*verstehen*" which means, simply, "to understand". Significantly, this is a *philosophical* term (as in the faculty of understanding, in Kant). So, it would be difficult for a German reader of philosophy not to read this as *also* meaning "had an insufficient understanding of women", and thus "of truth". Accordingly, this is also a jibe at the way philosophers think about understanding and truth. Now, this is not a particularly sophisticated or clever pun (there are better ones to come), but it contains a double meaning that carries significance. That is, the doubleness of the meaning itself means something, suggesting something complex, subtle or hidden in the midst of the apparently straightforward. In brief, it is not just the case that dogmatists are sexually inept, in some way, and that they had an inadequate philosophy of truth, but that *these two claims are intrinsically linked*. Nietzsche's puns are frequently charged with meaning in this way. We will return to this particular double meaning, and what light if any it sheds on Nietzsche's notorious writings on women, in our discussion of §§231–9. For it turns out that here in the first sentence, in what looks for all the world like a light-hearted and mildly offensive joke, Nietzsche is introducing one of his most central philosophical ideas.

Significantly, the sentence is also impossible to translate in such a way as to capture all its nuances. There are many translations of Nietzsche's book, all are fine, intelligent, professional; and they all translate this sentence slightly differently, putting a different spin on the idea. So then, if the idea turns out to be so central, we already have proof that Nietzsche cannot be as straightforward to read as, to many, he appears.

Thirdly, this trope of truth as a woman is already a complex internal and external reference. A variation shows up in §220, first of all. Also, to an educated German reader, it would likely be reminiscent of the last lines of Goethe's *Faust* II, which Nietzsche quotes much later in §236. But, it is certainly an echo of the trope of woman as wisdom in *Zarathustra*, Part 1, "On Reading and Writing" ("Brave, unconcerned, mocking, violent – thus wisdom wants us: she is a woman and always loves only a warrior"); and that very passage is used, slightly revised, as an aphorism to start off the third Treatise in *Genealogy of Morality*. In this book it would be quite impossible for us to track all of Nietzsche's allusions and cross-references; in any case the translations generally list many in footnotes or endnotes. However, we should certainly be aware of how Nietzsche's book, from its opening sentence (to the closing stanza of the final poem), is self-knowingly immersed in a pre-existing fabric of texts, thoughts, histories and beliefs, both personal and global.

A fourth observation is that the sentence begins as a hypothesis: *if* we make a certain claim, *what* then follows? Nietzsche frequently constructs his thoughts in this form. Later in the Preface, for example, he will make plentiful use of suggestive questions, "mights", "maybes" and "perhaps". This "hypothetical" way of working has a distinguished history in philosophy and science. For example, in philosophy we encounter it in the idea of a thought experiment that helps us to analyse the content of our concepts. John Locke (I have in mind especially the discussion of personal identity in *An Essay Concerning Human Understanding*) was particularly adept at such thought experiments. What, we might ask, are the consequences for our concept of a person's *identity* if he or she loses all memory, swaps bodies with another person, or whatever? In modern science, a different hypothetical form of working has become dominant. One hypothesizes some X in order first to analyse what empirical consequences it would have, and then to devise and perform an experiment to test for the presence of just these consequences. The presence of consequences does not prove X, but the absence of the consequences proves not-X. Finally, in Kant's *Critique of Pure Reason*, he describes a set of "ideas" that cannot constitute knowledge but only "regulate" it. That is, interesting insights might be had if we think of the observable world "as if" such ideas have objective reality.

Nietzsche's hypothetical method has something in common with all three of these, and especially the first and third form, but there are important differences. First, as here, the tone is often playful or mocking. And this suggests that the hypothesis might have a different purpose from Locke's serious attempt to explore particular abstract concepts. Secondly, Nietzsche's hypotheses typically do not target a specific concept but rather a particular *way of understanding* something. That is, they seem to be interested in opening up or calling into question a "world-view". So, here, Nietzsche is targeting a way of thinking about philosophy and the methods it employs to discover the truth. (Moreover, less directly, the targets here include the way in which philosophers think about gender in an ethical, biological or social way, as well as the general capacity to understand.) In respect to the implicit reference to Kant's notion of regulative ideas, we will have much to say later about notions in Nietzsche that seem to function not so much as straightforward truth-claims, but rather as provocations to thought or initiations of long-term projects (the famous idea of eternal recurrence might be one of these).

"Speaking seriously", Nietzsche continues. This confirms the jokey status of the first sentences, certainly. But there is also a kind of contradiction here. The "seriously" [*ernstlich*] echoes the "horrible seriousness" [*schauerliche Ernst*] earlier. The idea of seriousness becomes important later in the book. Already, though, we have a suggestive contrast. A contrast between, on the one hand, a seriousness linked to horror, and associated with dogmatists who may be nearing their "last breaths" and, on the other, a seriousness to be found in jokes and puns, associated (as we will soon see) with all that is living. Nietzsche wants to be taken seriously, on these *latter* terms.

"Speaking seriously", then, philosophical dogmatizing should be seen as childishness, no matter how "elevated" it may seem. For it is based upon superstitions or word play, the "seduction by grammar", or even upon a generalization of some particular human fact (e.g. a foible of the philosopher). Two things are to be noticed here. First, briefly, we have yet another inversion of the contrast discussed above: here, Nietzsche is being "serious" about childishness and play. How is such play to be distinguished from the jokiness characteristic of much of Nietzsche's writing? The obvious answer, and one we will see Nietzsche returning to, is that the play of the dogmatic philosophers is self-deceptive, not recognized for what it is.

A second thing worth noticing is the parenthetical comment on the "soul superstition" and associated concepts. This is an important theme for Nietzsche. He is here referring to the idea that the location of human identity is in an immortal and independent soul; that the soul is the seat also of consciousness and will, and thus (ideally at least) in control of the body, action as well as thought. These are indeed historically important ideas within the history of Christianity and philosophy (especially moral philosophy). What we need to notice is that, uncritically assumed, these certainly may be dogma or superstitions. However, they are also topics within philosophical metaphysics. That is, the truth or falsehood of the claim that the soul exists, and has such and such properties, is not always just assumed by philosophy, but *argued for*. If Nietzsche's claim that these are just superstitions is to be upheld, then he will have to demonstrate that all such metaphysical arguments are not neutral attempts to establish truth, but partisan attempts to give to prejudice the appearance of reason. So, at stake in Nietzsche's book are not just the particular claims philosophy has made (about the soul, for example), but the methods (such as rational argumentation) that philosophy has used to try to establish these claims.

We will skip quickly over the next couple of sentences, only making two quick observations: first of all, we have the "monstrous and terrifying grotesques [*Fratzen*]" as which "great things" must first stride the earth in order to "inscribe eternal demands into the heart". The image puts one in mind of primordial mythic beings (for example, the Titans in Greek myth). The next sentence makes clear, though, that Nietzsche is referring not to mythic figures so much as ideas, grossly and grotesquely distorted, that gradually become accepted as something like common sense. This introduces the theme of the *historical* origins of basic principles and laws – often, for Nietzsche, a historical origin that appears to be quite different to the character of these laws. If a basic principle is historical, in this sense, then it is also not "basic" in a traditional philosophical sense: it is not *a priori*, for example, nor an "eternal truth". And yet, just such a principle might be *taken to be* basic for some broad and comprehensive world-view (not just a philosophy, but a religion, a culture, a science, a way of life). Secondly, notice that this history and its contemporary effects is not something to be simply despised and abandoned (even were that possible), but is to be met "not without gratitude". But why gratitude? That is the topic of the rest of the Preface.

The last topic of the Preface begins by asking us to recognize that the most fearful and indeed dangerous "grotesque" was precisely an error of a dogmatic philosopher: Plato's "fabrication" [*Erfindung*] of the pure spirit and the Good as such. Nietzsche means the ideas of a spirit or mind that is able to purify itself of any engagement with the world of appearances and of human desires, and of an absolutely universal Good, that exists in itself independently of human affairs. Nietzsche explains that such fabrication meant "standing truth on its head" and "denying *perspective*, the basic condition of all life". We will return to these ideas later.

But now, Nietzsche says, "Europe breathes a sigh of relief from this nightmare and at least can enjoy a healthier – sleep". Again, this is a common form of joke in Nietzsche: the unexpected completion of a sentence with the long dividing dash to indicate comic timing. (We get another joke structured in this manner in the parenthetical comment about gunpowder and the printing press towards the end of the preface.) The overcoming of Plato's thought has not led to wakefulness, awareness, clear-sightedness, but just to deeper sleep. (See also *Zarathustra*, Part 1, "On the Teachers of Virtue".) Notice also that the sigh of relief echoes the "last gasps" of dogmatism. It is as if one way of thinking or living (dogmatism) has been suffocated so that now another (whatever is characteristic of recent, sleeping, Europe) can breathe while sleeping.

But, Nietzsche continues, this process of overcoming this error has also "cultivated" an enormous reserve of strength [*Kraft*]. And, "we *whose task* [Aufgabe] *is wakefulness itself*" are "heirs" to this strength. This idea of a reserve of strength is elaborated a few lines later with the "magnificent tension [*Spannung*] of the spirit". Attempts have been made to hide or remove this tension, this built-up strength – Nietzsche names Jesuitism and democracy as two. The latter might even be working, the spirit might no longer experience itself as "need". But "we" still feel, the "whole need of the spirit and the whole tension of its bow".

At the moment, it is impossible for us to investigate what Nietzsche might mean by this strength or tension; by the "task of wakefulness"; what it might mean to attempt to remove the tension through Jesuitism or democracy and a free press; or even what is the "need of the spirit". All these themes we will return to in the course of our discussion. It remains for us to notice the pronoun "we". We "free spirits", or "we good Europeans". (Certainly not "we Germans"; here, briefly and jokingly and later in a much more sustained manner, Nietzsche is always critical of the cultural and political state of his native country.) Nietzsche is addressing his readership as partners or potential partners in a future philosophical (and ultimately also moral and political) enterprise. His book, then, is not meant for just anyone, but for those who already feel this need of the spirit. This, in itself, is a curious idea. We tend to think of philosophical texts (and others too, such as scientific writings) as essentially open in the sense that given a certain degree of background knowledge (which is again openly available) anyone can read and understand them. Nietzsche's "we" suggests that his book is not open; there will be some people who are not meant to read it.

The Preface has introduced many of the major themes of *Beyond Good and Evil*, such as the nature of truth and appropriate strategies for "winning" it; the problem of establishing *historically* how ideas and, more importantly, ways of living arise; considering what might now arise to replace them; and the idea of perspective. It has also shown us several of Nietzsche's typical ways of working: the hypothetical mode of writing, for example, and the jokes and puns that are intended to be serious but not "clumsy". We have also observed how Nietzsche's writings participate in a pre-existing web of textual references. It is important to add that this is not just a fact about, or a strategy of, writing, but is also a philosophical theme. Again and again Nietzsche will tell us how the philosopher cannot separate herself from or even fully come to understand the conditions within which she works. This idea is part of the meaning of concepts like "going down", "entanglement" or the "untimely" (see §§ 26, 56 and 212 respectively). It appears in Nietzsche's Preface also in a subtle joke. The first syllable of the book is "Vor" meaning pre- or before, and this is said of suppositions. Before the book can even begin, Nietzsche tells us, we already find ourselves in a field of embedded suppositions.

2 "On the Prejudices of the Philosophers": *A Critique of Metaphysical Ground* (Part I §§1–23)

After the Preface, Nietzsche's book is divided into nine major Parts. These Parts are, by and large, of similar length. Each of the major Parts, however, consists of numbered sections that vary dramatically in length, from a single sentence to several pages. (Here, we shall reference these sections with the symbol § rather than referring to a page number. This is merely a matter of convenience; and it involves an irony Nietzsche might have appreciated, since the §-sign is so often associated with scientific or systematic philosophy, such as Kant's.) Now, this way of writing should be familiar to anyone who has read Nietzsche before. Most of his other books, although they may not have "major Parts", are certainly written as a series of variably short sections. This has a mixed effect upon us as readers. On the one hand, it makes Nietzsche eminently readable: he is brief, pithy, apparently without long arguments or developments to follow. On the other, though, this readability has a cost: it is more difficult to see, and thus all too easy to forget about, the relationships between sections. The reader struggles to understand how Nietzsche's writing comprises more than a series of observations. The only way to answer this is to go through the text patiently, looking for the links that turn a series of observations into a sustained philosophy.

§1

Part 1 is, in brief, a critique of a handful of basic metaphysical positions which Nietzsche sees as having a controlling influence in the history of philosophy, and which stand in the way of asking a *new* set of questions. One such new question given in §1 is *what is the value of the will to truth*?

Nietzsche, therefore, is picking up immediately on what was also the first theme of the Preface: truth. However, there is a small but all-important difference. Whereas in the Preface it appeared as though what was at issue was the nature of truth, the question now is of the "will to truth" and, in particular, of its value. The former is a fairly traditional question within philosophy; the latter, however, is not. Nietzsche is explicitly asking: why do we pursue truth, why do we think it is important? Let us put this way of thinking to the famous beginning of the Preface, "Presupposing that truth is a woman". Now the question of "why pursue truth" becomes "why (do men) pursue women?". Well, no doubt there are many and complex reasons for this! But *one* reason is of course: "to propagate the species, to continue life". This gives us our first clue to how Nietzsche will address the problem of the value of the will to truth: not truth itself, but this will *forms part of the conditions of life*, something without which life would be impossible. We have already seen, in the Preface, this notion of "condition of life". Whether by this Nietzsche means all life, life in general, or particular forms of life (e.g. the human), or something even more particular than that, is not yet clear. It will turn out that Nietzsche, depending upon context, can mean any of these three things by "life": there is an analysis of life as such, of human life, and of different peoples or cultures as essentially different "types of human life".

Since the title of the book so clearly references *morals*, and this section has introduced the notion of *value*, we should pause to consider in a preliminary way the difference. The question of the value of the will to truth is one of a series of such questions; another is the value of morality (this is stated very clearly in *Genealogy*, Preface §5). By this is not, evidently, meant the morality of morality. By a "value" Nietzsche means: something in the service of a particular mode of life; or, more or less equivalently, in the service of the will to power of a dominant drive. So, as we have just seen, the general answer to the value of the will to truth is: it is a condition of life. By "morals" or, more generally, the whole phenomenon of "morality" he means something much narrower. A morality is a value that expresses itself universally, as a command for all (and thus in terms of the language of virtues, vices, duties, rights, goods, evils, etc.), and also which is not transparent, not aware of itself as value (and thus cannot recognize the possibility of other legitimate values). We will return, on many occasions, to Nietzsche's analysis of both of these notions.

The dominant image of §1 is the Sphinx, a figure in Greek (by way of Egyptian and Near Eastern) mythology who asked unlucky travellers a riddle, and killed them if they failed to answer. The tragic hero Oedipus answered the riddle correctly, and in fury the Sphinx destroyed itself. The Sphinx, for Nietzsche here, is the will to truth: questioning and demanding answers. Significantly, within Greek myth, the Sphinx is always female. This metaphor thus, unsurprisingly, echoes the metaphor of truth as a woman from the Preface. However, although there is clearly a connection of some kind between these two metaphors, it is not so clear what it is, because here again what is at issue is the *will to* truth. In any case, figuratively, the problem of the value of the will to truth is to *put questions to* the Sphinx. Nietzsche ends the section by testifying to the "risk" of such a question: in the myth of the Sphinx, either the questioner or the questioned is always destroyed.

However, to ask the question of the value of the will to truth – however new, disturbing and risky this question may be – is nevertheless to ask a question. It is to demand an answer, a truth. Thus, Nietzsche's new question at least *appears* to be another manifestation of the will to truth. He wants to know, to discover the truth of, the value of truth. Is the question of the value of this will (Oedipus posing a question to the Sphinx) *included within* the general problem of pursuing truth (the Sphinx asking questions)? Thus the confusion over roles: "Who of us is Oedipus here? Who the Sphinx?" This is a general problem in Nietzsche. One of the most common conceptions of Nietzsche is a philosopher who denies the possibility of truth as the history of philosophy has defined it. From this first section it is already clear that Nietzsche is more complex than that characterization might suggest.

The first section to each of the nine Parts of the book is generally a statement about methodology, or at least a discussion of the difficulties involved in the particular enquiry. Nietzsche has told us that the problem of the value of the will to truth will be his theme; he is also telling us, by way of the metaphor of the sphinx, just what a difficult and dangerous question this is. However, the confusion over roles returns as a theme of masks, which as we shall see is in part an issue within methodology. Moreover, the implication that the questioner is also the questioned is a methodological point. This latter looks familiar: after all, did not Descartes begin by asking questions of his own mind, its contents and activities? Already in §3, it will become clear that Nietzsche's version of this structure is quite different from Descartes's. In short, although it doesn't look like it, here in §1 Nietzsche is setting out key aspects of his philosophical method. (In parallel, the last few sections in each Part often comprise a summary statement, draw conclusions, or move into another, deeper level of questioning – in any case they have the function of a climax and transition.)

§2, and discussion of perspective and interpretation

(Our discussion of this topic continues in §22.) Section 2 begins with another common device in Nietzsche: the false quotation. There is no attempt to deceive us, but Nietzsche is simply imagining how a previous philosopher (most likely one of the dogmatists from the Preface) would state and defend a position. In this case, the position is what Nietzsche calls the "faith in opposite values": that something which is described as X can have no relation (other than that of opposition itself) to not-X. This is assumed true of things that are obviously values, e.g. selfishness and self-lessness. But it is also assumed true of things that have an apparently value-neutral status, for example the transitory (constantly changing) and intransitory (unchanging). While we are at it, we may note a few other opposites that are of particular importance in Nietzsche: good and evil, obviously; truth and falsehood; freedom and necessity; consciousness and unconsciousness or instinct; fact (value-neutral or free) and value.

Why does Nietzsche, so early on in his book, latch on to the problem of opposites? Most obviously, to explain further the "beyond" of the title: to be beyond good and evil is to be beyond thinking them as exclusive and all-encompassing opposites. Equally obviously, Nietzsche sees the structure of oppositions as a basic type of rational thinking as in the logical truth "It is not the case that A and not-A". Accordingly, a critique of oppositional thinking might serve also as a critique of a traditional understanding of rationality. Moreover, in the content of these oppositions – that evil is fundamentally different from good, time from eternity, truth from deceit – are encoded dominant metaphysical or moral beliefs. These beliefs, Nietzsche argues, then organize all our more particular beliefs about what is good or what is truthful.

But there is also a general methodological point being developed here in the account of opposites. It leads us to an important distinction within Nietzsche. On the one hand, Nietzsche will often present us with arguments that are designed to show the impossibility of certain traditional philosophical ideas (for example, concerning the nature of truth), or the validity of others. He is, in other words, engaging in a perfectly straightforward manner with philosophy. Section 16 below is an example. On the other hand, Nietzsche also provides analyses of a broadly historical type concerning the origin of certain ideas. The origin may be psychological (e.g. fear or revenge), or it may be linguistic (we have already seen him speak of a "seduction by grammar"), or perhaps physiological (e.g. racial traits), social or political (e.g. class), or in the case of individual philosophers it may be some small twist of fate. There may be a necessity claimed for what is discovered in this analysis (that is, Nietzsche is not usually analysing in terms of historical contingencies), but it is not the logical necessity of an argument, but rather more like the causal necessity of a natural process. In this book, Nietzsche uses the name "morphology" (in §23) for this type of analysis; more famously, in his next book his calls it "genealogy". Such an analysis does not even need to investigate the truth or falsehood of an idea; rather, Nietzsche is interested in why people in large numbers – whole epochs, nations, or other groups – must believe it to be true.

Of course, that such a historical account of the advent of an idea can be given does not *in itself* count as an argument against it. A truth may have a chequered past and still be truth. However, it may be that a supposed truth has no other basis beyond (i) a historical compulsion of this type, and (ii) its coherence in a system with other ideas that also have such a historical basis (see §20). In which case, the analysis *as a whole* becomes compelling. If Nietzsche can show that the traditional philosophical techniques of argumentation are themselves held to be valid *only because of such a historical compulsion*, then at a stroke that would render any conventional argument concerning the truth unsound. The "faith" in opposites, here in §2, is just such a technique of argumentation; Nietzsche makes the general claim about logic explicit in §3. But how could one "show" this without assuming it? This is one version of the difficulty Nietzsche faces as a philosopher; and §1 made it clear that he is well aware of the problem.

The content of the invented quotation with which the section begins is relevant here. The reasoning is that the purity and absoluteness of a distinction could not arise from worldly events (such as human psychology, languages, or individual circumstances), but must arise "from the lap of Being". Nietzsche's point is that such reasoning uses the faith in opposites to prove the faith in opposites; this is obviously circular. However, given this, we ought to ask if Nietzsche should be understood to be thinking in terms of the distinction between philosophical argumentation and historical analysis that we outlined above. That distinction seems to be a version of the distinction between the transient and intransient. Perhaps philosophical analysis should be seen as, at best, one tool among others with no unique or special claim to be *the* method for establishing truth. Accordingly, for Nietzsche the specifically *logical* difficulty (developed in our previous paragraph) may be the least of his worries. Again, in §1 it was not just an intellectual puzzle as to which is Oedipus, which the Sphinx, but it was a matter of life and death. So here, the historical genesis of an idea has necessity, for it is related to the underlying conditions necessary for the existence of the type of life of the individual or group that believes it. Thus, here as elsewhere, Nietzsche employs the notion of a "value for life". To rigorously question such beliefs is "dangerous", as Nietzsche makes clear at the end of the passage, possibly even self-destructive (see the end of §23). We should note in passing, although there is no space to develop it here, that Nietzsche is not the first philosopher to look to historical development to understand not just the advent of but also both the necessity of and the nature of ideas. Before him, Hegel and Marx are the most famous examples.

Let us turn to one opposition in particular, that between fact and value. Above we distinguished between value oppositions and value-neutral oppositions. One of Nietzsche's claims here, however, will be that the second type of opposition (what above we called "apparently value-neutral") is ultimately built upon the first (value oppositions): there are no metaphysical claims that are "value-neutral". In short, the fact/value distinction – fundamental to much philosophical thinking (Hume, Kant, Positivism, etc.) – must be considered an effect rather than a basic axiom. The fact/value distinction should not be underestimated in importance. For example, it feeds into Kant's famous and apparently broader distinction between theoretical or speculative philosophy (dealing with knowledge, reality, metaphysics) and moral or practical philosophy (dealing with moral law and moral action). That distinction, which organizes the whole of Kant's thought (and much of German Idealism thereafter) is accordingly not fundamental, Nietzsche claims. So, when Nietzsche talks about values and interpretations (things that might seem to be related to me, as a subject), he will also be speaking about the nature of life, nature and reality (things we might suppose are independent of me). In what way he makes this connection is not yet clear, but we will investigate shortly.

Another claim being put forward here is that, in general, in all such cases of supposed opposition there is a hidden but constitutive inter-relation between the terms. Notice, however, that this claim, and the previous one too, are again hypotheticals rather than straightforward truth claims: "dangerous perhaps", Nietzsche writes. Let us make two observations here. First, given Nietzsche has been speaking about the value of truth – and asking (hypothetically) why not rather falsehood – perhaps this hypothetical mode is an attempt by Nietzsche to get around the complexities we noticed in §1. That is, the hypothetical mode means he is not in a direct logical self-contradiction when making truth claims about the will to truth. Secondly, though, this section is precisely about questioning the fundamental nature of opposites – or, in other words, about whether what is apparently contradictory really is so. Expressed metaphorically, we should be asking ourselves whether the distinction between Oedipus and the Sphinx is another of these opposites in which metaphysics has invested its faith.

In order to pursue all these ideas further, we must look at the elaborate analogy Nietzsche develops concerning perspective. Perspective would appear to be an important philosophical idea for Nietzsche, but here it is developed in association first with optics and subsequently with painting. The optical metaphor is fairly straightforward: what happens to be near us, what is in the foreground, appears larger, clearer. (Think about a stage set, for example, as viewed from the front row.) We estimate the size or distance of other things using this foreground. But then, what *happens to be near us* becomes the *standard* by which we judge other things. There is a mirror image here of the analysis of optical phenomena by Berkeley. Berkeley held that we tend to assert the existence of things in space, and of space itself, because we can see things laid out in space, near or far. But, Berkeley argues, in fact all we see are things larger or smaller, and we infer (illegitimately he believes) that this means they are arranged in space.

Within the mainstream tradition of drawing or painting (from the fourteenth to the nineteenth centuries, approximately) the image is generally organized as a perspective: that is it attempts to approximate, using mathematical methods, to what the visual appearance of a scene would be for an observer at a particular location in front of this scene. Now, of course, the canvas (or whatever surface) is flat and therefore the perspective is an illusion. Precisely because it is an illusion, the painter can use it to achieve certain effects: as in *trompe l'oeil*, where typically the painting gives the illusion of being part of the architecture. Or, again, as in the choice of a low ("frog") angle of perspective, which makes whatever is in the foreground of the image appear exaggeratedly huge and powerful (e.g. a king or general in armour astride his horse), and whatever is in the background not only far away but also small (a conquered army). It is this second type of illusion especially to which Nietzsche seems to be referring. The perspective (any perspective) contains within itself an evaluation: *this* is important, while *that* is insignificant. The perspective is then a motivation or justification to assert that something is the case. Not incidentally, "*Frosch-Perspektive*" also means a blinkered or narrow view. This is a perspective, in other words, that refuses other perspectives and indeed refuses to acknowledge itself as perspective and instead proclaims what it sees as truth in itself.

For Nietzsche, then, the *first* characterization of perspective, one that emerges from the elaborate optical metaphor, is as a way of valuing things that also tends to assert that this is not mere evaluation but fact. Although it can perhaps be resisted, this tendency is built in to the idea of "viewing" something (knowing something, gathering evidence about it, valuing something morally): that which appears always and necessarily appears perspectivally. Moreover, a perspective presents what appear to be opposites or widely separated phenomena. However (going back to the analogy), these things are right next to each other on the painted surface, at the same level and in close relation. Thus, Nietzsche writes that "perhaps" what is presented as true or selfless might, despite the appearances, be less valuable than the false or selfish. But valuable *to or for what*? Nietzsche answers: these "wicked" [*schlimm*] things might have the "higher or more fundamental value for all life". Again, we are back to the theme of life and its conditions. Recall that this came up in the Preface, precisely where Nietzsche mentioned perspective. It is becoming increasingly difficult to think of

notions like "interpretation", "perspective" or "value" as if they are attitudes of an *observer*. They are that only secondarily, as a consequence of
the nature of life and its conditions. It is the job of Nietzsche's historical
method to uncover the development of these conditions. Leaving behind
the optical metaphor, for a moment, Nietzsche's second and much richer
characterization of perspective is that it is in fact a characterization not of a
viewing or knowing subject, but of the basic nature of reality.

Accordingly, we might speculate, to overcome the problem of perspective would be to view a painting as a "flat" surface, as a "valueless" field of
relations among colours and shapes. That is, we must ignore the illusion of
perspective. This would involve working back through the manner in
which the painter created the illusion of perspective, taking this illusion
apart in order to see the canvas as actually flat. Such a "working back"
would be akin to Nietzsche's historical method for the analysis of the aris-
ing of values. However, even so, *optically* we would still be located in front
of the canvas, and whatever bit of the canvas was nearest would appear
largest. Quite apart from the illusion of perspective created by the painter,
there is and must be a perspective to our mere viewing of the canvas. This
elaborate analogy thus suggests a certain impossibility of a rigorous "overcoming" of perspective. (Nietzsche will return to the analysis of perspective
and value in §34.) In other words, considering this as an analogy of our
knowledge or truths, Nietzsche is claiming the rigorous impossibility of
fully eliminating perspective, and this is equivalent to the claim that the
conscious thinking of a philosopher might be driven by instinctive needs or
desires. Already in this section, however, we have another way: the will to
"overcome" perspective is already parasitic upon the belief in the
significance and fundamental nature of the opposition between truth and
falsehood. But this belief may be just a common metaphysical *perspective*.
What, Nietzsche is asking us, is the value of the will to overcome perspective? Nietzsche insists that a historically significant conception of scientific
objectivity would be the absolute elimination of perspectives, the elimination of all "prejudices". But this, he argues, is simply impossible: for one
thing, the belief in the value and possibility of truth is a perspective that
cannot meaningfully be eliminated in the pursuit of objectivity (see *The
Gay Science*, §344). Accordingly, the association of the problem of the
value of the will to truth in the previous section, and the problem of perspective in this one, together constitute the beginnings of a critique of
science (and likewise of philosophers in so far as they model their understanding of knowledge or truth on science). However, it is not just science
and scientifically oriented philosophy that fall into this trap: the moral
notion of selflessness and the political notion of justice or democracy, for
example, both depend upon a belief that is structurally similar to the belief
in the possibility of eliminating perspective.

However, Nietzsche *sometimes* talks about a capacity to remove oneself from a local sphere of prejudice and metaphysical error, in order to obtain a less "perspectival" perspective (§380 of *The Gay Science* is a good example; there, he calls this being the "wanderer"). He suggests that the condition of this removing oneself may be not an elimination of perspective, but rather a *comprehensive assembly of* perspectives. So, later in *Beyond*, §211, Nietzsche speaks of the philosopher having to "see with many different eyes and consciences". This might be an explanation of how the "wanderer" is different from the naive conception of sciences as perspectiveless (e.g. presuppositionless) (see also *Genealogy of Morality*, Third Treatise, §12). We should go back to the idea of "frog perspective" as "blinkered" and thus as refusing to recognize the possibility of other perspectives. To be sure, being aware of perspective as such (that is, being aware of the necessity of perspective in all seeing and knowing), and thus recognizing the range and diversity of perspectives, is not the same as overcoming perspective. But, it is at least a condition of the kinds of *new* perspectives that we described above. (Nietzsche appears to make this point below, in §5; and in §11 we will return to this problem.) Accordingly, in §186 for example, Nietzsche will talk of a methodology of observing feelings of value and differences of value. This method is impossible unless one is first willing to admit and understand phenomena within the notion of perspective.

Here, we should mention the question of the relation between an interpretation [*Auslegung*] and a perspective. In §14, for example, Nietzsche writes about physics as "world interpretation"; likewise in §22. The two notions have much in common, to be sure: both mean that something is viewed according to a previously accepted set of beliefs. Nietzsche *tends* to talk about "perspective" when he wants to draw explicit attention to the fact that these beliefs are related to the drives, values or will of human beings; he *tends* to talk about "interpretation" when he is thinking more in terms of the intellectual operation of understanding something *as if* it is this way or that. (Interpretation is thus related to "spiritualization", see §19.) However, on Nietzsche's account, every interpretation is also a perspective in so far as it is ultimately related to drives, values and will. In *Genealogy of Morality*, Nietzsche claims that the Third Treatise is an example of the art of interpretation (Preface, §8), an example of how he believes his own work should be read. This "should" does not refer to objectivity (the idea of "art" already makes this clear). Rather, he means that it should be interpreted by those who understand the idea of perspective, and indeed those whose own perspectives are already on the way to being realigned to the notion of the world as will to power; certainly not, then, the perspective of "modern man". We will look at the idea of interpretation again in our discussion of §22.

The section ends with the "dangerous" hypothesis that "perhaps" what appear to be opposites might in fact be entangled in a historical process of development. This is a "dangerous" perspective to take precisely to the extent that the faith in opposites might be a condition of life. Who will risk this dangerous "perhaps"? A new type of philosopher who is "coming". (This recalls the idea of the "goal" that ends the Preface.) This philosopher of the future will not just come to have philosophical knowledge about the inter-relatedness of that which appears to be purely opposite – because the suggestion of this whole section is that philosophical ways of knowing might be the problem, rather than the solution. On the contrary, she will also "somehow" have a "reverse taste and tendency". These last lines set out a new problem for the book to address. What could it be that would make a philosopher not only think differently but have this "reverse taste and tendency"? As we shall see, Nietzsche will propose nothing short of a revolution in the instincts and drives that make a particular form of life the type that it is. The new philosopher will have to be a new variety of human being.

§3

One of the additional oppositions mentioned above shows up already in §3: consciousness and instinct. Consciousness, Nietzsche claims, is not a grounding or original moment within mental life. Just as the moment of birth has no relevance for heredity – conception is the point where the genetic makeup of a child is determined and it is, in the analogy, hidden, microscopic, somewhat arbitrary – so becoming conscious of something has no relevance to it. Rather, Nietzsche claims, "most" of what is conscious philosophical thinking is "secretly guided, and forced into determinate channels", by instincts. This is a direct attack on what is generally seen as the tradition of Descartes in philosophy: the absolute transparency of conscious thought to itself serving as a ground of the philosophical enterprise. One implication of such a claim is that the various errors Nietzsche accuses philosophers of are not the product simply of ignorance. If a philosopher is "unconsciously" committed to a certain perspective and set of values, then coming to know this fact about him- or herself will not necessarily make any difference.

Section 3 goes on to make an additional, related claim: the apparently sovereign movements of logic are founded on valuations. By "sovereign" [*Selbstherrlichkeit* – there is a pejorative overtone of "self-aggrandisement"], Nietzsche alludes to the fact that logical principles seem to be self-justifying, not requiring further justification. Not just conscious thoughts, then, but the logical relations between thoughts – by which a philosopher appears to prove or disprove a proposition, for example – are instinctual. That is, Nietzsche goes on, the basic principles of logic are based on "physiological requirements for the preservation of a certain type of life". So, for

example, the fact that determinate thoughts are more valued than the inde-
terminate is grounded in what is necessary for the preservation of human
beings. (In this example, Nietzsche has in mind, among other similar
philosophies, Descartes's famous criteria of clarity and distinctness.) Such a
logical principle is "regulative" for us; it guides *our* conscious thought. This
is not unimportant, by any means, and perhaps not something that one
could or would even want to dispense with. Just like the deserved "value"
of the true or selfless in §2, Nietzsche's point is far from the claim that the
ascription of truth, selflessness or the employment of logic are useless.
Rather, that neither truth, selflessness nor logic are rigorously distinct from
their apparent opposites (falsehood or deception, selfishness, irrationality),
and that neither is the value that can be assigned to them. That is, neither
set is simply "good" and the other simply "evil". In any case, logical principles may in fact be "foreground estimates", exactly the conditions necessary
for such beings as we are. The phrase "foreground estimate" [*Vordergrunds-
Schätzungen*] is the same as was used (alongside "perspective") in the previous section to explicate the notion of value oppositions. Nietzsche is still
speaking of the general problem of perspective.

Behind the headline claims about consciousness and logic, Nietzsche has
made two important connections in this section. First, that an "instinct"
[*Instinkt*] can be (or perhaps is always) a "value" [*Wert*]. Secondly, the assertion of a value rests upon the conditions for the possibility of life.

The last sentence has given translators something of a headache. Let
us render it as "This would be to assume, namely, that it is not exactly
man who is the 'measure of things'." (It could also be "not man alone
who is . . .".) The "*nicht gerade*" (not exactly) echoes the "exactly" in the
previous sentence; here it probably has an ironic tone, implying under-
statement, such as one might say in English "a war zone is not exactly the
safest place to be". The reference is to Protagoras's famous statement that
"Man is the measure of all things". Nietzsche is suggesting that the analysis
of logic and its grounds includes the assertion that the true measure of all
things is not exactly man (the conscious, thinking, philosophical man) but
life itself *in man*.

§4

Section 4 picks up another key opposition: truth and falseness. The value
given to "truth", Nietzsche claims, may have little or nothing to do with
whether a judgement is in fact true or not. Rather, its value stems from
the extent to which, again, it is "life-promoting, life-preserving". And, he
adds, "we are fundamentally inclined" to believe that those judgements
most indispensable for life are both the ones hailed by philosophers as
the most "true" and, in fact, the most false. In parenthesis we have the

key example: "synthetic judgements *a priori*". This refers to one of Kant's most basic claims: that certain judgements can be isolated that are true *a priori* while being more than empty products of reasoning. Kant attempts to prove the existence and validity of such judgements by "transcendental reasoning": such judgements are the condition of the possibility of any experience of the world, and therefore (since we clearly do have experiences of the world) must be valid. Nietzsche's own position can be usefully seen as a subtle modification of Kant's. Such judgements, he argues, are conditions of the possibility of life, therefore valid *for us* in so far as we are alive, and therefore *deemed to be true* – whether or not they are true.

But Nietzsche's analysis goes one step further: the fact that a judgement is a condition of life, and therefore must be considered "true", not only makes it irrelevant whether or not it is true, but actually makes it more likely that it is, in fact, false. Again, the most false are the most necessary conditions. But this makes his way of thinking "dangerous". This is the case partly because any subversion or inversion of existing values will expose one to danger. More importantly, though, it leads rapidly to those giddy questions of §1: who is the Sphinx, who Oedipus? We are right back, that is, to those questions about the will to truth, and whether truth can be spoken of this will. By this line of questioning, we are beyond good and evil. We no longer take that opposition to be fundamental: it is only an effect of more basic processes of living and willing.

Notice the reference to "our new language": Nietzsche is not so much referring to a new philosophical language (a terminology, say). In fact, Nietzsche invents relatively few new terms; his innovations lie in the rehabilitation of old terms (e.g. freedom, instinct, life, will, power). The new language, then, is the unsettling new way of addressing familiar ideas, a kind of revolution *within* philosophical language, which turns these ideas on their head. Here, what is the familiar theme that is being turned on its head? It is that the falseness of a judgement is one of the few philosophically significant objections to a judgement. But, on Nietzsche's analysis, language (especially grammar) is one of the roots, or at least buttresses, of metaphysical error (see e.g. §17). So, the new language must not only struggle against old ideas, but even against language itself. This helps us to understand the importance of style and poetry for Nietzsche. The stylistic problem of philosophical prose, or philosophically directed poetry, is to find an *aesthetic* means of expression for what the old language had to pass over in silence. But, importantly, *language* is only half the problem. In so far as it borrows its manner of thinking from language, in so far as it employs concepts, abstractions, logical linkages, oppositions and systematic architectonics, then *thought itself* must be equally "narrow" in its perspectives. In *Zarathustra*, Part 2, "On Self-Overcoming", Nietzsche identifies the "will to truth" with "a will to the thinkability of all things"; that is, a will to the false constitution of the image of the world such that it is, top to bottom, thinkable (and thus, not incidentally, available for expression in language). So, the problem of the aesthetic means of expressing must at the same time be the problem of the aesthetic means of *thinking* – and indeed, of *existing*. Nietzsche writes, accordingly: "what meaning would *our* entire being have if not this, that in us this will to truth has come to a consciousness of itself *as a problem*?" (*Genealogy*, Third Treatise, §27). This whole analysis links to the themes of "masks" and "honesty" (the latter we will explore in Part 7), and also to our concept of "realignment". We will discuss the problem of Nietzsche's style again and often, and especially under §296.

§5

Although, in §3, Nietzsche made the claim that the consciousness of the philosopher is not in control of his or her philosophy (and thus in some sense "innocent"), in §5 he nevertheless takes philosophers to task for not having the honesty to admit that their philosophy is based on assumptions, whims or wishes. Philosophers make a "great and virtuous noise" about truth, but their claims are defended with grounds sought only after the fact. The rest of the passage is a venomous attack on Kant and Spinoza. The point is that even where philosophy *is* conscious, and not determined by hidden sources, even there it is dishonest and cowardly. This makes us suspicious, and is part of the reason why philosophy has been overshadowed by science recently (see Part 6). Not to be dishonest requires, Nietzsche says, the "good taste" or "courage of conscience" to admit the dishonesty to oneself, to others (perhaps as a warning), or to "mock" oneself. Not, notice, *to think otherwise*; this is not a call for philosophers to be honest about the truth, but rather to be honest about the deception. (Nietzsche's discussion of intellectual honesty and related issues continues throughout the book, most particularly in Part 7, "Our Virtues".)

§6

The analysis of §4 is continued in §6: all philosophy is only an involuntary or unobserved "confession" or "memoir" of its author. What produces [*ausmachen*] it (or "what it amounts to"), like a seed produces a plant, is the moral or immoral "intention" [*Absicht*]. In looking at the real basis of philosophies, Nietzsche claims, one will find, at one time or another, all the basic drives of human beings serving as the dominant intention. Each of these basic drives strives to be dominant – indeed, the notion of "drive" [*Trieb*] is, in part, defined by striving for absolute domination

[*Herrschsüchtig*]. A philosophy thus bears direct witness to who the philosopher is, in what "order of rank" [*Rangordnung*] his drives stand. There are, however, scholars who have a genuine will to knowledge that functions independently of (and not as the master of) other drives. Nietzsche will discuss such individuals further in "We Scholars" (Part 6).

We need to observe several new ideas in this passage. First of all, the close connection between a moral commitment or evaluation and the idea of "drive". (Given what has been said in the previous few sections, we can at least provisionally associate the notions of "instinct" and "drive".) Secondly, that such a drive is thought of as an intention – that is, it exhibits the properties of having a goal or end (see also the analysis of "will" in §19). This is a particularly interesting and indeed troubling claim since within philosophical thought the idea of "intention" goes hand-in-hand with consciousness or conscious willing. Here, though, we have an intention without a conscious "I" behind it; indeed, the conscious "I" appears to have intentions only derivatively, on the basis of its underlying drives. Thirdly, one key intention of any drive is to achieve mastery over other drives. This last characteristic Nietzsche famously calls the "will to power". The relative strength or mastery of drives within an individual organism (such as a philosopher) Nietzsche calls their "order of rank". "Rank" is here understood both in the sense of a position of authority and command (as in military rank), but also quality (e.g. a wine can be of the first rank).

§§7, 8

Section 7 appears to be rather a digression. Nietzsche gives his interpretation of a spiteful comment of Epicurus about Plato and his followers. The Platonists are merely actors, nothing genuine. This, evidently, Nietzsche takes as agreeing with his own description of philosophers above. Nietzsche finally asks: did, a hundred years later, the Greeks understand who this "garden god" was? (The school of Epicurus was set up in the garden of his own house in Athens; but the reference to god may be an allusion forward to the figure of Dionysus, who makes an appearance only at the very end of the book.) It would take us too far afield to try to understand what of Epicurean thought Nietzsche finds amenable to his own. Suffice it to say that, for Epicurus as for Nietzsche, the intellect is not something naturally sovereign or distinct from empirical sense and from the affects or feelings. Section 8 briefly reinforces and generalizes the claim of Epicurus: philosophy is a stage and there must be a moment where the basic "conviction" appears on it, like an ass. An ass is a stubbornly proud animal, though it has little to be proud of. For more on the analogy of a staged or ritualized mockery of the ass, see also "The Ass Festival" at the end of the fourth Part of *Zarathustra*.

§9

Section 9 continues the invective against ancient philosophy, this time the Stoics. The Stoics believed, broadly, that nature was organized rationally, and that therefore the proper way of life for a rational human being was to live "according to nature". Nietzsche attacks the conception of nature here. Nature squanders and is indifferent [*gleichgültig* – literally "of equal value"] without measure, is indifference [*Indifferenz*] itself as a power [*Macht*]. Notice that although marking the distinction is difficult in English, Nietzsche has used two distinct words for "indifferent". The first stems from "gültig", meaning to be valid, and thus meaning indifferent in the sense of being unconcerned about questions of validity, rank or value. The second derives from Latin, and means to distinguish or separate: so indifference in the sense of treating everything alike, without distinguishing. The two concepts are obviously linked for Nietzsche: the question of what values are valid for an individual has been said to be also his or her distinguishing characteristic.

Being itself without aim – and that means without a dominant drive and thus a dominant value – nature must appear utterly indifferent (in both senses) and as wasteful with respect to any aim. How, though, can indifference be a "power"? A partial solution is given in *The Gay Science*, §360. There, Nietzsche distinguishes between two types of cause: the one a quantity of built-up energy; the other a trigger that releases this energy in a particular direction. The important thing about this second cause is that it can be accidental, random and insignificant in size. It mimics, but is not, a decision or intention. If we apply this to the problem of nature as a "power", we can see that nature has a determinate and necessary *course*, an effective capacity that brings about events, but one that is quite indifferent (in both senses) and without real intention.

Life, however, must involve preferring and wanting-to-be-different, or other. This in two related senses: first, life itself wanting to be different or other to other instances of life (as in the biological notion of competition, and in Nietzsche's sense of wanting mastery). Second, life involves differentiating among other things, willing that some things be valued differently. So, Nietzsche continues, the truth of Stoicism (and indeed of all philosophies) is that they are actors and self-deceivers. Philosophies always aim to impose their values, even upon nature (though it is often thought of as independent of mind and will). This happens with all philosophies: as soon as it begins to "believe in itself" – take itself seriously – it "creates the world in its own image". And, he finishes, this cannot but happen because philosophy just consists of this tyrannical drive, the "most spiritual will to power". By "spiritual" [*geistig*], Nietzsche means concerning mind, thought or consciousness, as opposed to concerning physical states, actions, drives or instincts. Not that he is opposing these two absolutely (as in mind–body dualism) – far from it. But some drives are "made abstract and sifted" as he put it in §5.

The "will to power" is a key notion in Nietzsche. We will return to it in much more detail later, especially in §36 and the passages leading up to it. For the moment we can think of it as a general name for the fact that drives all who seek mastery: seeking to be different and assigning (and thus also seeking to impose) a value to that difference.

§10

The problem of the creation of the world in the image of the dominant drive that manifests itself in a philosophy is, in §10, modified into the problem of real versus apparent worlds. It is a problem that goes back also to ancient philosophy and, most obviously, to Plato. This problem, Nietzsche claims, occupies his contemporaries, who are eager, subtle and even "shrewd" [*Schlauheit*] concerning it. But, to interpret this eagerness as – except in exceptional cases, such as (as we saw above) the scholar, or the nihilist – a will to truth would be a mistake. (Note the standard joke-structure: the nihilists make their bed to lie on – and die. Nihilisim is anti-life for Nietzsche, and nothing could be more clear now than that Nietzsche is not a genuine nihilist, as he is often said to be.) There is here an unspoken alternative to the presumption that in this close attention there lies a genuine will to truth. The alternative must be rather: to think of the critical attention given to the real/apparent distinction as a pose for a philosophy that wishes to sustain this distinction at all costs.

There are also some contemporary philosophers, Nietzsche notes, who are "stronger [*stärker*] and more full of life", who treat the problem differently. Later in the passage he names these philosophers "sceptical anti-realists" and "knowledge-microscopists". (It is not clear who, exactly, Nietzsche might have in mind.) These philosophers argue against appearance and arrogantly use the word "perspective". Nietzsche could not, up to a point, agree more. Modern approaches to the pursuit of philosophy (especially positivism) are indeed to be rejected, but not so as to go backwards. Nietzsche accuses such philosophers of really trying to roll back the tide of modern ideas and go backwards to some previous faith. Where knowledge cannot be obtained, goes the old theological manoeuvre, there one must have faith. However, had such philosophers "more force [*Kraft*], flight, courage or artistic ability", they would will to go up and beyond [*darüberhinaus*]. They would attempt to live within the notion of perspective, rather than using it as a tool in the service of an old faith. Notice that I have translated "*Kraft*" as "force" rather than, as is more common, "strength". This is to mark a distinction from a different word for strength above:

starker, meaning stronger. *"Kraft"* is the technical term used within physics for "force". In various contexts, though, the two words can be used interchangeably, and it is unclear whether Nietzsche is making a distinction here, or just using two words to express the same idea.

It is worth noting a common tactic on Nietzsche's part: namely, to agree definitively with one part of someone's position, and disagree equally strongly with some other part. We will see this particularly clearly with respect to the figures of Socrates and Plato; and we have already noted it in the case of Kant for whom Nietzsche generally expresses contempt *while at the same time* employing Kantian ideas or types of argument. A related strategy would be to assign a simple property to something, and then, elsewhere, assign a different property to the same thing. (Nietzsche will do just this in discussing the Jewish and German peoples in Part 8.)

These approaches have two related consequences. First, it is dangerous to assert that Nietzsche himself either is or is not an X – where X is a type of philosopher, or a figure typically holding some position (e.g. a nihilist). Or, similarly, that Nietzsche himself either approves or disapproves of some X. There are too many possible approaches to an idea, period, people or philosophy for Nietzsche's relation to it ever to be simple. For example: he might be analysing it in terms of its historical dependence upon some basic metaphysical or moral prejudice, or in terms of a historical consequence; he might be diagnosing it as a particular kind of psychological or physiological condition (e.g. self-deception); he might be asking how it can be made use of to further certain ambitions (cf. the "gratitude" of the Preface); he might be employing rhetorical exaggerations to achieve certain effects; or, finally, he might be evaluating it as a *relatively* healthy or favourable perspective. This list is not exhaustive, and one can find examples of all these ways of considering philosophers, periods, peoples or ideas in this text. The basic rule of thumb is: because Nietzsche's approach requires us to synthesize complex pictures from many simple pictures, to quote Nietzsche is to misunderstand Nietzsche.

Secondly, it introduces a new methodological element to our reading of philosophy. There is no necessity to the assumption that philosophical systems are truly systematic, such that one must accept all or reject all. Rather, because the individual that produced them (and the intellectual environment from within which he or she wrote) is to be considered a collection of drives or instincts (though certainly one may be dominant for a time), so the product (philosophical texts) may consist of many voices. We may also consider this a warning not automatically to expect systematic philosophical rigour from Nietzsche's work itself – while at the same time not exempting us from searching for it. On the other hand, we get an apparently contradictory statement in §20: philosophical concepts are not in isolation, but exist in complex inter-determinations. These determinations, though, need not be of logical entailment, or even conscious deliberation. Moreover, they may cross the boundaries between philosophers of the most diverse kinds. For example, we have already seen Nietzsche suggest that there are moral beliefs at work in the basic preconditions of science. Similarly, we have just seen Nietzsche suggest that the most "modern" sceptics and scholars are secretly allied (it may be a secret even from them) to the most ancient theologians. Philosophies may indeed be *systematic* in nature, but by no means in the ways their authors believe them to be, or would even recognize as legitimate system. Philosophical concepts exist in monstrous networks of inter-determination that do not respect boundaries. Nietzsche is concerned to track these "monsters" wherever they may lead.

§11

Section 11 is a famous critique of Kant. This time, though, not Kant's moral philosophy, which was attacked in §5, but the "theoretical" philosophy. By this is meant Kant's account of the underlying conditions of knowledge and experience. Kant's analysis of these conditions took the form of a study of the principles governing the activity of the "faculties" – that is, the operations of the mind. Nietzsche's critique is simple: what is gained by claiming that one has discovered a "faculty"? Nothing, he answers. The real question of how something happens (how, for example, we come to assert that something is true) is not answered, just pushed back. The question is just repeated in a different form. He jokingly quotes the comic playwright Molière that opium causes sleep because of a "sleep-causing virtue" in it. This is not an answer, just a different name for the problem. (We will not here consider whether Nietzsche's famous critique of the notion of "faculty" in fact involves a misunderstanding, perhaps a deliberate one, of Kant's thought.)

However, the critique of Kant is accompanied by Nietzsche's description of German philosophy after Kant: youthful, full of energy and enthusiasm, looking for new faculties in the "bushes". We've grown up since then, Nietzsche claims – and moreover no worse injustice could be done to such youth and energy than to take it seriously. Nietzsche's new question, addressed to Kant's basic question of "how are synthetic *a priori* judgements possible?" is "Why is belief in such judgements *necessary*?" And the answer returns us to the problems of the conditions of life. Such judgements are not held because they are true – we have no legitimate entitlement to such judgements – nevertheless they must be believed in. They belong to the "perspectival optics of life" – a reference back to the optical metaphor with which Nietzsche introduced the general notion of perspective in §2.

However, Nietzsche is being disingenuous here. Although Kant famously expressed his basic question in terms of possibility, elsewhere he makes two claims that accord with Nietzsche's own. First, Kant argues that it is characteristic of a synthetic *a priori* judgement to be necessary in two different ways: first, the truth claim in such a judgement must appear to be necessary; secondly, such judgements are necessary for any experience and consciousness whatsoever. That is, such judgements are not ones that we sometimes make (or perhaps only philosophers make) but rather lie underneath *all* other judgements as their condition. Moreover, Kant argues that such judgements are necessarily true only for such beings as we are. In other words, although necessary for us they would look contingent for another type of being whose relation to the world was not just different from ours in some detail, but structured entirely differently. Kant's candidate for this other being, if it exists at all, is God. The divine intellect is not simply a magnified – even infinitely magnified – version of the human intellect.

The problem that Kant and Nietzsche have in common can be expressed in this way: "What is the thinking that can look outside the conditions of thinking, and judge what is necessary for it such that it could in fact be false or contingent?" We have already seen Nietzsche address this problem, for it is closely related to the problem of Sphinx and Oedipus. That is: "How is it possible for thought to look outside the value of truth in order to ask the question of the value of the will to truth?" The problem is the problem of the *outside*. Kant has an answer to this problem (although of course it may not be an adequate one). He distinguishes between natural knowledge – knowledge of things outside and within the mind – and transcendental knowledge – knowledge of *how the first type comes to be*. If transcendental knowledge reveals that all natural knowledge depends upon a distinction – between, say, how objects are in themselves, and how they manifest themselves to human beings – then it becomes possible to speculate concerning another type of being whose knowledge does not rely upon that distinction.

Equivalently, we find Nietzsche here apparently making a distinction between the kinds of beliefs that human beings must hold true, and knowledge concerning why those beliefs must be held to be true (because holding them to be true is a condition of continued life). The former, for example, would be certain metaphysical oppositions; the latter would be the answer to the question of what is the value of those oppositions. But the latter type of knowledge also makes possible speculation concerning types of being who would no longer have to hold certain beliefs to be true, perhaps because such beings were a different form of life; or just because such beings are able to hold themselves at a distance from such holding-to-be-true, and treat such beliefs mockingly or ironically, perhaps, or as gambits in a game, or suspend them temporarily. Please also have a look back at the discussion of perspective and interpretation in §2; and we will return to the discussion in §22.

§12

This section is about atomism, both the metaphysical version that dates to the ancient world, and the more modern version in the sciences of chemistry and physics. Nietzsche takes this theory to have been refuted, although one can still use it as a "handy tool or domestic convenience" – this is explained as meaning an "abbreviation". He ascribes the refutation to Boscovich (an eighteenth-century physicist). Significantly, he adds that Boscovich and Copernicus have been the most "successful opponents" of visual evidence. Again, we are back to the optical analogy: the blinkered perspective that takes what happens to be near (or most evident visually) for what is in itself true or valuable. The analogy is clearest in the case of Copernicus: visual evidence (basing one's assumptions on what is nearest and most self-evident) supports the Earth at the centre of the solar system, with the sun, planets and stars all moving around it; Copernicus argued against common sense for a sun-centred model. (It is sometimes asked "what would it *look like* if visual common sense suggested that the Earth does orbit the sun?" The only available (that is, observable) model for such a satellite is the moon, which is in a synchronically rotating orbit – it constantly keeps the same face to the Earth. If that were true of the Earth, the sun would not "move" in the sky at all. I mention this only because several passages in the book suggest Nietzsche had a keen interest in astronomy, if only as a symbol.)

Since it is a refuted theory so far as the explicit claims made by contemporary physics, Nietzsche continues, atomism is most dangerous when not explicit, when acting below the surface, as an "atomistic need". That is to say, when a mode of thinking with close analogies to physical atomism keeps showing up in other areas of thought. His key example is the Christian idea of the soul, considered to be atom-like in its separability, foundational unity, incorruptibility or immortality. Nietzsche then playfully adds an aside: "Just between ourselves" – as if no one who has no right to overhear were listening – we do not have to dispense with the idea of soul entirely. Rather, there are new non-atomistic accounts of the soul that might still be philosophically useful. His examples are: (i) a mortal, instead of immortal soul. Thus, a soul that is not atomistic in so far as it is not indestructible; (ii) the soul as the multiplicity of the subject [*Subjekts-Vielheit*]. Here, then, the soul is not atomistic in so far as it is not being identified with the logical subject of predication. We should compare Descartes's account of the substantial soul as the absolute and always identical subject of all mental predicates. Finally, (iii), the soul as the social structure of drives and affects [*Gesellschaftsbau der Triebe und Affekte*]. The soul is not atomistic because it is not unitary or simple. Notice, significantly, in the last of these, the intriguing implication that the concept of the social is more fundamental than the concept of the individual; Nietzsche is clearly no individualist in a straightforward sense! Here, these alternative models of soul are not further elaborated. However, one implication of the last two examples is clear enough: the apparent unity of the soul is *an effect of* a multiplicity, or of the inter-relationships, of drives or affects. We will return to these ideas often enough, and especially in our interpretation of §56.

The psychologist working with these new ideas is condemned to invention [*Erfinden*], or discovery [*Finden*]. This is a pun: the German originals of these two words have the same root; we have seen the same pun before in §11. Notice, however, that the sense of the pun as employed in §§11 and 12 is different: in the former, Nietzsche seems to be chiding those philosophers who followed Kant for not knowing the difference between invention (making things up) and discovery (noticing and describing what is actually there). In the latter, he seems to be claiming that a new psychologist – such as it would seem he himself wants to be – *will have to make things up*, and perhaps by chance this fiction will turn out to be true. However, it could be that Nietzsche's point concerns rather the intimate relation between discovery and invention. For example, in the scientific method we discussed in analysing the Preface, hypothesis precedes the gathering of evidence that might show it to be true or false. There is, then, a delay in time between the new idea (the hypothesis that is invented) and the ability to "know the difference" between invention and discovery, and thus determine the truth or falsehood of the hypothesis. This time delay – the hypothesis being too early or too late for truth – becomes an important general theme for Nietzsche, echoing the title of an earlier book: *Untimely Meditations*. Here, most obviously, we have the theme of the philosopher of the future, who is yet to come, the mere idea of which appears scandalous or mad in the present.

Moreover, looking again at §11, did not Nietzsche also chide "us" for taking too seriously the youthful exuberance of the post-Kantian German philosophers? It now becomes clear why Nietzsche has composed §11 as he has, with the emphasis not so much on the criticism of Kant's notion of "faculty", as on how Kant's influence is to be understood. Perhaps the real criticism is not of those who do not know the difference between invention and discovery, but rather of us, *who have come too late*, or have grown too old, and thus believe we know. The "new psychologist" will inaugurate a new period of youthfulness (compare §94). This theme of a *new* mode of youthfulness again clearly ties in with the notion of being "untimely", mentioned above.

§13

The brief Section 13 is a criticism addressed to Darwin and evolution theory. For Nietzsche, the core of evolution theory is the assumption that living organisms will to survive, both as individuals, and in the form of passing on inherited or new traits. Only then can the mechanism of "survival of the fittest" work as the engine of evolution. All living beings will to survive; it tends to be the case that those fit for survival do survive; therefore, over time, the traits that favour survival win out. This section argues that the drive to survive, to self-preserve, is derivative although common. More primordial is the will to power, which could just as well manifest itself in a self-*destructive* act of a *discharge* of strength. (See also *Twilight of the Idols*, "Skirmishes of an Untimely Man", §14.) When Nietzsche spoke about the "conditions of life" earlier, therefore, we should not hear this with entirely Darwinian ears. The issue is not *primarily* about the conditions of the survival or preservation of life – but rather the conditions for the existence of a certain type of life as will to power. Some types of life, to be sure, may concern themselves with survival. Often, however, Nietzsche will later tell us, those concerned with survival are not the fittest or highest, but precisely the lowest – and even then not because of survival *per se*, but because this is a way of attaining dominance. (See Zarathustra's "Prologue", §5: "His race is as ineradicable as a beetle; the last man lives longest".)

There is also a briefly made methodological point in this section. A general methodological principle is the "economy of principles" – economy here in the sense of being thrifty with. This is by no means unique to Nietzsche, and is related to what in philosophy is often referred to as Ockham's razor. In fact, in §11, we already saw Nietzsche criticizing Kant and his followers for violating just this methodological principle. By employing the language of "faculties" to try to solve epistemological problems, Nietzsche argued, Kant was a spendthrift with principles, questions, names. Plenty of everything – except any real answers.

In the particular case of "survival" as a drive, Nietzsche is warning about "*superfluous* teleological principles". A teleological principle would be one that describes something in terms of its end or goal. Thus, having survival as a goal would be a teleological description of life. Now, it may well be that the will to power is a teleological principle; power *looks like* the goal of all willing; and this would be *in addition to* the specific content of the drive (towards sex, artistic expression, etc.). But, since it includes within itself the possibility of manifesting itself as survival, at least we do not need to posit the goal of survival separately (and thus superfluously). (We will return to the question of whether the will to power is itself teleological in §36.) There may be another superfluous principle here, incidentally: following the work of Malthus, Darwin universalized the principle of the scarcity of resources relative to an expanding population, and this puts a pressure on population for survival. From Nietzsche's angle, though, it is only *because* there exists a particular form of life whose will to power manifests itself in a survival drive that *consequently* there will be scarcity of resources in nature. Scarcity is not a neutral description, but one that assumes a value. From the perspective of different forms of life, nature is "wasteful and indifferent beyond measure", and both "fertile" and "desolate", as we saw in §9.

§14

This section returns to physics, touched upon earlier with the problem of atomism. Here, Nietzsche is generalizing: all physics is a "world-interpretation" [*Auslegung*] and "-arrangement" [*Zurechtlegung*]. The second of these two terms is difficult to translate, but the main thing is to notice that again Nietzsche is playing with the common root: *legen*, meaning to lay something down. So, interpretation is to "lay out", and arrangement is to "lay down so as to add up to something". This interpretation and arrangement, as we might expect, is "*nach uns!*", meaning according to us, but with a suggestion of "in our image". This interpretation is contrasted with a "world-explanation" [*Erklärung*]. One way of thinking through what Nietzsche means by this distinction is to say that physics finds or even invents patterns in nature, but does not actually understand them. This idea of merely observing order in phenomena without pretending to explain it by reference to some underlying reality is indeed explicit in the nineteenth-century positivism of Comte, and no doubt Nietzsche has this in mind. However, what is interpreted and arranged is sensible data – what we see, hear, touch. And, we moderns have a basic belief [*Glaube*] in the validity of the senses – indeed, we believe that explanation itself consists of pointing to sensible evidence. From all this, it follows that in spite of the basic principles of positivism, this merely interpretative nature of physics is overlooked (even by positivists) and is thought to be explanation.

That is because the commitment to observable phenomena in positivism is not a value-neutral commitment; positivism is a spiritualized version of "eternally popular sensualism". We must hear a derogatory tone in "*Volkstümlich*" [popular]; this basic belief of our age is, Nietzsche claims, a fundamentally "plebeian taste". He contrasts it with the "*noble* way of thinking" [*vornehme Denkweise*] of Plato, who resisted the senses, and believed the way to solve problems and explain phenomena lay in "cold" "nets of concepts". (We have seen Nietzsche discuss, and apparently approve of, a similar resistance to sensual and specifically visual evidence in the section on atomism.) This distinction between plebeian and noble is important for Nietzsche – and indeed Part 9 is entitled "What is Noble?"

Notice, however, that Nietzsche is not siding with Plato; he is not a Platonist. The situation is very much like the discussion of the various forms of scepticism in §10. Nietzsche's relations to other philosophers are generally very nuanced. Nietzsche finds "noble" the resistance to the unthinking belief in the senses – it is as if Plato had correctly identified a problem – but finds the Platonic *solution to this problem* unsatisfactory. Moreover, the Platonic approach is not just different to the tastes of the modern age, but also unsuitable. The proposition that "Where man has nothing more to see and grasp then also he has nothing more to seek" is entirely valid for that future "race" [*Geschlecht*] of the future with "dirty" [*grob* – can also mean "coarse" or "rough"] work to do.

The biological term "*Geschlecht*" clues us in to what is at stake here: distinct modes of life, ultimately distinct dominant drives exhibiting their will to power. Thus, the belief in the senses, or the "resistance" to them, is a basic proposition necessary for certain modes of life – modes that Nietzsche has described with the terms "plebeian" and "noble". It follows that (to return to the notion of interpretation with which the passage begins) Platonism is no less a failure to explain, no less an interpretation, and finally no less an interpretation that is "*nach uns!*" – made in the image of a mode of life. It is only that its first gesture – its first instinct: the resistance to the senses – is what Nietzsche feels is most required now, and in the future he describes.

§15

Within idealistic philosophy (that of Kant and those following Kant), a "phenomenon" is that which appears to us as a part of nature, and accordingly dominated above all by the concept of cause and effect. But others (this is an idealist position, though not Kant's) argue that the external world is a product of our sense organs – the world is an effect, sense organs the cause. But, if the sense organs were a part of that world then our sense organs would be the cause of themselves. Assuming, Nietzsche concludes, that the "*causa sui*" – something that is the cause of itself – is absurd, then he has just performed a *reductio ad absurdum* on idealistic thought. (That is, he has shown that the position has absurd consequences and therefore cannot be true.) If the sense organs are not phenomena, then they cannot be causes (because they do not belong to the order of natural things). So, the world is not a product of our sense organs.

But what then are we to conclude: perhaps that the external world exists *only as sense*, sense appearance without a "that which appears as sense" behind it? "Sensualism, therefore, at least as a regulative hypothesis, if not as a heuristic principle." "What?", Nietzsche writes, in mock horror at his own idea. Such a sensualism – as a regulative or heuristic claim, not as a *truth claim* – would be akin to the "flattening" of illusory perspective in §2. The external world might *appear* as though it has depth but actually, like the painting, it is only a flat surface of sense. Accordingly, the last question "the external world is not a product of our organs – ?" is a tease. The world *is* a product, in the sense that the illusion of an independent and substantial world is created by the "perspectival optics of life"; the world *is not* a product, however, in the sense that it *is not at all*, if by "world" we mean substances, causes, discrete bodies – that is, the world populated by the metaphysical entities Nietzsche has been discussing throughout Part 1.

Does this not contradict Nietzsche's apparent approval of the first instinct of Platonism: to resist the senses? Moreover, how does this "sensualism" relate to plebeian sensualism alluded to in §14? Nietzsche's reply, we can speculate, would be that surely it is possible to be *something like* a sensualist, in the above described manner, without also having to be the *slave* of the senses. Back in §14 we read that the charm of Plato's way of thinking is felt by those who may have had stronger and more sensitive sense organs but who "knew how to find a higher triumph in remaining masters of their senses". Sensualism, as a hypothesis, is not in itself a metaphysical- or value-commitment by the Nietzschean physiologist, but is employed as a tool. Moreover, it may have a further instrumental value in so far as it leads to a revised notion of appearance. This notion of "leading to" should remind us of the distinctively Kantian idea of "regulation" (see our discussion in the Preface); and, indeed, Nietzsche uses the term in this section. (We will discuss Nietzsche's notion of appearance more closely in §34.)

Of more general interest here is that sensualism and positivism, although in themselves indicative of a plebeian taste and interest, are nevertheless part of the broad historical movement of Europe's Christian-Democratic culture becoming exhausted. In direct analogy to their instrumental use within philosophy is their furthering of the historical process by which this old culture will finally be able to overcome itself, and something else emerge. Thus, as Nietzsche says in the Preface, we should be grateful. The analogy between the philosophical self-overcoming within an individual soul, and Europe's self-overcoming of its inherited forms of life, is not an accident. Accordingly, for Nietzsche, there is a tight relation between philosophical methodology and metaphysical critique, on the one hand – this is primarily what he is up to here in Part 1 – and the social and political questions he turns to later in the book.

§16

This section is primarily an argument against the Cartesian tradition of philosophy. Descartes, who posed for himself the possibility of a truly radical scepticism, argued that there was one thing about which he could be absolutely and immediately certain: that I think (a proposition which, he felt, contained also the proposition "I exist"). Nietzsche, however, argues that there are any number of subtle and difficult questions that would need to be answered before Descartes's immediate certainty could be accepted. More seriously still, there is a *contradictio in adjecto* – a contradiction between the adjective "immediate" and the noun "certainty". In order to be certain of something, Nietzsche argues, I have to know what it is. And this knowing must involve the process of comparing it to something else that I already know – in this case, comparing what I am doing *now* with what I know to be "thinking", in order to be certain that what I am doing *now* is, indeed, thinking. Thus, this arrival at certainty is a mediated process. Accordingly, more generally, what is certain could never be so *immediately*. (However, at this point at least Descartes can reply: it does not matter what I am doing – whether thinking, feeling willing or whatever – because what is immediately certain is that I am doing something, and that is enough. Nietzsche would have to reconstruct his argument to deal with "doing" in general rather than thought in particular.) This section inaugurates a series of reflections in the subsequent sections on thinking, willing and associated notions.

§17

In this section, Nietzsche is developing a common theme in his work: the relationship between grammatical or other linguistic structures, and commonly (and tightly) held beliefs. In this case, the fact that "I" is a pronoun and "think" a verb that attaches to it, as its activity, is seen as one key reason why otherwise perceptive philosophers continue to believe in the kinds of Cartesian ideas we discussed in §16. In contrast, Nietzsche asserts that "a thought arrives when 'it' wishes, not when 'I' wish". Even when we try to empty the "I" of content and say merely that it or something thinks, that is too much, and already an interpretation of the process inspired by grammar.

Nietzsche makes a link back to the problem of atomism. He writes that the "older atomism sought for every 'force' that effects, that lump of matter wherein the force resides". Atomists thus felt compelled to trace force back to the "earth that remains" [*Erdenrest*, see §12] – matter or substance that is the seat of force but itself unchanging – being unable to conceive of force otherwise. In other words, the basic grammar of propositions (subject and object) influenced an interpretation of the physical world that exhibited a similar "grammar": substance is subject, force and its effect is the object. This is a particular manner in which physics generally is an interpretation "*nach uns*", according to us or in our image.

This analysis is an example of Nietzsche's broadly historical method: to focus less on the truth or falsity of an idea, but rather on the conditions that led to its emergence as a dominant idea. (Please see the discussion above under §2, and again below under §23.) In this case, the condition is the common, underlying grammatical structure of a set of languages. As we explained in §2, this historical analysis does not necessarily serve as a disproof of the idea, but is at least calling it into suspicion. Likewise, we should think about the conditions under which we can become "accustomed" to do without the grammatical subject "it", and what implications this may have.

§18

This curious little section concerns free will. Nietzsche is not interested here in arguing for or against free will. Rather, he slyly assumes that it has been refuted many times over. But, refuting it once again is not a mark of weakness or obsession – rather, of the feeling of strength. Again, as with atomism (§12), we might suspect that the reason for this is that the "theory" of free will lives on surreptitiously as an assumption, in other discourses as an analogy, and as a refuge. Thus, the capacity to raise oneself to a whole-hearted refutation of it must mean also possessing the strength to abandon this assumption and the "refuge" it provides. Nietzsche will go one better: provide a discussion of the will that completely sidesteps the problem of *proving* either free will or determinism as traditionally treated. This discussion is §19.

§19, and discussion of affect

Just like the "I" that thinks, the will is not immediately available to inspection, as even Schopenhauer (who had been one of Nietzsche's philosophical heroes earlier in his career) believed. The "will" is only one word (there is the influence of our language, again), but actually an extremely complex set of phenomena. Nietzsche lists four constituent elements.

First, the will consists of a set of feelings [*Gefühle*]: the feeling of the state away from which (the state I am in now that I will be changed; e.g. hunger), the state towards which (eating or satiated), and the feelings of this away and towards. Moreover, there is a habituated feeling of the muscles, even without their actual movement. Secondly, in every act of will there is a "commanding thought". This thought is not separable from the willing, but is integral to it. Thirdly, the will is above all else an "affect" [*Affect*] of command. What is often called free will is the consciousness of the "affect of superiority" with respect to someone or something that must obey. The fourth component is that in willing we are both commanding and obeying.

As in obeying, we feel compulsion, force, necessity. But these passive feelings are ignored (or externalized – as when I say "my body is feeling tired today") because, as we saw earlier, there is a deeply held belief in the unity of the "I". This leaves only the affects of superiority and command. For that reason, one believes that the willing suffices for the action, that there is indeed no difference between willing and acting. This is equivalent to saying that the will is free, not constrained or at least capable on its own of overcoming constraints. In willing one thus "enjoys an increase in the feeling of power that accompanies all success".

In short, the body (including what we call the mind) is a social structure of many souls (that is, many drives, desires, needs). And, as in any "well-constructed and happy community . . . the ruling class identifies itself with the successes of the community". There is, then, the deceptive (but also useful) appearance of a single, unitary will substituting itself for the complex relations of feeling, thinking, commanding and obeying within the "social structure" of the self. Accordingly, for Nietzsche, the phenomenon of willing is necessarily a moral phenomenon: that is, it concerns itself with the "relations of domination under which the phenomenon 'life' arises". Note that there is a similar discussion of will in *The Gay Science*, §127; there, interestingly, the thought of the simplicity and effectiveness of will is explicitly ascribed to "the oldest religiosity".

Incidentally, it is worth asking whether Nietzsche has in mind a clear-cut distinction between "feeling" and "affect". Why, that is, is the "affect" of superiority or command not classed with the first group of feelings? The word "affect" is a particularly tricky one in the history of philosophy. The tradition of thought that Nietzsche seems to be employing here defines affect as a disturbance or "stirring" of the soul caused by a relation to something outside it, and which tends to lead to, or indeed already is, action (Nietzsche's examples in *The Gay Science* passage cited above are "defence, revenge, retribution"). So, here, the first group of feelings are (or at least appear to be) neutral or "objective" presentations of *definite* states or movements. Feelings do not immediately give rise to action. On the other hand, the "affects" involve values, and in particular the value of "superior to" and "this is what must be done" (i.e. this is the good) – such a valuation is in itself an action, even if in other ways it is "passive" (like "defence"; and see §192). The affect also has an object – that is, it is directed to something, in this case to "what must obey" – but an object interpreted relative to (in this case superior) force. While a feeling is a feeling of X, the affect is "directed to" its X; it is in other words a particular manifestation of a drive or of its relation to other drives. Then, later, that part of us which obeys is said to manifest itself again in "feeling": that which feels constraint is not feeling *its own* evaluation, *its own* will to power. So, although "feeling" might appear to be the more fundamental, immediate datum, this is an illusion. "Feeling" appears to be value-neutral, and disengaged from will, only because it has been interpreted in that way. A feeling is an abstracted part of a reaction to a basic affect. Talking about the "affects" or the "system of the affects", then, is an account of how the human organism responds to its environment, whether physically or intellectually, but in any case characterized by "valuing".

On the other hand, the affect itself is a spiritualization of the *immediate* evaluation of the will to power that constitutes a drive. We will have to return to the idea of spiritualization, but for now we can say that it means: the evaluation that constitutes a particular drive "raised" to consciousness as an idea, and the idea appearing "in itself" and independent of its origin. Here, the idea is that "I command" and the affect of commanding (perhaps even the affect that this commanding is right or just), which we can detach from the whole problem of a complex of forces, and a particular situation, and think of as "free will" and my consciousness of freedom. Although there is in this spiritualization a detachment of the idea or affect from its relational origin, Nietzsche wishes to argue that that which we call "freedom" is actually a disguised relational affect of having power over this or that.

In §21 below, Nietzsche turns to the notion of "unfree will", a will caught in the net of determinism. The point is similar there, but it leads him from a discussion of the affect of freedom to the metaphysical problem of the nature of causation.

§20

Although he is not yet using the term, the idea of "spiritualization" dominates §20 too. Ideas appear to be separate, but are actually part of a primitive or primordial system of interrelated ideas. All philosophers "discover" – in fact merely remember (the reference is to the idea of *anamnesis* in Plato) – some aspect of this system. Accordingly, the "family resemblance" of Western philosophies goes hand in hand with the commonness of grammar of Western languages; and philosophy outside these bounds will look "into the world" differently. Nietzsche encourages us to ask: what lies behind these determining grammatical functions? "The spell of *physiological* value judgements and racial conditions" – what we have been calling a particular mode of life. There is a two-way reinforcement here: a language and its grammar emerge because of the physiology of a group or type (see also §268); the language, however, subtly influences belief systems that strengthen the type (thus the idea of "breeding").

Nietzsche also takes this analysis to be directly opposed to the empiricism of Locke, for whom the individual (not to mention the class or race!) was "blank" prior to its exposure to empirical sensation. That is, for Locke, if we look differently into the world that can only be because individuals or groups have had different experiences. For Nietzsche, in contrast, there is a physiological inheritance that tends (innately, if you will – as is suggested by the reference to Plato) towards a particular manner of interpreting the world, and itself (see for example §264).

§21

The idea of *causa sui* – to be the cause of oneself – is (as Nietzsche has already claimed) an outrageous absurdity. Here again it is equated with the idea of free will. One "exonerates" God, the world, one's parents and ancestors, one's culture or race of one's actions and indeed one's being – and takes sole responsibility for existence, as if "to pull oneself out of the swamp of nothingness and into existence, by the hair".

But there is a similar and still more common mistake, which is to reject such free will in favour of an "unfree will". The problem here is that we "reify" cause and effect. These are useful concepts, to be sure, but interpret rather than explain. The guilty party here is science, who thinks of a cause as a separate "thing" that pushes until some *thing* else emerges, the effect. In the "in-itself", Nietzsche claims, there is no separation of these, no "following from" according to some law of cause and effect – no rule of law at all. Like the free will, the unfree will is a mistake and a myth: it is rather a matter of strong and weak wills. (See *Genealogy*, First Treatise, §13 – there Nietzsche argues that will is and must be willing; that is, it is expenditure and relation. It is a metaphysical mistake to separate the potential (I am free, I *can* will) from the actuality (I will).)

So, then, these ideas are interpretations – which means evaluations of the order as which the world is viewed. An evaluation is a function, the key function, of a mode of life. Therefore, the question naturally arises for Nietzsche: what kind of person would feel the need to believe in freedom or unfreedom? Those who wish to take responsibility for everything belong to the "vain races"; they condition themselves to feel the affect of command. Those who wish to take responsibility for nothing are weak and driven by an inner self-contempt. Nietzsche singles out socialists as his key example of the latter. Note, though, that socialism has its "good taste" (but also note the inverted commas) which makes it "astonishingly attractive".

§22, and discussion of perspective and interpretation, part 2

This section returns to natural science, especially physics. Nietzsche again accuses science, in so far as it speaks of "law", of being merely interpretation and, indeed, bad interpretation. We raised the notion of natural law in the previous section. Significantly, Nietzsche's own professional training was in philology – a term not much in use any more but which meant the scientific investigation of the history and meaning of texts and of language. A philologist, then, would consider herself an expert in the science of interpretation.

We must ask why Nietzsche considers this notion of "conformity to law" a "bad" interpretation of the "text" of nature? First of all, Nietzsche seems to insist that nature is not a "text" in the first place. The notion of the "book of nature" is a venerable one in the history of philosophy and science. Perhaps Nietzsche means by this that nature is not analogous to some kind of written document, not a set of signs with meanings. That would be to humanize nature (this humanization is mentioned again later in the passage), to treat nature as if it were related to, or a product of, the human. Consequently, even to think of nature as a text for interpretation is already to interpret badly. But, there are two other reasons why this interpretation is "bad" that take us back to the problem of perspective in §2. First, there is a general principle (although it is not directly stated here by Nietzsche) that *any interpretation that does not understand itself as interpretation is by that very fact a "bad" interpretation*. We have already employed this principle, for example in looking at the first sentences of the preface and asking what makes a dogmatist dogmatic; we will look in more detail at this point shortly. Moreover, Nietzsche insists that this is an obvious case of an evaluative perspective influencing the reading. The idea of a law of nature, a law that deals equally with all natural objects – that is a modern notion of democracy or democratic justice that has been imposed upon nature. This should remind us of the discussion of Stoicism in §9, and the "*nach uns*" of §14.

Someone else could interpret the "same phenomena" differently (notice that Nietzsche most certainly does not say "same text", although he does later say "read"). Nature is the "tyrannically ruthless and relentless execution of power claims". This interpreter would envision the "the without-exception and the unconditional in all 'will to power'". And this would be so vivid that any expression of this other interpretation in words (in a new text) would be insufficient – it would be "too human". Again, nature is so inhuman that not only can it not be understood as a text (texts are what human beings write and read), but any text that tries to capture this inhumanness could only do so by way of the detour of metaphors based upon human phenomena (e.g. tyranny, ruthlessness).

Nietzsche continues, however, by saying that this other interpretation would agree with "you" (he is still addressing "you physicists") that the world has a "necessary" and "calculable" [*berechenbar*] course. Within the physics of Nietzsche's era, nature was understood to be "necessary" in that every natural object was determined to act in accordance with universal laws; the same laws also rendered the events of nature "calculable" – that is, one could predict outcomes. (Because of more recent theories in physics, such as quantum mechanics and complexity theory, this is no longer so appropriate a description of the basic understanding of nature in physics). By "law" is meant a description of the basic and universal constitution of nature. It is the universality that perturbs Nietzsche here, not least because universality in combination with law makes the whole a ridiculous analogy of morality. The world, as this *other* interpretation would have it, however, is also necessary and calculable, not because of "laws", but because of the complete lack of laws so that "every power at every moment draws its utmost consequences".

"You", the physicists, will feel compelled to object that this, too, is only an interpretation. "Well then, so much the better." Better, because by treating it as an interpretation you are at least accepting the basic principle of interpretation or perspective. Better, again, because you will likewise be accepting the related proposition that nature or the world are not "texts", and that interpretive texts written about them are irredeemably human documents.

Nevertheless, does Nietzsche wish to place these two (and any other) interpretations side-by-side, and treat them all equally? That would be to evade the question of their truth. On the one hand, as we saw already in §1, Nietzsche is indeed interested in truth much less than in the *value of the will to truth*. These two interpretations would be case studies in understanding how certain kinds of truth claims – and even the belief in truth itself – benefit certain forms of life. So, we could become dispassionate spectators of various types of interpretation, various perspectives, and thus various ways in which life can be structured by the domination of one drive's will to power. We would collect and catalogue these perspectives and treat them all equally. But this very passage warns us against the idea of such equal treatment, as being a plebeian, democratic instinct. That is to say, the "dispassionate" or objective study of perspective would be to interpret the problem of perspective *according to a perspective*: namely, the perspective typical both of modern, democratic, European man, and of physics with its absolutely universal laws. In discussing §1, we argued that there was an interesting problem, perhaps a paradox, in Nietzsche's approach – one that he acknowledges. This is the problem of how one makes truth claims about the value of the will to truth. Now, we have encountered a mirror-image of this problem: how does one make value claims about the truth of values? Or, this same problem expressed in the terms we were using just above: how should one interpret the various interpretations of the world?

This raises a problem for Nietzsche's notion of a "typology" of morals and values, proposed at the beginning of Part 5. Nietzsche's solution is that such an assembly of data might well be a start; the problem is that on its own this scholarly activity would make possible but would not constitute even an asking of the fundamental question of morality. Accordingly, he praises the virtues of scholars thus far and no further, in Part 6. Also, there is a relation between this moral, democratic idea of equality in the collection of data on perspective, and the seeing with "many eyes" we discussed under §2 above. Again, the former may be the condition of the latter – and for that we should be grateful – but it is not the same as being the new philosopher towards which Nietzsche is working. Similarly, the sensualism Nietzsche discusses in §§14–15 is not a metaphysically satisfactory solution to the problem of appearance, but might lead toward one.

There is an important additional difference between the two interpretations of nature or the world sketched in §22, and this is the "principle" we spoke of above. Nietzsche argues that the first interpreter, the physicist, is self-deceptive or deluded. That is, he is unaware of the fact that his moral values are conditioning his view of the world (and, indeed, that his underlying physiology is conditioning those moral values). Accordingly, he is unaware that there is a contradiction: the very "objectivity" and "universality of law" that he demands in science is belied by the subjective and parochial values he imposes upon nature. Moreover, the first interpreter *could not* become aware of this: it is an ontological impossibility for the type of being he is *thoroughly or authentically* to acknowledge the perspectival nature of his world-view. Without an alteration in the basic structure of his drives, he would at best be "acting" the acknowledgement of perspective. The idea of the "actor" – someone whose works and words reflect values that they do not, cannot, actually hold – is an important concept in Nietzsche's book (see especially §205).

The second interpreter, though, is under no such illusions. To the extent it is possible, at least, she is fully aware of the physiological underpinning of her moral beliefs, and of how these in turn make necessary a certain way of understanding the world. But just as the first interpreter's blindness or "frog perspective" was no accident, but a product of the type of organic being he is, so here this lack of illusion is also no accident. This philosopher has realigned her whole understanding of herself and the world to the notion of will to power. *And she approves of all this*: there is no contradiction between values, modes of interpretation and the interpretative result. Her mode of life is the ground of her values – and thus of her interpretations – as it is ultimately the ground of any set of values and interpretations. Accordingly, the phrase "she is fully aware" is saying too much: the Socratic injunction to know oneself is already an interpretation of what it means to know and be a self. What could it matter if I happened to be *conscious* of the physiological ground of my evaluations? What benefit would accrue if I sought them out, even assuming that is possible? Rather, the point is whether there is a thorough realignment of my organic being and my interpretations. "Honesty" is meant primarily *ontologically* rather than epistemologically.

However, *life itself cannot be valued*, Nietzsche insists (*Twilight of the Idols*, "The Problem of Socrates", §2; and "Morality as Anti-Nature", §5; the reasoning is given in "The Four Great Errors", §8). Life cannot be valued because it exists as a valuing. This suggests that beyond the notions of health, nobility, honesty, affirmation and realignment, an interpretation could no more be true in an absolute sense (understood as a view from "outside", objective or selfless, or consisting of a concept "of the whole") than a living being could also be dead. Do perspectives and interpretations then become infinite in number? Perhaps, Nietzsche answers; but the point is not their number. Rather, the points significant for Nietzsche are *differences* of interpretations on the order of rank, the rootedness in physiology and human types, the fact of interpretation as a basic structure of spirit, and finally, as Nietzsche puts it elsewhere, that we "cannot look around our own corner" (*The Gay Science*, §374). Note in "corner" an echo of how the whole problem of perspective was introduced in §2. (See also §1 of the Preface of the *Genealogy*. Also note in both passages the decidedly Kantian flair to the arguments; they should remind us of the Paralogisms in the *Critique of Pure Reason*, especially A346 = B404.) It *may* be, then, that Nietzsche wishes to assert the view of nature given in §22 as factual (or that it is as factual a description as can be given). Any other account is false, an error. But short of that it is *certainly* the case that he espouses the virtue of self-honesty in the second interpreter; and indeed approves of what we called the "realignment" that would have to be involved in affirming a dangerous interpretation. The next section reinforces this, turning from physics to psychology, and addressing precisely the problem of honesty and realignment that we spoke of above.

We have shown that the notion of perspective is clearly linked to something like morality, in so far as it always involves values and evaluations. We have also shown, with the discussion here of science and knowledge, that it has huge epistemological implications and, alongside these, methodological implications. Concerning the latter, it leads Nietzsche to consider a historical, developmental account of ideas and the belief in them. (The very next section, §23, picks up this idea.) Finally, Nietzsche here is again clearly suggesting that perspective and value are rooted in his underlying conception of life (and more broadly still, nature) as will to power. That is to say, perspective is nothing short of a way of characterizing the nature of reality. This has been suggested, but not yet fully explained; for this, please see the discussion of will to power attached to §36 below.

§23

We begin with the claim that "all psychology so far has got stuck in moral prejudices and fears". Nietzsche defines psychology as a morphology, and as a *"doctrine of the development* [Entwicklungslehre] *of the will to power"*. By "morphology" is meant a science concerned with the *form* of its object (animals, plants, but also cultural forms; Nietzsche may have Goethe's notion of morphology in mind here). So, in this case, the "doctrine" is of the particular configuration reached by the system of drives or instincts and their manifestation in evaluations. A key example of this would be the democratic instinct and its manifestation in the presuppositions of physicists. The second part of Nietzsche's definition deals with "development" – change over time. This morphology of development is a brief attempt to explain this method. (Please also see our discussion of §2 above, where some of the basic ideas of this method were introduced.) So far in the book, we have had a handful of brief treatments of development: for example, the discussion of machinists and bridge-builders of the future in §14, or, still more clearly, the "family resemblances" of Western languages and philosophies in §20. However, these examples do not really show well what Nietzsche has in mind by "development". In brief, he is referring to the historically articulated and generally repressed relationships between apparently different, unrelated, or even opposite states, as described in §2. In particular, the development of a will to power that takes as its apparent ideal the "good", from out of what it itself would define as the evil. Nietzsche is interested in the developments themselves, but this general morphology would comprise a study of the *forms of development*; we will be better able to discuss further what this might mean later, and will do so under §259.

Such a psychology is new, not having been tried or even thought of before. (Notice the further reference to the problem of texts and the meaning or intention behind them.) This developmental, morphological psychology is what Nietzsche will call "genealogy" in his next book, starting with its title: *On the Genealogy of Morality*. Interestingly, though, in that book Nietzsche draws what even here looks like an obvious conclusion. This "psychology" is a tracing back of cultural artefacts, beliefs, philosophies, to the development into relatively fixed forms of the will to power of underlying drives. Then, this "psychology" is not psychology at all (or at least not at first), but "physiology" (see *Genealogy*, First Treatise, §17 note).

One reason, perhaps, that this new "psychology" has not been tried before is that the psychologist has to overcome herself. That is, overcome the "resistance in the heart" – her own deeply held prejudices – and risk a feeling like sea-sickness. Nietzsche means overturning prejudices against, for example, the complex inter-relation of good and evil, or how many affects typically seen as wicked are in fact part of the condition of life. Nietzsche adds, interestingly, that such affects would have to be enhanced [*gesteigert*] if life is to be enhanced. That is, if there is to be a further development of the will to power, towards the philosopher of the future, then these (apparently wicked) conditions of life will have to be strengthened.

There are many good reasons for turning back from such overcoming, but (keeping with the metaphor that began with "sea-sickness") Nietzsche tries to whip up enthusiasm for a "dangerous" voyage that will sail right over and past morality. Perhaps this sailing past will destroy the remainder of our moral prejudices – thus curing our sea-sickness. Dangerous, but "what do *we* matter?" compared to the "profounder world of insight" opened up. The "what do *we* matter?" means three things; first, what does our previous moral identity matter; second, what sacrifice is too great for the new type of being towards which our investigations might contribute; third, it is not primarily or exclusively a question of coming to *know oneself*, as we argued above in discussing "honesty" in §22. Notice that Nietzsche is tentatively proposing not just a difficult journey (sea-sickness), but a *dangerous* one that might *transform the psychologist* and lead to a different world. In other words, it might be possible to offer resistance to, and to overcome, the "innate" physiological value systems and dominant interpreting drives of one's being. It might be possible, then, not just for humans as a species to develop into new forms of life – but for individual human beings to also make such a journey of realignment, at least in part. In so far as our individual projects are relevant at all to the philosophy of the future, this result is significant; although in any case "what do we matter" as individuals, rather than tokens of a type.

As its title suggests, this Part has been a critique of widely prevalent metaphysical assumptions. A few years later, reviewing his career, Nietzsche calls *Beyond* a "critique of modernity" (*Ecce Homo*, "Why I write such good books", "Beyond Good and Evil", §2). This sounds as though *Beyond* is entirely negative in character. Although in *Ecce Homo* he distinguishes sharply between the "yes" saying and the "no" saying aspects of his project, things are not so simple. First of all, even the dominant critical tone of the first Part gives way to a positive characterization of some new philosophical adventure (in §2, for instance). And this must be the case, for a critique of *values* (a critique that is not concerned just to point out rational inconsistencies, say) is possible only if we have already had a glimpse of the conditions for new values. Secondly, the very next Part is a characterization of the "free spirit" who opposes and strives to change this "modernity". Indeed, we will see throughout the book the theme of the close relationship between being a philosopher who is of "today" (working with or against current philosophical problems) and one who is of "tomorrow".

3 "The Free Spirit": The Philosopher Realigned to Will to Power (Part 2 §§24–44)

Part 2 is entitled "the free spirit". Of course, we have just seen Nietzsche attack the conventional philosophical ways of understanding the notion of "freedom", so we will need to address the question of how he intends we understand "free" now. But we have seen this phrase before, and as early as the Preface: "we free, *very* free spirits". The free spirit anticipates and prepares the way for that new type of human being that Nietzsche calls the "philosopher of the future". That is to say, "we" prepare for the being that realigns itself to thinking of itself and the world in terms of will to power. The term "realign" is mine, not Nietzsche's, but seems appropriate to describe this process of overcoming hinted at just above in §23. It is a project of the knowledge of will to power, but also a project of physiology, of becoming a being that can affirm its own dominant will to power.

§24

As we have seen Nietzsche claim before, certain errors are a condition of life. We are devoted to these errors in so far as we are devoted to life. Here, Nietzsche is attempting to describe something of the nature of these errors. They *simplify*, thus making everything "bright and free and light and easy". We have seen some of these simplifications before. For example, in the analyses of atomism or cause and effect, Nietzsche speaks of them as a convenience, but not basic principles. The will to knowledge does not merely go astray, Nietzsche argues, but is founded upon a will to "non-knowledge" [*Unwissen*]. And the knowledge that arises on this foundation is not the opposite of non-knowledge, but its refinement [*Verfeinerung*]. Despite this deep foundation in errors, it is possible to "devote" one's "eyes" to see these "wonders". Similarly, later in the passage, despite even our language being infected by errors, "here and there we grasp it and laugh about it".

The light-hearted delight of this section contrasts sharply with the danger and sea-sickness that ended the previous Part. Both, though, concern the adventure of learning to see differently. We must ask how are these contrasting tones to be reconciled? The realignment to the will to power, we suggested above, must involve a revolution in the instincts and desires that make up one's form of life. But the result is still life, and thus (Nietzsche argues) still necessarily bound to the simplifications and falsifications that are necessary for life. It is only that this new, realigned life is one that no longer feels the need to resist its own nature – moreover, a life whose still present essential falsifications, which are any life's condition, do not *also* falsify, disguise or repress its realignment to will to power. The joy Nietzsche speaks of here is the simple joy of being alive, once life is released from the self-imposed burden of taking its mistakes so *seriously*, from treating them as truths, or not recognizing the necessity of perspective. Given this rapid oscillation of danger and laughter, it is not surprising, then, that the very next section turns to the "serious" problem of being serious.

§25

Section 24 was joyful [*fröhlich*], since it spoke of the love of life – but now Nietzsche offers a serious word. (Incidentally, "joyful" is an important word in Nietzsche: the same word makes up the title of the book usually translated as *The Gay Science*.) The serious word addressed to philosophical colleagues is, in effect, *don't be so serious*. Don't find yourself "posing" as defenders of some truth. "In the end you know well enough that nothing can depend upon whether precisely *you* are proved right, and moreover that no philosopher so far has ever been proved right." Instead, flee, behind masks and subtlety [*feinheit*], into the garden (like Epicurus). And, choose the "good solitude", not the role of the poisonous outcast (like Spinoza) who is a "degeneration" [*Entartung*]. We should notice here the use of the term "mask", although we have seen the concept before under headings such as disguises and deceptions. Nietzsche will return to this idea very frequently; our challenge will be to understand how what appears to be a fairly simple idea can take us to the heart of Nietzsche's conception of method, style and even responsibility (see especially our discussions under §§284 and 296).

Nietzsche is describing a double danger. First, that those who devote their eyes to seeing the underlying error of all knowledge might be tempted to advocate and defend truth. This would be to espouse the philosophy of the future using the standard techniques of the philosophy of the past; it would be to grasp the perspectival character of knowledge in every case except one's own. But Nietzsche has been telling us that these techniques (and even language itself) are *implicated* in falsehood. So, however it is that the philosopher of the future (and the free spirit) will live and speak, it is not in this "serious" way. Secondly, those who choose not to become truth's advocate in the open might nevertheless wage a war from the shadows, and become poisonous, solitary degenerates. We will see this notion frequently in Nietzsche, namely the degeneration of a figure who is not quite strong enough to live thoroughly according to their insights (e.g. §§29–30, 203).

§26

The theme of solitude is continued in this section. "Every select [*auserlesen*] human" tries to deliver [*erlösen*] herself from the crowds, to where she can forget the human rule, because she is its exception [*Ausnahme*]. There is one exception to this behaviour of those who are exceptional, and that is someone whose stronger instincts take them into the thick of this "rule". And this person is the "knower" [*Erkennende*] in the great and exceptional sense. Such a person (the exceptional of the exceptional) will feel disgust and sympathy [*Mitgefühl*], but take on [*aufnehmen*] all the burden and displeasure upon herself. The heavy-handed repetition of "exception" has been preparing us for a pun: here we have "*aufnehmen*" (to take up or receive) instead of "*ausnehmen*" (to except; literally to take out or remove). The exception to the exception takes up with the human rule, and goes "down" or "in". "Disgust" of this going down or in is an echo of the "sea-sickness" of §23 (nausea, especially because of smell, is a common metaphor). With the idea of going down, Nietzsche is also echoing the famous opening passage of his *Thus Spoke Zarathustra*, in which Zarathustra after years of refuge in a cave in the mountains, decides he must now go down, among men. Moreover, the language of deliverance and of taking on burdens is heavily religious – and this again echoes the deliberately biblical style of *Zarathustra*. What the language here does not echo is the additional destructive sense of the related passages in *Zarathustra*: there, "*untergehen*" (literally, to go under) also means to sink, be destroyed. This sense, however, can be found in §23 with its "what do *we* matter?".

The knower must go down or in because the human rule is more interesting than the exception. The long and serious study of the "average" human is required of every philosopher, although it is not pleasant. However, there are shortcuts: the cynics (Nietzsche means both the ancient

Cynics, and more recent philosophers who fit this mould). These are "common souls" who nevertheless approach "honesty" [*Redlichkeit*], who see the "average" and the "rule" in themselves but also have the spirit to speak or write about it. Similarly, there are cases where a kind of genius is inexplicably attached to an "ape's body". Someone who speaks "badly" of human beings (seeing the motivation for all actions in hunger, sex, vanity) but without any bitterness or indignation [*Entrüstung*] – that is, without any sense that seeing such motivation in human beings is false, an insult, or at best a defect. Such people must again be listened to, as they are hugely informative about the human rule; certainly, much more informative than those who try to cover up such information by being indignant. Indignant against whom? Against themselves, perhaps, for giving something away – or, as a "substitute", against the world (Plato and Platonic Christianity are the obvious candidates for world-denigration as far as Nietzsche is concerned), God (perhaps Nietzsche has the often bitter deism of Voltaire in mind), or society (Rousseau would be the obvious example). What is not yet clear, however, is why Nietzsche believes not only that the average case is more interesting, but also why it is a necessary object of study for the philosopher.

§27

A playful, personal section, using Sanskrit words to be deliberately arcane; the section is about the difficulty of being understood. The upshot is that when one lives among those who live differently, who move like frogs, tortoises, or the slow waters of the Ganges, then one is grateful whenever these others show any subtlety [*Feinheit*] of interpretation. However, there are friends who, because they know themselves to be friends, are too lazy to be subtle. Such friends should be given some space for their misunderstandings, and laughed at. The next section will serve to explain Nietzsche's theme here. However, we should not miss the brief but important introduction of the theme of the friend; a theme that becomes increasingly important as the book proceeds.

§28

What moves like a tortoise has a quite distinctive "tempo" in its *style*. Thus this section is a commentary on the ideas of §27. Style here is not just a linguistic phenomenon – just as, indeed, Nietzsche has said that language itself is not. Rather, they express "the average tempo of its [a race's] 'metabolism' [*Stoffwechsels*]". From the tempo of style Nietzsche is led to the problem of translation, which is effectively equivalent to the philologist's problem of understanding. Without the ability to reproduce the tempo, even "honest" [*ehrlich*] translations are vulgarizations and almost falsifications.

The mention here first of "race" [*Rasse*] and then of metabolism is not just metaphorical. In so far as Nietzsche's account of perspective, for example, rests on the question of the drives and instincts of life, it should not be surprising that a great deal of his thinking concerns physiology. Characterizations of racial differences have a long and very dark history, certainly; and Nietzsche is not above contributing to it. However, it would be a mistake briskly to label Nietzsche a "racist" of some kind. First, it must be said that his use of the concept "race" is very imprecise, swerving from a kind of ethnography to broad European national characteristics (just below, but also and especially Part 8); and it is also rarely essentialist, since he also talks of historical developments from out of social causes. The language used is imprecise as well: as often as Nietzsche speaks of race he also talks about forms, classes, species, peoples and so forth, all of which suggest a broader sense of difference and identity than the merely racial. Finally, Nietzsche does speak of racial types, but he is not a "supremacist" or advocate of racial "purity". The philosopher of the future is a *new* "type" of human being, if anything a new pan-European mode, and is not a return of any previous type. I mention these things to ensure we do not prejudge Nietzsche according to a reputation that he only partly deserves.

The Germans are incapable of a *presto* tempo (the nationalist politics of Bismarck is dismissed, then, as just plain slow-witted). Lessing is an exception, but even he could not hope to keep up with Machiavelli, Petronius, or Aristophanes. (All, notice, *southern*, from Mediterranean lands; this contrast of north and south within Europe is a virtually constant theme of Part 8.) Under Plato's death-bed pillow was a copy of Aristophanes, Nietzsche tells us. Aristophanes, whose tempo reflected a Greek mode of life to which Plato "said no" – but which Plato also needed in order to endure life. Reading this together with §27, which seems very personal, we can guess what Nietzsche does not say: that the one whose style will be misunderstood because those who move like tortoises cannot but misunderstand it, is Nietzsche himself. And, by extension, that there must be something about the philosophy of the future which has to proceed at a *presto* pace. It is difficult, then, not to return to the early sections of this Part, and think about those philosophers who are enjoined not to lose their joy and humour. The philosophers of the future, the ideal of free spirits, do not just think and speak differently, but live differently.

§29

Only very few can be "independent" [*unabhängig*], the prerogative of the strong. But, even with this right, should someone attempt independence who does not have to, that would be very dangerous. He might lose his way in a labyrinth and be torn apart by conscience [*Gewissen*]. (The reference is to the myth of Theseus and the Minotaur; see also §295.) This also takes us back to the sea-sickness of §23 and the disgust later. "Conscience" here is a feeling by which we know when we have violated our deepest prejudices. (In the *Genealogy of Morality*, Nietzsche gives extended account of the historical genesis of conscience, particularly "bad conscience". The point here is broader.) This event (being torn apart by conscience) occurs so far from ordinary human events that it is impossible for others to feel sympathy. And such a one – something of him has survived, note – cannot return, cannot go back to their pity [*Mitleid* – sometimes also translated as "compassion"]. This of course is a warning – much like those we have seen before – concerning the dangers of the philosophical approach Nietzsche is suggesting. What is new here is the impossibility of return; it appears that return is not so much impossible as that the agony of returning to their pity would be unbearable, even compared to being torn apart by conscience.

Why? The theme of pity is usually directed the other way. The "higher human" ought not feel pity for those who are incapable of keeping up (or even for themselves, their former selves); to feel pity would be a sign that one has not reconceived one's moral and emotional universe in terms of the will to power. Here, it is the reverse: to be the object of pity of average humans would mean accepting their judgement that one is at or below their order of rank. It would, in short, mean not being independent. We will return to Nietzsche's thoughts on pity often, and especially in §202.

§30

This section continues the theme of pity (or rather its absence) and related ideas. "Our highest insights" (Nietzsche is again speaking on behalf of free spirits) must sound like foolishness [*Torheit*] or even, in some circumstances, crimes – when heard by those who are not constituted [*geartet*] or predetermined for them. We are back to "our new language" in §4 and in general the "untimeliness" of Nietzsche's ideas. This use of the first person plural is fairly common in Nietzsche, as in "we free spirits". All this has connotations of a kind of intimate group of readers and thinkers, the initiates. The "we" is often confronted by a hostile or uncomprehending "they". Nietzsche's point, then, is that the distinction between "us" and the rest is not arbitrary, nor based on something contingent like knowledge or learning, but based upon the type of human being we are. Accordingly, the discussion that follows concerns the distinction between "exoteric" (*for* those outside a select group, or *judged by* the standards of those outside) and "esoteric" (*only for* those inside). Nietzsche insists that the difference is not inside and outside (as if it were a question of geography, or one's contingent circle of acquaintances), but rather above and below – that is, an order of rank. There are heights of the soul from which the tragic does not have a tragic effect, and were all the world's woes wound up together, it would not compel pity. So, similarly, what nourishes a higher man is poison to another type – so also with some books (like Nietzsche's perhaps). Only a higher type degenerating might descend so far as to be revered as a saint (this should be compared to the end of §29).

This passage helps us to understand the earlier one about pity, but more significantly it reinforces just how comprehensive a claim Nietzsche wishes to make in relation to the idea of an order of rank. By "order of rank" Nietzsche means very crudely that hierarchy of "natural masters" among humans, and those "naturally mastered". This condition of master and mastered, however, is not a historical accident, but is founded upon one's mode of life. "Mastery", significantly, does not have to be political, social or economic (and very often is not); it may mean a position of influence over values in the arts, for example; it may mean nothing "exoteric" at all. Here, the order of rank determines one's interpretation of truth, crime, nourishment, tragedy, books, sainthood, courage, and even smell. And, accordingly, Nietzsche's examples here cover a deliberately wide range of possible attitudes: the philosophical, aesthetic, the sense of justice or virtue (that is, political and social attitudes), the religious, and the physiological. Ultimately, order of rank has to do with the strength and health of the will to power of one's drives, and thus also with the physiological and spiritual capacity for the type of advancement of the human that Nietzsche has been discussing. Being high up in the order of rank is equivalent, for Nietzsche, to the idea of nobility.

§31

This is another apparently personal section, giving a narrative of personal development. The key points here begin with the "art of nuances" [*Kunst der Nuance*]. The merely young say yes and no too quickly, having the worst taste ("the taste for the unconditional [*Unbedingt*]"), and judging without "art" – unlike the "real artists of life". This yes and no "falsifies" people and things into appropriate objects for their "wrath and reverence". That is to say, too eager to praise entirely, or reject entirely, the young revalue their world such that it merits praise or rejection.

Later, the not-so-young suffer disappointments, and turn on their earlier selves. "Indeed, one feels good conscience as a danger, as if a self-veiling and weariness of subtler honesty." Still, one is "partisan" [*Partei*], *against* youth. Later still, one realizes this too was still youth.

Why "still youth"? Partly, of course, because it is still an unsubtle yes and no: one is still "partisan". But also because in turning on itself, the not-so-young exhibit the signs of self-loathing that is characteristic of the indignant, which Nietzsche discussed at the end of §26. This self-loathing will be a common theme in the analyses to come. Finally, it should be recognized that a proper response to the unsubtle errors of youth is not a rejection of youth, but an appreciation of it as youth, as a level of creative energy that, in a modified form, one might try to recapture. Thus, this section is not (as it might appear on first reading) advocating an abandonment of youth, but on the contrary a recognition that every increase in subtlety and insight is a product of youth, towards a better youth (see the poem at the end of the book). Here, we should think of Nietzsche's treatment of the *initial youthfulness* of Kant and his immediate followers in §11, as opposed to its subsequent influence. The "real artists of life" are neither merely young, nor merely older; they are nowhere or "untimely" in the ages of man. Nietzsche is using the characteristics of "youth" and "experience" in a curious mixture as a provisional new language for the new kind of philosopher he is anticipating.

§32

The discussion of individual development now shifts into a discussion of the historical development of the evaluation of actions. There are five stages distinguished here. First, we have a (prehistorical) youthful stage, in which the value of an action is judged in terms of its consequences. Secondly, Nietzsche then considers the whole of the historical period as a gradual development of the view that the value of an action lies in its origin. There is a link here, he claims, to the period of the rule of aristocratic values and of good breeding. Thirdly, at some point, however, a disastrous new idea emerged, which identifies origin with intention. That is, with the conscious aim that the one who acts has in mind at the time of action. Accordingly, there would have to follow the injunction to "know thyself". The high point of such a philosophy is Kant, who demanded that will be fully and transparently rational in its intent in order to be moral.

Nietzsche then calls for another change (the fourth stage), based upon a more profound understanding of the human organism. Among us "immoralists" there is the suspicion that "the decisive value of an action lies in what is precisely *unintentional* about it". The intention is like a sign or symptom, requiring interpretation, and on its own tells us almost nothing. The job of performing this new shift, of overcoming this morality, is the secret work that has been reserved for "the subtlest and most honest, and also the most malicious [*boshaftest*], consciences of today, as [they are] living touchstones of the soul". Note, though, that the result is not altogether different from the aristocratic morality of "origins". But this new period has to be named "negatively"; the fifth stage is a new situation in which the beyond good and evil can be asserted positively.

There is a great deal to discuss concerning this important passage. But let us begin by looking at the parallels with §31. Again we have stages. In the personal development, there is an initial stage of youth that externalizes its values, seeking confirmation in a world it has reformed in its image. So, in the prehistorical, which searches for the value of an action in external consequences but which still has to judge those consequences in terms of values it already holds. Then, there is the not-so-young stage that begins with disappointment and demands a self-examination. Its earlier errors seemed almost "deliberate blindness" – that is, intentional. Accordingly, it learns to detest itself. Similarly, in Nietzsche's potted history, we have skipped over the stage in which origin is important, and moved to intention. In the intentional stage, conscious will takes responsibility for action; it can now praise itself but, given the impossible standards set for moral action (as e.g. in Kant), tends towards self-loathing.

What is skipped over in the story of personal development – what must be *still youthful* – is the aristocratic stage. In §31, it is marked only by the sentence on "the real artists of life". Here, the yes and no of youth are refined perhaps, but above all acknowledged as perspectives that originate in the organic self, not as conscious will but as the nature of that self. It is *this* youth that Nietzsche wishes to set forth as a challenge to our "old" ways of thinking. The "extra-moral" stage will begin by philosophers, through their subtle analyses of the drives and prejudices of the human organism, recovering through *knowledge* what was known by *instinct* during the early moral stage of human history. But the name "extra-moral" is only a beginning, Nietzsche tells us without further explanation. The name of the subsequent, future stage will have to reflect the internalization of this knowledge that has been realigned to the will to power. The fifth stage is akin to the noble, but prepared for by the free spirits.

The parallel between these two narratives of development – the one of an individual, the other of the whole history of moral beliefs – is informative. It helps us to understand the process of self-overcoming by which the philosophers of the future can arrive. This self-overcoming is an overcoming of a historical development that has sedimented itself in the self, and indeed also of historically determined modes of understanding "youth", "development" and "maturity". The individual is a "microcosm" of the larger, historical or indeed natural process. We have seen something like this before (in §15), and will again in the famous, closing two sections of the book.

§33

One element in this self-overcoming is avoiding the error of self-denial. This takes two forms: first, a morality the ideal of which is altruism, that is, the devotion of oneself to others; second, the aesthetics of disinterestedness, according to which proper attention can be given to the aesthetic object only if other forms of attention (desire, moral approval or blame) are excluded. Kant's aesthetics is the primary reference for the latter. Such attitudes are too "sugary" not to be met with caution. We might suspect that this self-denial is an extension of the self-loathing Nietzsche discussed in §31. And, referring now to §32, if there is something disastrous in the assumption that value lies in the intention of an act then presumably there must be something equally disastrous in the mirror-image of that assumption: namely, that one has the intention of annulling all intentions.

Two significant observations can be made here. The first should be obvious by now, but is still worth pointing out: all values are, at bottom, equivalent for Nietzsche. Whether something is valued because I consider it morally good, or beautiful, useful to me, or the object of my desire, these are just variations on the central evaluative function of all drives. However, this is not to claim that the effects of each are all the same. Nor is it to say that there might not be interesting psychological stories to tell about *why we consider such values to be different*. For example, Nietzsche would be interested in an analysis of why a philosopher like Kant was so adamant that moral values were quite different from other types of value.

The second observation stems from the first, and concerns what appear to be two particularly prominent levels of philosophizing in Nietzsche. On the one hand, we have the fundamental analysis of the nature of drives or instincts as will to power, and the thinking of the living body as a complex interaction of drives. For lack of a better word, we can call this Nietzsche's *metaphysics*. On the other hand, we have the psychological or historical analyses of the *spiritualization* of these drives into various concepts, conscious values, or ways of understanding self and world. For an example of the latter, although Nietzsche does not here give us this story, in this section we could imagine him providing some account of how a drive became spiritualized into the aesthetic principle of disinterest. In this book, in the next part, Nietzsche names what he is doing a "natural history"; in §23 it was "morphology of development"; in his next book, he will call it "genealogy". Now, we noted the difference between these two levels earlier in our discussion of §2. There, however, it could not yet be clear how the two are related. How one interprets Nietzsche as a philosopher, overall, depends to a remarkably large extent on which of these two modes of thinking one takes to be the most distinctively Nietzschean. Here, in this book, we are trying to occupy a middle ground, and uncover the intricate and necessary inter-relationship between the two.

§34, and discussion of appearance

Together with §36, this is an important section in that it contains statements of some of Nietzsche's most characteristic "metaphysical" thought. Actually, though, much of the material here we have seen before: such as the suspicion of the transparency or "immediate certainties" of consciousness, the dismissal as mere prejudice of the belief in the fundamental opposition of truth and falsehood, or the idea that perspectival evaluations are a condition of life. The significance of the passage may lie in the way Nietzsche relates all these notions. Let us initially focus just on what appears to be new.

The section opens with the proposition that whatever philosophical standpoint one takes "today", the "erroneousness" [*Irrtümlichkeit*] of the world "in which we believe we live" seems obvious. The world is held to be basically otherwise than how it appears, and perhaps even basically deceptive. That is, separate from our purported knowledge of it, the world *in itself* has a deceptive quality. This passage is often quoted out of context as if it is a statement of a basic belief of Nietzsche's (e.g. on the back cover of the de Gruyter complete works). The context, however, makes it clear that he is speaking of a strong trend among philosophers "today", and this trend forms part of that crisis or tension we have seen him discuss so often. It is also a sly reference to the "malevolent demon" in Descartes, who systematically deceives me about the external world. By the end of the passage, Nietzsche will write of himself thinking differently with respect to deception. In short, to believe that if there is not truth then there must be deception is to remain committed to traditional metaphysical oppositions.

So, the passage must be read ironically or at least as not in Nietzsche's own voice. In contrast to this opening proposition, we are then asked to imagine a philosopher who claimed that thinking or spirit were responsible for this falseness, for falsely inferring things about the world. Such a philosopher would have found an "honourable way out", taken by every *advocatus dei* (God's advocate). (This last phrase is a joke on the expression "devil's advocate", which is the curious role within the Catholic process of conferring sainthood, designating the official who argues against canonization. Nietzsche is also referring to philosophers such as Leibniz whose *Theodicy* is a kind of defence of God.) Such a philosopher might be considered a God's advocate because he defends God against the charge of creating an essentially false (or, indeed, essentially evil) world. But, in this case, we would at long last become suspicious of thinking itself, as having played on us the "biggest prank" ever. What is the prank? Not merely to have consistently misinterpreted the world, but to have held out the hope that, if only we were rigorous or objective enough, this falsification could be *overcome by thinking*. Thus, starting with the next sentence, Nietzsche appends the critique of the transparency of consciousness to itself, which would be a first condition of any possible overcoming of thinking's falsification by thinking.

Either, then, the world is in itself false, or else human thinking is irreparably falsifying. We have no reason to believe that Nietzsche feels these are the only choices. Nevertheless, something very interesting has been said: Nietzsche has diagnosed the beliefs of contemporary philosophy and shown how their inner problems lead to a crisis. We have seen him speak about this crisis on several previous occasions, most notably in the discussion of the pent-up "magnificent tension" of the spirit in the Preface. Significantly, then, the kind of philosophical work that Nietzsche sees himself engaged in has been *prepared for*, and even has an inevitability about it. Just as a psychological or historical story can be given that describes how previous belief systems arose from basic drives, such a story can be provided even for Nietzsche's own thinking. He does not exempt himself from the kind of analyses he gives of others. That is, the kind of "suspicion" that he writes of a few sentences later is a perfectly "natural" development in the spiritualization of the drives from out of this crisis. The philosophers, who are the "most duped" beings on earth, now appear to have the duty of suspicion. Why, Nietzsche argues, should we be enraged at being deceived or cheated, since the evaluation of truth higher than appearances is a mere "moral prejudice"? Moreover, feeling cheated is even more absurd if it is the case that perspectival evaluations are the basis of the possibility of life, and thus indirectly of thought.

Let us suppose, Nietzsche argues, that one could completely eliminate the "world of appearances". Then, it follows there would also be nothing of "truth" remaining either. (Compare this to the point Nietzsche famously elaborated in the section "How the 'True World' Finally Became a Fable" in *Twilight of the Idols*.) Why does this follow? Truth *conceived of as a representation of reality* assumes the idea of representation, and with that idea also assumes the possibility of falsehood *in representation*. Should the "world of appearances" be abolished, then so is the possibility of false representation, and with it true representation. All that remains is existence.

Nietzsche then repeats the suspicion of the opposition of truth and falsehood, and hypothesizes in its place "gradations" or "shade" of appearances, different "values" [the French word *valeurs*]. This last term is explicitly borrowed from the language of painters – significantly, just as Nietzsche borrowed aspects of the problem of perspective way back in §2. Now what is meant by this curious idea? The most straightforward interpretation is

that Nietzsche is arguing against the *strict or absolute* version of the opposition, and that rather there are degrees of truth or falsehood. It is difficult
to understand what this might mean, however, without referring to at least
the *ideal* of absolute truth. But, would thinking in terms of truth ideals be a
substantive step forward?

More interesting would be to think about what the idea of appearance
would mean if separated from the notion of an underlying reality and thus
of representation. There is appearance, Nietzsche might be saying, without
something "in itself" that appears. A fairly standard philosophical view
of perception is that over there is an object (an apple, say), and over here
me with eyes and nervous system; the apple is "in itself", and so am I.
There is a relation between us (of emitted or reflected light and optics,
of nerve impulses interpreted by me as an image), which is appearance.
But appearance is *always consequent on* the existence of both the apple and
me. Suppose, however, that what comes first is the appearance, and only
subsequently to it do we say "apple" and, indeed, "me". That is, only subsequently do we interpret the appearance as a representation of something.
Appearance, thought of as relation prior to things related, would indeed
be a notion of appearance that was no longer thought of in terms of the
opposition of true and false – because it was not representation of anything
in itself, by the activity of thinking *in itself*.

Let us return to the idea of "*valeur*", in painting. An example of this
would be the notion of a tonal value, which refers to the position of a
"tone" on multiple scales (scales of light to dark, red to blue or some other
spectrum, scales of colour saturation, purity, luminosity or opacity, etc.),
and also relative to other adjacent tones or within the painting as a whole.
At first sight, this *initial* sense of the word "*valeur*" appears to be quite
different from the idea of value or evaluation that Nietzsche has been using.
However, notice that the allusion to painting is more than just a convenient metaphor. As we discussed in the context of perspective, painting
(at least prominent traditions of painting) is concerned to create the *effect*
of representation. So, there are tonal values, singly and collectively, and
these are interpreted as a representation of reality. The situation is directly
analogous to the new notion of appearance discussed above. Moreover,
notice that even the tonal value does not exist "in itself". Rather, its being
a tonal value is constituted from outside itself by other values around it, and
by the multiple scales (colour, saturation, luminosity) within which it is
situated. According to our new analysis, appearance – now one that is not
referred back to some thing in itself – cannot be objectified as a kind of
thing. Its thingliness – the fact that it appears as *this* tonal value – is always
already a product of relations. Nor are these relations on absolute scales
of opposition (such as truth and falsehood, assuming as we did briefly
above that it even makes sense to think of this as a scale). Nietzsche is

arguing that, if by "thing" we mean anything metaphysical such as substance, self-identity, or the ability to be a cause, then *there are no things*.

We had a first glimpse of this notion of appearance in §§14–15. There, Nietzsche spoke about "sensualism" in a deeply ambiguous manner. First, sensualism was labelled plebeian, and contrasted with the noble attitude of Plato who distrusted the senses instinctively. On the other hand, though, Nietzsche suggested that sensualism was necessary as a "regulative hypothesis" in order to overcome idealism. In our discussion we tried to show the consistency of these two points. The sensualist places his trust in the mere data of sense, he values it highly as such; the idealist denigrates it, again as such, preferring to place her trust in what does not appear. But to value appearances as such, either positively or negatively, is absurd: as we have just discussed, that which appears, appears *as value*.

Now, we must try to understand these ideas in conjunction with those in §22, where Nietzsche wrote "every power at every moment draws its utmost consequences". There it was a question of understanding how the course of events could be necessary and calculable without being subject to universal laws of cause and effect. At the time, we left the meaning of this "every" unanalysed – perhaps it was a different way of talking about universality? Now, though, we can see that the "every" power and moment relate to the notion of appearances and entities as relations. To isolate one drive or instinct and to discuss or measure its will to power is nonsense. There is no "one" power – that would be again to employ a metaphysical category such as substance, which has an essential unity – there are rather fields of power (where "field" is understood on a close analogy with the concept of field – magnetic, gravitational – in nineteenth and twentieth-century physics). Or, as Nietzsche has expressed it several times now: there are "communities" of drives. Power is always a power relation: a relation of dominating, withdrawing, reacting.

"The world", in so far as it is something that concerns [*angehen*] us, is a "fiction" [*Fiktion*], then. Does this mean that the world, in so far as it does not concern us (that is, in itself) is not a fiction? On the contrary, such a world could not even be a fiction, because it would not be appearance at all. The *idea* of such a world might be a fiction (here we should again compare Kant on regulative ideas of reason). However, Nietzsche's concern is with appearance; the world, as appearance or as it concerns us, is a fiction. Does this not seem a rather extreme or over-dramatic form of words? Let us return to our understanding of appearance. This fiction only exists in so far as the forces that make up the world have power relations with the community of drives that make up "us". These constituting relations appear as tones or gradations. This appearing *subsequently* allows a world that seems to be thing-like (nature, for example), and an "us" that also seems thing-like (you and I), to appear *as fictions*. So, Nietzsche's form of words would be misleading if he were calling *appearance* "fiction". But he is rather calling the world that appears a fiction – by this is meant that its seeming independence of us as a thing-like existence, which might or might not be represented truthfully in appearances and ultimately in our beliefs, is a fiction. Similarly, our seeming independence and substance-like status as individual minds or souls, which can form representations of a world while being outside it, must be a fiction.

Accordingly, Nietzsche continues: does not an "original author" [*Urheber*] belong to a fiction? By this could be meant a creator of the world, of course. But Nietzsche could also be referring back to the opening sentences of the section. There are those today who believe that either there is a natural "principle" of deceptiveness, or that the "spirit" is responsible for the falsification of the world. Someone, surely, must be responsible for this fiction. But, Nietzsche counters, the "belongingness" together of the idea of fiction and author may be part of the fiction. Subtle gradations of power relations are appearance without there being something (behind appearance) that appears. That is, the "appearance" of there being (indeed, having to be) something in itself (such as nature, human minds, or God) that could be held responsible for the fiction is *derivative* with respect to the appearance. The world, *and "us" with it*, is a fiction. Accordingly, truth, as the adequate representation of the world by us, must also be a fiction. Section 35 expands upon this last consequence.

The passage ends with a series of questions that radiate outward from the problem of authorship. "Are we not allowed to be a bit ironical with respect to the subject, as we are with respect to predicate and object?" This then leads Nietzsche back to the now familiar theme of the conditioning of grammar (and of "governesses" who teach us grammar as children). Consider the proposition, "the author writes the fiction". Nietzsche is saying that we have learned now to question the object of this proposition "the fiction", so shouldn't we also question the subject: "the author"? But, of course, he does not say "question", he says "be a bit ironical". Irony is a rhetorical function in which the speaker says one thing but (more or less obviously) intends a different meaning. The difference signalled by irony could be subtle, a matter of mere tone, a playing with assertion and lack of seriousness. Now, broadly speaking, fiction is certainly ironical in that the author of a novel may write "This happened" but really means something like "let us pretend that this happened", or "*what if* this happened?" However, here it is not the author who is being ironical, but us (we free spirits) who are being a bit ironical *about the author*.

This is a statement of method. Having put forward the thesis of the non-thingliness, or non-substantiality of appearance and of world and self too, Nietzsche cannot then reintroduce substantiality by saying that the author (of the world) does or does not exist. For one thing, he would be forced to use the subject–object grammatical form to argue that such a grammatical form has no validity; this is at least awkward, if not impossible. If we take seriously both Nietzsche's thesis that grammar influences metaphysical *beliefs*, and the thesis that everything is appearance not substance, then an assertion such as "There is no author of the world" is a kind of performative contradiction. The assertion has to assert the formal possibility of the existence of something *other than* world as appearance, and must therefore assume at least the intelligibility of the "world" being a substantial *effect*, in order also to assert that this possibility is not fulfilled. In brief, the assertion "there is no author of the world", although apparently just negative, seems to assert far too much *in its mere propositional form*. This situation is not a genuine paradox, but it certainly illustrates the kinds of issues Nietzsche has in mind when elsewhere speaking of the importance of a "new language" or of style in philosophy.

Thus, a more adequate philosophical approach might be *irony*, a kind of necessarily *indirect* philosophical project. Such irony has much in common with conventional irony, but takes on a more radical structure: this form of irony asserts one proposition but intends not to assert at all, that is, *to withdraw the proposition as a straightforward truth claim*. This assertion and withdrawal is not simply a cancellation (as if the philosopher had never said anything at all); rather, it has an effect. The act of assertion is a provocation and intervention (the second interpretation above), and also an expression of the realignment of the philosopher to will to power. Such irony takes us back to §24 and "laughing" (which must be different both from arguing for or against, and from ignoring) at science (and see §27). We should recall also the perilous "seriousness" and martyrdom to truth that must be avoided in §25, and the copy of Aristophanes that was under Plato's pillow. This irony, as a kind of lightness of approach, a withdrawal of conventional philosophical seriousness, has been a constant theme throughout "The Free Spirit". The origin of its validity as a philosophical approach is named in §24 as the "joyfulness of life".

§35

A distinction is being made between, on the one hand, truth or the search for truth (i.e. the will to truth, from §1) which "has something about it", and on the other hand being too human about the search for truth. Being too human is characterized as "searching for truth in order to do good". In order for this latter action to be possible, truth and the search for truth themselves would have to be good (according, presumably, to a fairly traditional sense of what is "good"). Or, at least, that truth is value-neutral with respect to our conceptions of the good. What Nietzsche has been telling us, however, is that the very constitution of the notion of truth is value-laden.

Moreover, that the will to truth is a spiritualized mode of the will to power, and thus is fundamentally evaluative in nature. Nothing is found, then, because the very act involves a kind of contradiction in terms.

The implication is not that truth or the search for truth are impossible, strictly speaking. Only that one must not be too human – one must perhaps even be *inhuman* – about truth. To be inhuman about the search for truth would mean not to expect or care if truth aids one to do good. Moreover, this would involve not thinking of truth as a type of accurate or adequate representation of the world. Not only because this separate, represented world is a "fiction" – as §34 said – but because its fictionality is constituted by the fact that such an approach overlooks appearance as power relations and thus as *intrinsically* evaluative.

§36, and discussion of will to power

Were it not for the many layers of hypothesis and supposition, this section would be straightforward. It would be among Nietzsche's most unadorned statements of a new metaphysical position: an ontology of nature based upon will to power. But it is not straightforward, because riddled with "assuming this" or "supposing that".

Thus, we have two basic ways of interpreting the passage. First, we could read it as an unadorned, straightforward statement. The "suppose"s would simply be appropriate caution, as if Nietzsche were saying "I haven't yet but I will try to prove that . . .". Secondly, we could read it as a set of wildly speculative, sharply intervening thrusts at basic ideas within natural science (cause and effect, and the "mechanical" model of the interaction of atoms). The purpose of these thrusts would be to show the fragility of the basis of such science, the fact that it is (to all intents and purposes) a "fiction". That is to say, the purpose of the interventions is *not* seriously to propose an alternative metaphysical model. "Intervention" is not Nietzsche's word; however, the underlying notion is not an anachronism on my part. On the contrary, it has a rich history in the concept of "dialectic" – please see the discussion of "style" under §296 below.

However, using the approaches we have been discussing recently, we can see that these two "basic ways" of interpreting the section *are not actually different*. First of all, one of the implications of the metaphysical model that Nietzsche seems to be putting forward is precisely the questioning of the traditional characterization of truth as adequate representation. But a metaphysical model *would be* just such a representation: *there* is nature, and *here* is mind or spirit, representing the former in a conceptual model. Nietzsche would be coming close to speaking of nature in terms of universal, natural laws – something he warns us about elsewhere. Therefore, seriously putting it forward as a model would again involve a contradiction in terms.

Moreover, it is only because we contemplate this metaphysics as a truth that we encounter *within it* the problem of representing truth. This entanglement should remind us of Oedipus and Sphinx in §1. The proper response to this conundrum, though, is not silence, scepticism or even nihilism, nor is it a kind of mysticism, in which we posit something unsaid and unsayable just beyond the reach of any philosophy; rather, it is laughter. As Nietzsche forewarned us at the end of §34, we must be "a bit ironical", enjoying a kind of youthful laughter and even foolishness. When the philosopher has (to use the expression we have been employing here) realigned himself to the will to power, truth is not a representation of an objective something, but an expression of an underlying joy of life. In so far as it engages with what the philosophical tradition considers truth (or, for example, those founding metaphysical oppositions Nietzsche discusses in §2), this joy will be shaded towards a lack of seriousness or irony. Laughter is, as Nietzsche puts it in the "Attempt at Self-Criticism" added to the *The Birth of Tragedy*, "*this-worldly* consolation".

To pursue such lines of thought further, we need to lay out what metaphysical propositions Nietzsche appears to be putting forward. The chain of suppositions that makes up §36 has this four-part structure:

1. Suppose that what is given to us as real (that is, "appearance" in the sense of §34) comprises our "desires and passions" [*Begierden und Leidenschaften*], our drives and nothing else. Thinking is only a relationship among these drives. That is, thinking is not a representation of these drives or of the world; rather, thinking is inside or at the level of the drives. It is part of the "fiction" that these relationships among drives should seem to be independent of the drives and have representational or intentional content. These last claims are extremely important, since they so clearly distance Nietzsche from the broadly Cartesian belief in the fundamental distinction of natural, material, extended things from mind or spirit. Nietzsche is quite happy to talk about thoughts, souls, spirits – and indeed "spiritualization" is a very important concept as we have seen – but all such talk needs to be understood within this anti-Cartesian framework.

2. Within this supposition, consider the hypothesis that this "real" would also suffice for an understanding of the so-called mechanistic or material world – that is, the natural world as typically understood by physics. That is, this material world holds the same "reality-rank" [*Realitäts-Rang*] as affect. This idea of a reality rank is a curious one; we are more used to this notion of "rank" in the expression "order of rank", which describes the relations of dominance between the will to power of drives. It makes more sense when considered in relation to the claim immediately preceding: that this understanding of the

material world is not a deception. Not, that is, of a derivative class, which is subsequent to some genuine "real" level. So, we should think of "reality-rank" as meaning that the material world is understood at the same depth of understanding, in the same fundamental way, as affects. Indeed, this way of thinking suggests that the material world is a more primitive form of the world of affects. The material world would not be inorganic (opposed to life as inert stuff) but instead proto-organic. All drives and functions associated with life are here in a synthetic unity, before separating, branching out (e.g. into special-ized organs), forming into living beings. (For the methodological point Nietzsche makes here, see §13.)

3. Suppose further that the "real" drives of (1) had to be understood as will to power (that is, suppose that this is the only appropriate way to define "drive"). Let us pause here to summarize what we have dis-covered, thus far, about what Nietzsche means by "will to power". Will to power would define the basic character of drives, and in turn define the basic character of life. We have seen Nietzsche make just this claim above in, for example, §6. Now, a drive is to be understood as will to power; its primary function is to exert itself over and against other drives, to achieve mastery or dominance by consolidating the affective value of the relation between drives. The function of a drive is to discharge itself as mastery, expressed as the affect of command, wealth, power, creativity. Its function is not to preserve itself (as we saw in §13), although self-preservation might be a means towards this discharge (waiting for the right moment, for example), or a product of it (where factual dominance puts in one's control the conditions of one's preservation). Furthermore, survival or self-preservation appears to be a teleological principle – survival is a goal, an intention, that organizes all activity leading up to the attainment of the goal. Initially, the will to power might appear teleological too: power is a goal or intention of a drive. And, indeed, Nietzsche sometimes uses the concept in just this way. But, to take this language of teleology too seriously would be a mistake, Nietzsche would argue. Will is a relational concept (we saw this in §34); there is will only in so far as there is a power relation, that is, a relation of dominance or being-dominated. What appears as an *additional* intention of a drive, then, appears so only because we have already falsified matters in isolating the drive from its will to power, that is, from its relation. The *telos* appears only because we have first misunderstood will. Nietzsche analyses this falsification in §21.

So, in brief, this new hypothesis is that all organic functions can be "traced back" to will to power. This includes of course thought itself and thus philosophy (§9). These are will to power spiritualized; that is, "abstracted and sifted" to the level of ideas, models of the world, explanations, general laws or principles. This spiritualization may serve to disguise will to power, but it can also serve to enhance it, by raising its dominance to a universal relation at the level of ideas. We have also, in §14 for example, suggested that for Nietzsche the characterization of a will to power as strong or weak, healthy or unhealthy, active or reactive, distinguishes types of human beings and, in particular, the "noble" from the "plebeian" type. The will to power can permit distinctions among types of human life (nobility and plebeian, perhaps among other, finer distinctions), and thus also an analysis of the interactions of these types. Moreover, as we have just been reminded, it becomes spiritualized in various ways. All of these are broadly *historical* events. And therefore the study of will to power as the basic character of life is not only a subject for biology (and, as we see below, also physics) but also psychology and *history*. Thus above Nietzsche defined psychology as a "morphology" of the development of the will to power (§23); this point becomes, in his next book, the famous notion of "genealogy".

4. Then, hypothesis (2) not only attempts to think "inorganic" nature as proto-organic, a primitive form of will, but more fundamentally as will to power. That is, if will to power is the basic form of all organic drives, and if material nature is proto-organic, then the final hypothesis would be that the will to power is the basic determination of all "efficient force" [*wirkende Kraft*]. By "efficient force" Nietzsche is referring to the basic model of cause and effect employed by mechanistic physics; such a model takes one of Aristotle's four causes and makes it primary. The efficient cause ("efficient" understood in the sense of "having efficacy"), for Aristotle, is the previous thing (or things) that functions as the agent that brings about the cause. The will to power model, Nietzsche is proposing, can adequately and fully replace the efficient cause model of mechanistic natural science. We have seen a similar claim already in §22, where Nietzsche used it to reinterpret concepts such as calculability in physics.

These are the four nested hypotheses Nietzsche puts forward. The last sentence of the passage contains a curious expression that we should stop to consider. Nietzsche writes that the "will to power" constitutes "the world seen from within [*Die Welt von innen gesehen*], in its 'intelligible character' . . .". Now, the second of these notions takes us back to Kant and the idealistic tradition that followed him: the intelligible character of the world was the world "in itself", distinct from the manner of its appearance. Nietzsche puts it in inverted commas to indicate that, of course, he does not buy into this distinction – the fact that he claims that the world *could* be viewed in its intelligible character is already proof of this, and shows that Nietzsche intends to define his position by its difference from Kantian idealism.

The first notion ("seen from within"), however, reminds us of several important claims. First, the point made just above about the material world and our affects being of the same "reality-rank". This certainly repeats the idea of an understanding of the world not merely as secondary appearance. However, what we did not note above is that this comparison also says something about the affects. Traditionally, affection is often classed along with sensations and feelings as a derivative mode of representation, a type of image or picture of some more fundamental state of affairs. For Nietzsche, affect (as the affects of command or superiority in §19) is a first order state of affairs, being the relation among the will to power of drives. From this idea we might speculate that, for Nietzsche, to "see from within" is not to "see" at all – in the sense of forming a derivative image *of something else*. What it means to "see" here needs to be reunderstood along the lines of affection, as a first order reality. Not only what is seen, *but the seeing itself*, is "within". Secondly, "seen from within" recalls the notion of appearance without that which appears. This is another way of expressing the above point. Using the idea of affection, Nietzsche is attempting a philosophy of appearance that does not require the structure of representation (or, as we will discuss later, the structure of a *subject* that represents to itself some *object*). Thirdly, "seen from within" also should remind us of the idea of thought as the inter-relation of drives. Again, rather than thought being a distinct type of thing that may or may not accurately represent some other real thing, Nietzsche is trying to understand thought as "within" the real – that is, at the level of the will to power of drives and of the relations of drives. Thought and affect are thus closely related; thought might even be affect "spiritualized".

Thus, the attack on truth as representation can be approached from a different direction as well. Rather than a property of a thought, truth is to be understood as a state of being or a mode of life. In particular, truth is the state of realignment: to be truthful is for one's dominant will to power to reveal itself immediately in affect and thought. Nietzsche discusses this notion under the heading "honesty". It is made thematic in Part 7, but the notion of honesty has appeared frequently in the book already (e.g. the end of §32). By contrast, because the will to power of humans lower on the order of rank is always initially reactive and spiritualized in such a way as to disguise, misrepresent, devalue or at least redirect will to power, then it is an *ontological* characteristic of the plebeian that they "lie" (see for example, §260), even in believing in truth. The world "seen from within" is not a *thought*, but the affective state of a new type of human being.

§37

We should ask ourselves why it might appear, as Nietzsche asks mockingly, that God is refuted [*widerlegt*], but the Devil is not. First of all, because the origin of life is immanent to nature, a function of nature, rather than being created, while the other-worldliness of Platonic Christianity often associated material nature with evil. Moreover, one might be tempted to describe the will to power as wicked or evil – which would eliminate God's presence (popularly, the presence of Good) from the world altogether, in favour of the Devil. Immediately, though, Nietzsche replies: "on the contrary!" [*Im Gegenteil*]. Now, the contrary would be that the Devil is refuted and God not – is this what Nietzsche means? Recall that this is all to "speak popularly" rather than philosophically. And "who the devil is forcing you to speak popularly"? This last joke is significant: it is the devil who, if anyone, is forcing you to speak and understand the situation so unphilosophically. If there is genuine "evil" to be found here, it is with those who take such popular ways of speaking seriously. To be "Beyond Good and Evil" is also to be beyond the opposition of God and Devil too. (However, Nietzsche does use the notion of evil when he wishes to be provocative, and perhaps ironic too. In general, for example, he will often argue that an advancement of the human type would be possible only if humans became more "evil" rather than more "good"; at such times, the terms are being used for types of beliefs, but as these beliefs are evaluated by conventional moralities.) Still, Nietzsche does not say "not at all" or the equivalent; he says "on the contrary". This is because, as we shall see later, there is an account of the divine in Nietzsche, and it is extremely significant. The clearest example is near the end of the book, in §295.

§38

The French Revolution (only a century prior to Nietzsche writing) has been so often interpreted that the text has disappeared under the interpretation. Could this happen again? (This is a teasing question, incidentally – while many Europeans might have worried that the *Revolution* could happen again, Nietzsche is worried that the *interpretation* could.) That is, Nietzsche is asking: could a "noble posterity" misunderstand the past in order to "make gazing upon it bearable"? As far as Nietzsche is concerned, this has already happened: we (European philosophers, theologians, psychologists) have indeed misunderstood the origin of will, life, good and evil, in order that we can interpret them in a more agreeable way. "And this very moment, is it not, in so far as we comprehend this – thereby past?" A new philosophy can emerge that no longer misunderstands this past. But, has this philosophy emerged *because* we comprehend our previous mistakes? Nietzsche has rejected the philosophical significance of comprehension, consciousness, or self-knowledge. So, we can safely assume here that "comprehension" is merely a delayed sign ("thereby past") of some other more basic change.

§39

Few would argue that something is true merely because it makes people happy or virtuous. But we still forget that making unhappy and making evil are not counter-arguments, either. It might be that what is most true is precisely what is most dangerous, and even that "strength of spirit" could be measured by how little it requires truth diluted or veiled. Here is an echo of one of Nietzsche's basic claims: that falsehoods might be conditions of life. It follows that truths would be dangerous. There is also a very close echo of Nietzsche's early book *The Birth of Tragedy*, in which he discusses Greek tragedy as a revelation (but a necessarily veiled one) of dangerous truths.

Certain *parts* of truth are more readily uncovered by the evil and unhappy – or even the happy evil, of whom moralists prefer not to speak. Hardness [*Härte*] and cunning [*List*] provide the best conditions for strong, independent spirits or philosophers than those softer conditions that produce scholars. Hardness is understood in the sense of adverse conditions – precisely those conditions which, on more traditional ways of thinking, are not conducive to life; cunning is an important concept to which Nietzsche will regularly return. Notice also that one characteristic "rightly prized" in the scholar is the "art of taking things lightly" – which is not at all far from the account we have just seen Nietzsche make of the free spirit who laughs and is full of joy. These small subtleties are worth noting, lest we believe Nietzsche is simply praising one type and denigrating the other.

The final unGerman trait of the philosopher as "free spirit" is to be without illusion, able to see clearly what is – like a banker able to make a fortune. Prior to the analogy with a banker, this description is perfectly compatible with an ordinary sense of objectivity or dispassionate observation. It is the connection to the banker, no doubt, that interests Nietzsche – with the connotations of shrewdness or cunning, power (at least financial), acquisition rather than mere observation, and with an overtone of exploitation. Moreover, as is well known, Christianity for centuries discouraged the lending of money for interest ("usury"); for this reason, money-lending and thus banking became associated with the Jews. By choosing this particular analogy, Nietzsche is having a sly go at German anti-Semites. To be sure, banking requires shrewdness and may involve exploitation – a typical anti-Semitic slander – but these are precisely the properties of the free spirit. Notice finally that the image of the banker accords well with the economic metaphor Nietzsche uses frequently in his work. We will return to discuss this metaphor at a later stage.

§40

This section is about "masks" [*Maske*] – a theme we have seen several times before (e.g. §§25, 26). A mask is obviously a way of hiding, of disengaging from the world. Moreover, it is an accretion of misinterpretations that grows around a person or event (as with the French Revolution in §38). But, more significantly, a mask is also a way of precisely *engaging* with the world on simplified, already understood, controllable terms. Here, Nietzsche introduces the idea of mask through the notion of "shame" [*Scham*]. Significantly, this word also means the external genitalia; we'll see Nietzsche later using this connection more directly (for example, at the beginning of Part 4).

A shame is what one wants to hide. The significant point Nietzsche is making is that we should not just think of the shameful as the bad or degrading things. Even a god can have shame, and what is most shameful is not the "worst" it is simply what is not appropriate for others. "It is not only malicious cunning [*Arglist*] behind the mask – there is so much good in cunning [*List*]." Moreover, it might be that the best mask might be the opposite of what is hidden. Certainly, we are familiar enough with the figure of criminality or perversion hiding behind respectability; but Nietzsche is talking of something "precious and vulnerable" hiding behind the crudest of behaviour. (The reference to rolling in a barrel is to Diogenes the Cynic – whom we have mentioned before; this is a wine barrel, though, so it is likely Nietzsche wants us to think of Dionysus too.) In accordance with Nietzsche's notion of an order of rank, there will be truths that are just not *for* others, that must be hidden – and it is likely also that these truths will be experienced *initially at least* as shameful or wicked, for example the kind of twists on conventional understanding that Nietzsche discussed in §23.

To be sure, there is an autobiographical element to this passage: Nietzsche's genteel public persona was famously at odds with the radical and scathing ideas in his books. However, as we have discussed previously, the notion of mask is an important element in Nietzsche's methodology. The mask is a description of the essential nature of the relations between those at different heights on the order of rank. As an instrument of such relations, the mask not only protects the one wearing the mask, but also the "friends" on the outside. In Nietzsche's striking and beautiful phrase, such a man "instinctively needs speech for silence and silencing [*Schweigen und Verschweigen*]". But we have already been warned not to take the *protective* dimension of the mask as its only virtue. In §26, the one who remains secreted away is not the stronger one who is destined for knowledge. To go down and inside, Nietzsche explains there, will require "much disguise". Thus, the mask is an instrument by which the philosopher engages with her contemporary world, in order at least to investigate it. However, the sections that follow will subtly expand upon this idea. Section 41 will make clear, with its notion of "tests", that the mask must remain strategic and mobile if it is not to become a trap or prison. Then, §44 will conclude with a list of masks that are clearly no longer defence mechanisms but precisely techniques for achieving certain ends. What those ends are, however, will not become clear until §61 and the idea of a "comprehensive responsibility" for the development of the human type.

The profound spirit needs a mask, hiding even from his closest friends. The notion of friends who are not yet close enough, not yet confidants, is a common one throughout the book, and culminates in the last stanzas of the poem with which the book finishes. And even if the mask is not put on deliberately, one will form anyway, based upon the "false" or "shallow" interpretations of every step or sign of the profound spirit. Wearing a mask, then, is at once a choice and a necessity; this is an elegant way of signalling the idea of realignment.

§41

This passage suggests certain "tests" [*Proben*] for those who would be and remain independent, and are destined for "command" [*Befehl*]. These are tests not only in the sense of indicators of those who are truly independent (i.e. in the sense of a medical test), but more importantly "trials" or "ordeals" through which one must pass in order to emerge as independent. It is a lengthy list: the test of not remaining "attached" to [*anhängen*] friends or nations, to pity for those "higher men" who are crushed by circumstance, to a science [*Wissenschaft*], to "detachment" itself [*Loslösung*], or to a virtue such as hospitality or liberality.

The first repeats the theme of the friends who are not confidants that we saw in the previous section. The theme of pity is one to which we shall return, but will not detain us here. "*Wissenshaft*" has a broader meaning than "science" in English, which has tended to become conflated with the "natural sciences": rather, it refers to any objective discipline of learning. Nietzsche does not write about remaining committed to "science", but rather to "a science" or even to "one science". This is an attack on specialism that will become more explicit in Part 6. Nietzsche seems also to be implying that the free spirit should wear sciences as masks – to be assumed for a time, but then abandoned for a different mask. The test of detachment reinforces this point. Recall the figure of the one destined for knowledge discussed in §26: one must go down and into (as Zarathustra). That is why, above, we emphasized that a mask is not only a mode of hiding, but also a mode of being engaged, that is a particular way of entering into a community with others. So, to remain with one mask (such as one science, or one virtue) is to risk becoming attached to detachment. The final item in the list presents a puzzle: the test of not remaining attached to one's generosity – for "rich souls" wish to "spend" themselves. (This is again an echo of the opening of *Thus Spoke Zarathustra*, in which Zarathustra wants to give away of himself; he is a full cup that wants to flow out.) Recall that the will to power is the basic feature of all drives; it exists as the desire to command and impose itself. Nietzsche's suggestion is that this "command" need not necessarily take the form of literal command or the inscribing of laws on tablets, it might also take the form of a generosity: of one's wealth or strength, perhaps, but also of knowledge. Rich souls must *also* conserve themselves. With that, we have come full circle: from the test of isolation and withdrawal above, to the test of exhausting oneself in generosity. It might appear that Nietzsche is trying to indicate an Aristotelian virtuous mean. More likely, though, just like with the language of "youth" and "maturity", he is attempting to re-understand these concepts so that they are no longer opposites.

§42

Nietzsche's proposed name for a new breed [*Gattung*] of philosophers is "attempters" [*Versucher*]. There are several significant puns here: in German as in English, the word is closely related to "tempt"; and in certain contexts Nietzsche clearly has this meaning primarily in mind. At such times the word is typically translated as "tempters". To tempt is to remain independent, but to somehow also draw others along, not by intellectual argument but by seduction. With this, Nietzsche is again hinting at the *responsibility* of the free spirit and especially the philosopher of the future (cf. §295). Moreover, the word can also be translated as "experimenters", that is, in a broadly scientific sense. These philosophers will experiment, in order to pursue the ideal of a new mode of philosophical life. Finally, of course, we have just had a section of "tests" or "trials", which were temptations from which one must attempt to pull away – bringing all three meanings together.

§43

Will these coming philosophers be "new friends of truth"? Probably, but certainly not dogmatists. The latter Nietzsche here defines as the assumption that one's truth is also a truth for everyman [*Jedermann*]. The word means both "everyone" in a straightforward sense, but also the figure of Everyman in Christian morality plays. Moreover, it carries the notion that, in English, might be expressed as "the man on the street", meaning a common person, one of many. Thus, when Nietzsche claims that this universalization of truth is the secret wish of all dogmatists, this means not only the traditional philosophical claim that truth, to be truth, should be universal, but also that precisely the truth to be elevated in this way is a plebeian, herd truth. Note that this is a rather broader definition of "dogmatist" than is usually the case, in line with Nietzsche's treatment of the topic in the Preface.

It is easier to accept this point as Nietzsche articulates it a few sentences later: what is good for one is not necessarily good for another, and even the notion of a common good is (in some way) impossible. That there is no strictly universal sense of the good has become a relatively familiar claim among moral and political philosophers. Moreover, Nietzsche claims, the attempt to present a universal good is always a sign of "bad taste". Let us for the moment also accept Nietzsche's thesis that a truth, as a perspective, is always evaluative (that is, always contains, or even is constituted by, *its* good). Still, it remains apparently difficult to accept his next conclusion, that one can be a friend to truth while acknowledging that truths need not agree. "My judgement [*Urteil*] is *my* judgement" Nietzsche imagines the future philosopher saying. This is an expression of unique and privileged ownership – and thus a denial of the "easy rights" of others to my judgement, unless perhaps they are of my "order of rank".

One way of understanding this would be to argue that the kinds of truths Nietzsche has in mind are not the ordinary kind: a person's telephone number, the price of a pint of milk; perhaps also not straightforward objective descriptions of a natural science type: the mean temperature on the surface of Venus, say. Rather, it is those truths that implicitly or explicitly involve an evaluation (an assertion of the good) that concern him. In that way, the easier-to-accept non-universality of the sense of good would be equivalent to the non-universality of truth. Thinking this way about Nietzsche has some merit, but is ultimately implausible.

To show this, we need to take into account two additional claims. First, that any assertion that X is the case, that this proposition is true, necessarily involves the idea of a proposition or thought *representing* some state of affairs in the world, but being different from it. And this, in turn, involves an interpretation (Nietzsche believes an unjustified one) of the relation between thought and world, or between language and world. In brief, we interpret the world (and ourselves) in such a way that statements about it appear not to involve interpretations (that is, appear to be fully objective or simple statements of fact). That is why he so frequently attacks the distinction between subject and object in grammar – because this grammatical function subtly influences us to distinguish the subject (the "I" that thinks or asserts) and the object (the "world" or state of affairs asserted about). If, moreover, this interpretation also involves an evaluation, then Nietzsche can legitimately claim that all truth claims are fundamentally evaluative.

Secondly, truth is not a representation at which an "I" could arrive, or which an "I" could assert, for the "I" is a social structure of drives. To the extent that one says "I" simply, there is *already* falsehood and misrepresentation. Rather, truth is a function of the relation among drives. That is why truths are always evaluative, but here there is a further implication. That which is said to be the "truth" is not something I have proved, or my opinion, belief, or assertion, but is *primarily my state of organic being*, or *the manner in which I live* which has made itself be known *in that living*. Accordingly, that which is false is *a state of organic being which inherently prohibits itself being known as such*. Truth or falsehood lies fundamentally at the level of existence, rather than at the level of representation or expression in language. It is: being known to itself as will to power. Here, obviously, the knower and the known are not separate (certainly not as subject and object). The free spirit, and the future philosopher is, in this sense, "realigned to" the will to power. Their thought, mode of living and acting, are manifestations of an "honest" will to power. We will return later to the theme of "honesty".

§44

This is a long section, which serves both to sum up Part 2 and introduce Part 3. Broadly, we need to notice two things. First of all, Nietzsche distinguishes "us" (the free spirits) from the future philosophers who are certainly this, but also something more. Nietzsche does not consider himself one of the future philosophers, but as their prophet, so to speak. More immediately important than this distinction, however, is to distinguish both from those who might also call themselves "free spirits" or "free thinkers". Nietzsche describes two classes here: first, thinkers of the democratic or even socialist ideal, who conceive of themselves as freed from previous non-democratic forms of society. Secondly, he discusses the "free thinkers" who conceive of themselves as free from the constraint of dogmatic and especially religious forms of thought. Principally from the discussions of "prejudices" in Part 1, we have already seen versions of the arguments that Nietzsche, quite sweepingly, gestures towards here. In brief, *either* this new freedom is to be evaluated not as progress, but negatively. That is, it is another step in the domination of the "herd", plebeian values, and away from independence, "solitude", the free spirit, and a philosophy that is realigned to will to power. Moreover, it is a step towards promoting just those conditions (the opposite of dangerous, high tension) under which higher types are least likely to emerge. *Or*, for the other modern type with whom the free spirit might be confused, this "freedom" is an illusion (the free thinkers have replaced one type of dogmatic faith with another, which is *functionally equivalent*).

The last thirty lines or so are an energetic and rhetorically brilliant description of the free spirit. Notice that most of these characteristics are not permanent or essential qualities, but mobile and nimble commitments or strategies ("at home . . . as guests", "occasionally"), what Nietzsche elsewhere calls "masks". Most of the ideas we have discussed already in different contexts: the attack on prejudice or dependency, the importance of gratitude, curiousness and probing in dark places, misers although also appearing to be prodigals, and so forth. So, here we will make just a few observations.

Being at home in "many countries of the spirit", though only as guests, reminds us of the notion of masks as controlled forms of engagement, and of the seeing with "many eyes" that occurs later (§211) but that has already been discussed above in §2. "Dependency" refers us not only to the notion of "independence", but also to the tests of attachment (the roots of the words are the same). "Fore- and back-ground" echoes the recurring image of perspective. To that Nietzsche adds playfully "Fore- and back-souls", which presumably refers again both to the idea of masks, but also to the distinction between the basic drives of a living being and the merely surface phenomena, such as thought or intention, which might be aligned, or might be disguises. With the "sometimes proud of tables of categories", Nietzsche unexpectedly welcomes Kant among the free spirits. He also suggests that Kant was providing a morphology or typology – a science of forms, though not one that was historical. Notice also the metaphors of midnight and noon, which we will speak of again for they are important particularly in the poem with which the book ends.

We should not miss the parallels with Kant. Part 1 is an attempt to puncture metaphysical illusions as constitutive (this is what Kant called "dialectic"). Part 2 is, in part, an analysis of what that type of being must be such that it could make that attempt (this is analogous to what Kant called "analytic"). Part 2 is an analytic of the free spirit. In this regard, we should note that the list of attributes with which §44 ends has (depending upon how one divides up the complex, run-on grammar) twelve elements, collected in four groups of three (these could be identified as location, affection, strategy, and defence). This is exactly the structure of Kant's famous table of categories. Of course, lest we get too carried away with the seriousness of this, being proud of tables of categories is only one of the "categories" of the free spirit – a Kantian approach, then, is one mask, among others.

Finally, although Nietzsche again stresses that the free spirits are not the philosophers to come, yet again the two classes may have the characteristics and virtues that Nietzsche lists in common. This raises the question of what the philosophy, and philosopher, of the future must be like. If we are hoping that the question will be pursued or even answered soon, the title of the next Part – which I will translate as "The Nature of Religion" – does not appear promising. However, in a surprising way, it is to the "ideal" of the future philosopher that Part 3 is ultimately devoted; and thus §44 serves as a transition to the next stage of Nietzsche's thought.

4 The Nature of Religion: Beyond Nihilism, Towards the Immanent Ideal (Part 3 §§45–62)

"The Religious Character" would be an equally suitable translation of the title of this Part [*das religiöse Wesen*].

§45

Nietzsche begins by setting out the task, and the problem of that task. The task is to "hunt" down the range of human experiences so far, and its "as yet undepleted possibilities". Immediately, the title of this Part, and the question of the philosopher of the future raised at the end of Part 2, make more sense. Future possibilities will reveal themselves at least partly in and through an understanding of the range "so far". If only, Nietzsche writes, there were helpers and companions for this hunt, but there are none. Scholars may have good eyes and noses, but not for the "great hunt" and its dangers: there they lose "*ihr Spürauge und ihre Spürnase*" (their eye and nose for traces). In addition to hunting metaphors, the language also suggests the detective. One would have to have a profound, wounded, monstrous [*ungeheurer*] conscience for this task, and then also the malicious spirituality [*boshafte Geistigkeit*] that can arrange and put into formulas. We should note immediately that the being above and surveying below of this spirituality is not first and foremost a height characteristic of objective and abstractive science, but the height of the order of rank.

There is a little joke at the end of the section, as Nietzsche rewrites his description of the agreeable vice of curiosity in conventional religious language.

§46, and discussion of the "Slave Revolt in Morality"

This section sketches out Nietzsche's infamous account of the origin of Christian values. Christianity consisted of a "slave revolt" in the sphere of values, which was a "revaluation" [*Umwertung*] of ancient morality. There is of course not one ancient morality – and nor is there one Christianity, as the first sentences make clear. Nietzsche describes the system of values of the rulers of Rome as free spirited, self-confident, tolerant, smilingly care-free. Such values are subjected to a "bold inversion" [*Umkehren*] so as to be understood as wicked, decadent, lazy and unruly, and thus requiring ruth-less and cruel sacrifice. In this inversion, the slaves become "masters". Spiritually, they are masters over themselves, having tyrannically sacrificed themselves – this of course makes them slaves to themselves as well, as Nietzsche makes clear in §195, and to value that slavery as a mark of super-iority in the eyes of God. Further, morally, they appear superior to their political or social masters. Nietzsche will return to key parts of this story throughout the book, but for the moment let us make a few observations on the passage.

First, what is meant by "revaluation"? This is an important concept in Nietzsche; and a term he uses to describe his own project. We have certainly seen the idea before in the book, most notably right at the beginning, with the question of the value of the will to truth. The value of this will was so deeply assumed that it was almost not noticed that it involved values at all; to raise the question is to begin a process of revaluation. Revaluation means to raise the question of value where previously it had not been possible to ask it, and partly thereby to shift comprehensively the manner in which basic and existing acts or states are evaluated. It is important not to miss the fact that Nietzsche thereby *admires* the work of early Christianity, an achievement of the spirit almost without parallel. He hopes that his own work will achieve something like this revaluation.

Secondly, what is meant by a "bold inversion"? Given the similarity in the construction of the words (revaluation: *Umwertung*, inversion: *Umkehren*), one might be forgiven for thinking that these concepts are similar for Nietzsche. But there is an all-important difference. An inversion *turns upside down* an existing moral order; it is like a negative image of that order. The result is still dependent on the original for its structure, for its basic distinctions. That is why Nietzsche speaks of it as an act of "revenge" – because it is a *re-action*. A revaluation, although necessarily beginning in the midst of some existing moral order, marks a definite break and involves newness or creativity.

Thirdly, what is meant by "the unconditional"? The slaves, Nietzsche claims, wanted and understood only tyranny (absolute subjugation under a single power). Similarly, they wanted and understood only the unconditional, that is, simple, universal and absolutely binding laws. Because of this, they detested the nuanced, free-spirited, cheerful Roman disposition. There is also a link to theology here: an omnipotent God is understood as an unconditioned being – for example, the *causa sui*. Thus, Nietzsche is implicitly drawing a link between the unconditional in morality and the positing of an unconditioned, single and all-powerful God. But why only tyranny and the unconditional? Because the slave's whole existence consists of his being dominated; the will to power of his drives is constantly a reaction to rather than the dominant and effective force. The slave may desire freedom, but neither knows nor understands it. For the slave, existence simply means being under tyranny. The inversion of values then flips the evaluation of this being under tyranny from something bad to something good. Everyone's existence *should be* tyrannized, unconditional, and thereby suffering. This idea of a *structurally necessary* slavery is developed further in §§194–5.

Fourthly, "French Revolution". If we look back to §38 – the discussion of how the French Revolution disappeared under the interpretations placed on it – we can now see what Nietzsche was driving at. The Christian slave revolt and its inversion of values "hid" itself, disappeared under the mass of commentary, justification, the "prolonged suicide of reason", as Nietzsche expressed it earlier. Rather than seeing sacrifice as a form of self-tyranny, it is seen as an act of love; rather than notice the reaction and revenge in this moral inversion, it is seen as the appearance *for the first time* of the true moral code, the true way to value things. The "revolt" was awesomely successful. So, the moral system is no longer simply a Christian phenomenon (nor a Jewish one), but characteristic of all modern European culture. (Although one has to read between the lines a little here, this point is made in §§194–5.) It is this forgetting or covering-over that we moderns are just beginning to realize.

Nietzsche's discussions of the "slave revolt" obviously are intended as a historical critique of Christianity and its moral principles. However, they also have several specifically philosophical targets in mind, but none more so than the famous "master–slave dialectic" in Hegel's *Phenomenology of Spirit*. Nietzsche's terminology is not quite the same, but the connection is clear nevertheless. In Hegel, consciousness finds itself divided between master and slave. The split results in a kind of alienation and the impossibility of fulfilment – especially for the master, who is alienated from the material and permanent grounds of what he enjoys. The overcoming of this division in consciousness consists of growth towards a new form of consciousness that does not suffer from this particular form of alienation. The passage in Hegel was of huge significance for political philosophers throughout the nineteenth century, Marx most obviously. Nietzsche's relation to this famous analysis has two revealing aspects. First, the "split" between master and slave is not, as it is for Hegel, simply a function of the structure of each consciousness in its relation with the other. Presumably, there will be some masters and slaves that arise from accidental forces in history. Someone will find themselves to be a slave; someone else a master. This situation just doesn't interest Nietzsche. He is interested in those types who are essentially masters or slaves, because their modes of life are essentially active or reactive. Rather than being parts of a divided or duplicated consciousness, master and slave are different types. Secondly, for Hegel, the overcoming of this difference is a progression to a higher spirituality. Such "overcoming" Nietzsche sees only as the triumph of the virtues created in the slave revolt. Higher spirituality, for Nietzsche, can only mean becoming *more master*.

§47

Nietzsche is here criticizing Schopenhauer and Richard Wagner (two former heroes of his) for their relation to a particular religious theme: how is it possible for the will to be denied? That is, particularly: how can a wilful person, self-serving to the point of sin, suddenly become a saint, in which all will is annulled? There is something, Nietzsche says, miraculous about this sudden change of a basic state to its opposite. A miracle cannot be analysed, is not subject to natural scientific investigation (e.g. in psychology). This is because it violates the basic principle of all thought: the inviolable faith in opposites (§2). However, we have seen Nietzsche subject this faith to a critique. Here, he will similarly say that there is no real opposition, and therefore no miracle that cannot be analysed. Seeing this conversion as an opposition and miracle was an error of interpretation. To borrow a Kantian notion, the opposition leads to an "antinomy" – an explicit contradiction – in this case, a psychological change that cannot be analysed psychologically. Psychology thus does not merely stop, but is "shipwrecked". Overcoming the antinomy requires an analysis that exposes the original contradiction as involving a misunderstanding, or being merely appearance.

§48

Reflections on how different European races have a different basic, physiological relation to religion, and accordingly also to the lack or loss of faith. Nietzsche then quotes from Ernest Renan and records his curious admiration for the passage, that has "truth standing on its head", and how elegant it is to have one's own "antipode". Note that, one section after renewing the critique of oppositions in the sphere of *the objects of* science, religion and morality, Nietzsche is happily speaking of "antipodes". Nietzsche's first response to the passage was to fall into its trap, and wrathfully oppose himself to it absolutely; the later response is appreciative, nuanced, no longer a simple "yes" or "no". This is an important, if indirect, point: the fact that we must abandon our faith in absolute oppositions does not mean there are no differences, but rather that they have to be understood and interpreted differently, with a sense of their complexity and historical genesis.

§49

Nietzsche contrasts an ancient Greek religion of gratitude [*Dankbarkeit*], which is "noble" [*vornehm*], with a religion overrun with fear character-istic of a later period of "rabble", when Christianity was around the corner. Note also that there are two words often translated as "noble" in Nietzsche's text: *edel* and *vornehm*. We have seen the first of these quite often (near the beginning of the Preface, for example); and Nietzsche tends to use it fairly generally, for something involving some distinction or spir-ituality. Nietzsche has reserved the second word for something more specific, and ultimately something "higher": for that aristocratic being and morality that he often seems to espouse (see e.g. §14). It is this second word that occurs in the title of Part 9. The Preface was also where we first encountered the notion of gratitude; we will return to this idea shortly, above all in discussing §56. The gratitude, significantly, is not towards a god or gods, but explicitly towards "nature and life". This whole passage is hugely important, because it is now clear why the noble philosopher of the future *must* be understood within the context of such a religious outlook.

The theme of fear links to the Renan quotation of the previous section. However, this is a relatively new element in the analysis of Christian religion, and we need to understand how the notion of fear is connected to the earlier notion of revenge. Nietzsche will return to the significance of fear in §59.

§§50–51

The first of these sections provides a breezy list of various types of "passion for God". The suggestion is that this passion is something base dressed up as something holy. This whole section serves to set up the problem of the true saint in the next section.

The "most powerful humans" have bowed before the saint. Not because self-conquest is a miracle in the manner discussed in §47, but because it demonstrated a "superior force" that sought to test itself in this self-conquest. In effect, then, the most powerful honoured their own will to power in honouring the saint. The form this self-conquest takes in the saint may well be a "neurosis", a kind of illness, but it was nevertheless a manifestation of power. Surely, though, this desire could not be for nothing; there must be a reason, a great danger or enemy here. This, presumably, is the origin of the error of interpretation that sees the saint in a traditional religious sense, as an instrument or intimate of God. Note, at the end of the passage, another frequent device in Nietzsche's prose: the unfinished sentence. It may be incomplete because Nietzsche feels he has already said "enough" or too much a few sentences previously, because there is something he does not want to or cannot say, or even something he is playfully pretending not to want to say, because it is too scandalous or too revealing. These are all possibilities. In fact, we know that in the saint the powerful received an intimation of the will to power. So, perhaps the unsaid here is that what the saint signifies has changed: the external will of God is replaced by the will to power. Nietzsche will develop this point further in §53.

§52

This section contrasts the Old and New Testaments, and the "taste" for each. Nietzsche portrays the former as like a vast, ancient architectural ruin, before which we stand in awe "of what humanity once was". Or rather, we stand in awe unless our taste is for the New Testament, which is the taste of small souls and "domestic pets" of Europe. Accordingly, to have stuck these two together, and pretend they are one book, is a profound literary sin.

§53

"Why atheism today?" It is important to realize that this opening question is not intended as a call to atheism, but rather as a historical and cultural question. Why, precisely today, is there a strong trend towards atheism? Nietzsche gives the answers in joking fashion.

The last sentence proves a sting in the tail: theism (belief in a God) is declining, but the religious instinct is growing. What does this mean? Two things. First, that although overtly theistic beliefs may be declining, implicit beliefs that *originated in* religious beliefs still remain and grow. Here, Nietzsche may be thinking of the metaphysical and ultimately moral "prejudices" he discussed in Part 1. These may owe their origin historically to religious beliefs or theological analyses, but in one form or another still organize all of modern thought about physics, psychology and politics. Significantly, these prejudices also still organize that form of belief called "atheism" (see *Genealogy*, Third Treatise, §24). Atheism is or can be a form of dogmatism. Secondly, that a new type of religion is emerging, one that worships will and life. This second idea was first, though indirectly, suggested in §51. With the dramatic change in object, of course, there must also be a dramatic difference in the nature of "worship". Nietzsche provides one description of such a difference in *Genealogy*, Second Treatise, §23. There, he writes, "there are *more noble* ways of making use of the fabrication of gods". Nietzsche will pursue both of the above alternatives in the remaining sections of this Part.

§54

This section continues the attack on the subject–object distinction, and accordingly a belief in the soul that, so far as Nietzsche is concerned, has organized both grammar and a great deal of the history of philosophy. We have seen many of these points before, for example in §§3 and 34. There is an explicit tie-in between this belief and Christianity. More recently, though, Nietzsche admits, modern philosophy has been anti-soul and therefore anti-Christian (although not necessarily, as we saw in the previous section, anti-religious). This anti-soul philosophy commenced in the asking whether thought might be the condition of the "I" – that is, as in Kant, the appearance of the I is an *effect of* the synthetic activity of thought rather than its substantial basis. The soul and the subject had "*merely apparent existence*". (Nietzsche then compares this idea with the Vedanta school of ancient Hinduism.) Interestingly, then, after the attacks of Part 1, it is Kant who is credited with "admirable perseverance and cunning [*List*]" in producing a philosophy that begins to break the stranglehold of previous beliefs. As with so many things, Nietzsche's relationship with Kant is much more complex and appreciative than it first appears. We should also re-emphasize that, although Nietzsche argues that modern philosophy in its scepticism is *to this extent anti-Christian*, it remains the case that Christian value judgements organize modern thought and life (e.g. in the notion of democracy). Accordingly, Hegel – who certainly participated in this general attack on the simple soul concept – nevertheless appears to be complicit in the slave revolution, on the analysis we gave of §46.

What is meant by "merely apparent existence"? There are several possibilities, all of which agree on Nietzsche's main point here: the non-substantiality of the "I" or "soul". The subject could be a phenomenon and not a thing-in-itself, employing Kantian thought, meaning it is *real* but not metaphysically foundational. Or, the subject could be a mere epiphenomenon, a kind of irrelevant by-product of real processes. Nietzsche seems to come close to this second idea in §17. Finally, "appearance" could be meant in the sense Nietzsche uses it in §34, that is, apparentness without either substantiality or a representational relation to substantiality. Section 56 below will give us good reasons for taking the discussion here in this third sense.

§55

Nietzsche tells a brief story of religious cruelty. We should note how familiar these compressed and sweeping narratives – covering thousands of years and/or vastly different modes of thinking – are becoming (e.g. §§32, 46). Read in isolation, such passages are rarely satisfying, because they leave out so much detail and analysis, and raise but fail to answer so many questions. We should, therefore, feel bound to read them as fragments of a richer and much more complex account of the history of religious and moral psychology. However, we should also ask what is gained by this decision to present the history in fragments. One possibility is that the effect is more polemical, more scandalous, because what is lost in complexity and subtlety is gained in the boldness of assertion. Another, which is compatible with the first, is that it allows Nietzsche to organize his thoughts around issues, rather than around the history itself. So, here, a fragment of the history serves his analysis of the particular theme of sacrifice; while in §32 a different fragment serves the idea of the extra-moral values of the free spirit. In his next book, *The Genealogy of Morality*, Nietzsche temporarily drops the strategy of giving the account in fragments, and instead devotes whole chapters to particular historical themes (above all, asceticism, which is also mentioned here in half a sentence).

Here, cruelty is identified with sacrifice, which links this section back to §46, another fragment of the overall picture. The history moves from a sacrifice of others *to* the god, to a sacrifice of oneself (this is the particular notion treated in §46), to a sacrifice *of* the god. But this last stage divides into two entirely different phenomena for Nietzsche. On the one hand, this is the sacrifice of Christ on the cross, part of the inversion of values that characterized the Christian slave revolt. But, on the other hand (and this is what Nietzsche stresses, but playfully, almost as if the obvious Christian reference had not occurred to him), it means giving up on any transcendent god as a part of religion, and worshipping only things that would remain: stones, stupidities, gravity, blind fate, and (for this is what the others amount to) nothingness. That is to say, preferring to worship a godless universe. The double meaning of this last stage, the fact that it has a double meaning and that the history of spirit could divide at this moment, is important: Nietzsche indeed uses it as an image to sum up his whole thought in the final stanzas of the poem at the book's end. The self-sacrifice of the second stage had (or at least was represented as having) purpose: one sacrificed one's will and instincts in order to be closer to God. The third, last stage of cruelty and sacrifice is a higher cruelty because it is a denial to the self of even this comfort or consolation, and has been reserved for the coming new "race" [*Geschlecht*] of human beings, the philosophers of the future.

§56, and discussion of Eternal Recurrence

The last, highest rung of cruelty discussed above seems to have two *further* outcomes. The first is what Nietzsche here calls "pessimism" in a particular nineteenth-century, half-Christian form that he finds in Schopenhauer. The second, however, is an "ideal" that has passed through pessimism, or which has been "delivered" from pessimism. This second form is achieved by thinking the most world-negating pessimism to its depths, and "perhaps thereby" having one's eyes opened to an "inverse ideal [*umgekehrtes Ideal*]". Notice first that in the "perhaps thereby" Nietzsche is once again refusing to commit himself as to whether the capacity to acquire this new awareness is within one's power (at least to the extent that thinking pessimism through to its depths is). Nietzsche after all has been offering a consistent critique of the extent to which an "I" is at the ground of the individual will. Rather, becoming a free spirit, still more a philosopher of the future, seems primarily, though perhaps not exclusively, a question of physiology and "race".

"Inverse" is the same word Nietzsche used in §46 for the revaluation of values of the Christian slave revolt. We paid considerable attention to this word there for it seemed to help us to distinguish an essentially positive from an essentially negative revaluation. Here, however, Nietzsche would appear to be undercutting the earlier point. However, he most certainly does not say that this new ideal would be *formed by way of* a mere inversion (for example, an inversion of pessimism); on the contrary, if anything it is the pessimism, as world-negating, that is reactive. This point is reinforced by the description of this new "ideal": "the most highspirited, alive, world-affirming human" – someone who has not only come to accept what is ("the whole play and spectacle"), but who affirms and desires it, to all eternity.

This is the first treatment in this book of one of Nietzsche's most famous ideas: *eternal recurrence* (or "eternal return"). This is a controversial notion in Nietzsche's work. The two most common and obvious interpretations of it are as follows. *Either* it asserts that in reality all events that constitute the order of the universe repeat themselves, in the same order, in a vast cycle, forever. This is a cosmological or metaphysical claim. One of the most complete versions of an argument to this conclusion can be found in entry 1062 of the *Will to Power*. Or it asserts that there is something significant about the kind of person who could genuinely desire that the universe *should* repeat itself in this manner. This is a claim about a new and remarkable type of human psychology. In Nietzsche's writings, taking the published and unpublished together, there is considerable textual evidence for both these interpretations. And they are not incompatible, of course: the first invites one to respond to its truth, raising the possibility of the second; the second does not preclude either the truth or falsity of the first. Given the distance Nietzsche is at pains to establish between himself and any straightforward truth claim about the natural world (witness the torturous set of nested hypotheses in §36), it is not surprising that the cosmological version is found mainly in his notebooks. There, evidently, Nietzsche allowed himself to wear temporarily, but with enthusiasm, the mask of a cosmologist.

In this passage the psychological interpretation appears most natural, for the ideal is of a human being who "wills" this eternity. The issue is only of a capacity for willing and joyfully affirming, and not of the truth of the object of will. However, at that point, our interpretation becomes more complicated. This new ideal, possessing the virtues of realignment and thus honesty, could not presumably affirm a state of affairs that did not accord with her basic way of understanding her own existence. For Nietzsche, a noble psychology lives out an existence realigned to the will to power, to the truth of nature. The problem of truth and cosmology, then, "returns". (This is presumably the insight discussed in §59.) Now, this human not only wills that he returns, and not only that the whole "play and spectacle" returns, but something more. Fundamentally, he wills the endless return of "he who needs this spectacle – and makes it necessary: because over and over he needs himself – and makes himself necessary". This passage will require some unpacking.

First of all, there is a pun both hugely important and difficult to translate. "To need" translates "*nötig haben*"; while "to make necessary" translates "*nötig machen*". In other words, "*nötig*" can mean both a need and a necessity. At some cost we could therefore translate the passage as "he who requires this spectacle – and who makes it required: because over and over he requires himself – and makes himself required". This is clearly a very strong sense of "need", which entails that something is a *condition of* something. So, while "need" means necessary as a condition of something else, "necessary" perhaps means something that *itself* could not but be. That is one significant contrast Nietzsche is bringing out – bringing out in order to put in question – in his pun. Another, though, is between (i) the passivity of having a need, having something as one's condition; and (ii) the activity involved in "making necessary". This second contrast seems to echo the notion expressed only a few sentences previously: between merely accepting what is, and willing its eternal return.

In order to understand Nietzsche's thinking here we need to introduce an important additional premise: that all events (the execution of a will to power) are reciprocally connected in an entanglement of conditions. This would appear to be a Nietzschean adaptation of a fairly traditional metaphysical idea – it is a common theme in Leibniz, for example, in most post-Newtonian deterministic philosophies, and also in Darwin. Because of Nietzsche's attempt to rethink the idea of cause and effect, however, we can recognize the influence of previous philosophical accounts of determinism, but we must not simply conflate Nietzsche's notion with this tradition – even if Nietzsche himself sometimes employs this notion in a deterministic, Laplacian manner. We have not come across the notion of the entanglement of conditions in *Beyond Good and Evil* yet, at least not explicitly, although there have been analogues in §§2 and 20. We have, however, put the notion to work in our discussion of §34 – it seemed to be required in order to understand what Nietzsche meant there by "values" in a painterly sense. However, Nietzsche does make this claim explicitly often enough in other writings – for example, and in the context of a discussion of eternal recurrence, in *Thus Spoke Zarathustra*, Part 3, "The Convalescent", and again in Part 4, "The Drunken Song", §10. It is easy to see how such a notion of the entanglement of conditions might be important in an attempt to prove a cosmological version of eternal return: such a premise would seem to guarantee that the same *whole* course of events would follow each time *da capo*, from the beginning. There is good reason, therefore, for asserting that, for Nietzsche, a belief in eternal recurrence must entail a belief in the entanglement of conditions (and possibly also the reverse, although this is less clear).

One implication of this notion of the entanglement of conditions is that one cannot want just oneself or one event to return. Any attempt to isolate objects or events in this way is metaphysically illegitimate. The will must want *also* the whole sequence of things and events, or nothing at all. And this is the crux of the matter: for not just joys but also sorrows, agonies and unmerited joy must be willed; not just those who are worthy, but those who are stupid, crass, or criminal. The willing is absolutely indiscriminate, without the capacity for its values to intervene; nor is there a transcendent God whose plan will give the whole, which may in itself appear valueless, a final purpose. It is this indiscriminate willing of eternal return that Nietzsche had in mind in the previous section in writing "to sacrifice God for the nothing". To turn away from or negate the world, as the pessimist of earlier in this section does, is a reaction to this nothingness – it is an inability even to come to terms with, much less affirm, it. The capacity to affirm life and existence in this manner would, Nietzsche believes, form the ultimate touchstone of how noble, how "of the future" a human being is. The most well-known treatment of the notion of eternal recurrence as a touchstone is *The Gay Science* §341, where it is termed "the heaviest weight" that would "transform or possibly crush" one.

Let us return to the last, disjointed phrases of the passage. This new ideal shouts *da capo* to "he" who needs and who makes necessary the spectacle. One way of understanding this first part, employing the notion of the entanglement of conditions, is that "I" exist as the being who has emerged out of past and present conditions, and "I" am also an unavoidable condition that makes it such that the present and future could not but be. So, what appeared at first as a contrast between passivity and activity now seems to be a way of understanding how an individual being is involved in the entanglement of conditions, as a kind of channel through which fate occurs. But, on Nietzsche's analysis, this is true of all entities, including a "stone", to use one of Nietzsche's examples in the previous section: for a stone too is conditioned and is a condition. Who, then, is this "he" who, most fundamentally, is willed in willing eternal recurrence?

Nietzsche continues: "because over and over he needs himself – and makes himself necessary". Another layer of thinking is added. At first, this just sounds paradoxical, especially if we are still thinking in terms of activity and passivity. In order to understand Nietzsche's thinking here, we should recall a few of the notions that were employed in the build-up to this section. First of all, two sections previously, in §54, the idea that the "I" or "soul" is not a basis but an effect of, an appearance emerging from, synthesizing activity. Similarly, recall in §12 that Nietzsche argues that the concept of the soul needs to be rescued from Christian dogmatism, but not necessarily abandoned. In its place, and among other notions, Nietzsche described the soul as the "multiplicity of the subject [*Subjekts-Vielheit*]". The "soul" is not a thing, but an effect of the gathering together of affects and thoughts, as the drives play themselves out across time. This would explain why Nietzsche feels it necessary to say "was and is" above – that is, signalling a span of time – and why here he makes the pun on *nötig*: to need and to make necessary. This synthetic activity first makes possible the appearance of an identity or wholeness that spans time.

It becomes clear that the idea of a channel of fate is, at best, a foreground approximation. The individual being is not essentially or originally *one*; it is a community of drives and a synthetic construction, spanning time. The individual being (their soul or identity) is not simply there with respect to past and future conditions, but is *constituted as having an identity in so far as it is collectively a channel*. (See also *Twilight of the Idols*, "Skirmishes of an Untimely Man", §33.) This identity is an appearance in the sense Nietzsche uses that term in §34: neither appearance as objective or universal truth, nor appearance as deception. This soul's identity, properly speaking, is precisely the manner in which it – whether constant or metamorphosing, spanning time – is a channel. Again, however, this would be true of all entities, at least those capable of synthesis – all humans, then, including the "stupid", drawing again from the list in §55.

If we now turn back to the issue of realignment, a new concept that we employed especially with respect to Part 2, we get an important result. In §56, the philosopher has had his eyes opened to this new ideal; and §57 speaks of "spiritual sight and insight". What is at stake here is a knowledge that is also an affirmation, that is also willed. "He" whose eternal return is desired is constituted not only as one who needs and makes necessary the whole spectacle but *also himself* – that is, who is not only a channel for fate but whose whole existence – including knowledge, insight, will – is to be this channel. (It is in this sense that Nietzsche asks famously "For what is freedom? That one has the will to assume responsibility for oneself" (*Twilight of the Idols*, "Skirmishes of an Untimely Man", §38).) This would be what we called "realignment": to be as will to power and as the *knowledge of* will to power. Here, though, we see that this "to be" is itself a function of will to power playing itself out in the entanglement of conditions. The synthetic gathering of affects and thoughts that makes up the identity of this being does not involve misinterpretation, misunderstanding, reactive evaluations – but rather is the spiritualization of its being a channel of fate. Zarathustra addresses his soul: "Where would future and past dwell closer together than in you?" (*Zarathustra*, Part 3, "On the Great Longing"). Past and future meet, in the present but also by way of the long journey of eternity, in and through that being whose existence is to be, and not to deny, that meeting. (One would deny that meeting, for example, in the belief in freedom as a *discontinuity* between past and future.)

However, we have so far neglected the fact that this passage occurs within the context of a discussion of the nature of religion. Now, someone with a little knowledge of Nietzsche might have stopped thinking about religion after the earlier passages on the "neurosis" of Christianity. Nietzsche's account of religion and the religious character would have been seen as entirely critical. But §51 introduced a noble sense of religion; and §53 made it clear that Nietzsche is distinguishing between religion and theism. The end of §56 returns to the problem of religion. How so? A being that makes the spectacle, and himself, necessary sounds like a variation on the standard formula for necessary being – that is, God. For example, commonly rehearsed versions of the cosmological argument for the existence of God end with a necessary being that can explain the existence or origin of a series of "contingent" beings – that is, beings the existence of which can only be explained through *other* beings. Nietzsche, however, refuses the distinction between necessary and contingent being. We have already seen him (e.g. in §21) attacking the notion of a self-caused being as an obvious metaphysical absurdity. For Nietzsche, everything is contingent in the sense that any thing exists only through other things – and as we have seen, ultimately only through *all* other things. Only the titanic, total system of things and events, repeating itself over and over, is necessary; here, "necessary" in the sense of not needing anything outside itself. That is, not needing a creator, designer, and so on, that transcends, stands outside or above, the whole cyclical spectacle of the cosmos. (Even to say "not needing", though, may be saying too much; see our discussion of §34.)

Thus, the last line of §56 should not be the surprise that Nietzsche pretends it is: "What? and this would not be – *circulus vitiosus deus* (God as a vicious circle)?" This is an explicit acknowledgement of the religious tenor of the language of necessity Nietzsche has been using. Nietzsche is asking whether the total system, forever returning on itself in a vast circle, is not how we should understand "God". This, of course, would be a curious version of pantheism: God exists in everything within nature or the cosmos. Moreover, God exists entirely immanently to nature or the cosmos, there is no transcendence in the sense we used this term just above, but *only to the extent* that this "nature" eternally recurs.

However, Nietzsche is not asserting such a pantheism. Any pantheism is still a theism, and Nietzsche appears to be working towards a sense of religion that is entirely distinct from theism. If we were to "freeze" the total system and treat it as a being (God), that would be to think of recurrence as a vast recording which simply is, in itself, and is played again and again. Such a recording would have a definite starting point, an initial state of affairs that is the cause of all the others. It would then also make sense to contemplate a point "outside" the system, from which its totality could be viewed (standing *alongside* the path of time, observing its shape, as the dwarf does in *Zarathustra* Part 3, "On the Vision and the Riddle"). Given Nietzsche's critique of the received metaphysical notions of cause and effect, identity and substance, this cannot be what he has in mind. (On this notion of the eternal recurrence taking on the appearance of being, see *Writings from the Late Notebooks* 7[54]. Moreover, on the relation between eternal recurrence and pantheism, see 5[71], §7.) If this were Nietzsche's point, the past would not concern me, except as "how I came to be"; and only the beginning would an object of gratitude, everything else only an instrument of its power. Moreover, the future would be conceived of as an effect of my action or inaction, and not something I need or towards which I should likewise feel reverent gratitude. Rather, for Nietzsche, every moment is a beginning at which the ideal (the "he") must shout "*da capo*". Thus, what is the past is a further future; what is future is the condition of my past and present. Accordingly, the key figure here – what is divine – is not nature or the total system, but rather the ideal: "he" who needs and makes necessary. Such a being recognizes and indeed wills himself, along with the whole spectacle, recognizing no essential distinction or negation between self and spectacle. For, this being is *fully integral to and in concert with that system*, right up to his most abstract spiritualization. The self, then, contains "more" than a stable and repeatedly recognizable "I" – spans more, reflects more, completes the whole of existence – but also, of course, is much "less" – it is insubstantial, precarious, evanescent, broken open (see §295).

Significantly, it follows also that what Nietzsche means by "ideal" must be quite different from traditional moral or philosophical usages. He becomes so concerned that his reader will misunderstand this point that, at the beginning of *Ecce Homo*, he repudiates the notion of ideal altogether (*Preface*, 2). "Ideal" [*Ideal*] is associated with having "idols" [*Götzen*]; there is no pun in German between "ideal" and "idol", but there is, importantly, between *Götzen* and "*Gott*" – God. At that last stage of his thinking, he prefers to use only the term "type" [*Typus*] of human or life, the point being that the other-worldliness, or the anti-natural, connotations of "ideal", are extremely dangerous. Moreover, in so far as Nietzsche's work is a historical and metaphysical critique of conceptions of "world" and "nature", then this dangerous notion of ideal is a key part of the *problem* and not of the solution. Here, although Nietzsche uses the term, this caution and modified meaning is recognized in two clear ways. First, in so far as the notion of eternal recurrence does not amount to a vicious circle made God. Secondly, the "new ideal" is not in any way outside or opposed to the total system of nature, but rather that being that is *most integrated within it*. It is this immanence of the ideal – immanence to nature, but also its immanence to those whose ideal it is – that must be understood here.

One implication of this is what Nietzsche elsewhere calls "*amor fati*" (love of fate). In *Ecce Homo*, "Why I Am So Clever", §10, Nietzsche writes: "My formula for human greatness is *amor fati*: that you do not want anything to be different, not forwards, not backwards, not for all eternity. Not just to tolerate necessity, still less to conceal it – all idealism is hypocrisy towards necessity – but to love it . . ." (and cf. *Gay Science* §276). This means the love of one's fate, a saying "yes" and of showing utmost gratitude for everything that has made one the particular channel of fate that one is (that which appears as past), and for all the implications of being this particular channel (that which appears as present). In the *Ecce Homo* passage, we can see an important echo of the present *Beyond Good and Evil* section: in both cases, one moves beyond a Stoic acceptance, towards enthusiasm, joy or love. In both cases, there is an indifference or equivalence to "forwards" or "backwards" – between needing and making necessary. In brief, *amor fati* is the attitude that Nietzsche's new, "opposite" ideal has to the belief in eternal recurrence.

The next section (§57) begins by speaking of a growing sight and insight. The sight and insight that grows in strength is "spiritual", though. What has been learned from §56 is not eternal recurrence as a metaphysical doctrine (although as we pointed out, there is evidence for interpreting Nietzsche's idea in this way). The insight is not into nature so much as into the nature of spirit and in particular into its as yet unexperienced possibilities (as Nietzsche put it in §45). So, we have recognized a new ideal: a new type of human being who can substitute a religion of gratitude for one of faith, and do so on the grounds of the willing of eternal recurrence and *amor fati*, and whose gods appear as dangerous temptations to further, immanent self-overcoming, joy and laughter, without reserve (see §295). This is an "insight" rather than a belief among others, because only such a new ideal is capable *not only* of affirmation of eternal recurrence *but also* of a mode of existence that does not systematically falsify itself and its world as do the "prejudices" of the philosophers in Part 1. Being capable of affirming eternal recurrence is, then, the ultimate "test" (cf. §41) or touchstone for a kind of being that is capable of conceiving of itself without either metaphysical or moral prejudice.

§57

We have already spoken above about the opening words of this section. It is important now to consider the notion of "distance" or "space" that grows with insight. Metaphorically, it is not difficult to grasp a number of the notions Nietzsche pursues. The new insight releases us from the narrow, low-angle viewpoints that he has been criticizing since §2. Similarly, it deepens our view, so that we no longer form our truths on the basis of "foreground approximations". However, the distance and space also echo the religious themes: our view is opened up to past and future, and to the whole system of nature. Distance should also remind us of the order of rank (which, as we have seen, is often described in terms of keeping at a distance; Nietzsche will use the expression "*pathos* of distance" in Part 9). The new insights allow us to understand for the first time the vast differences among supposedly "equal" human beings. Nietzsche finally develops the metaphor into a distinction between the restricted understanding and range of motion of children as compared to adulthood. Notice also the theme of *amor fati*: we should see (perhaps) all the previous concepts, and battles over concepts, as playful "exercise" for a new way of thinking. Future philosophers will be grateful even for the mistakes and horrors of the past, for they have made that future philosophy possible.

Significantly, this does not mean that the philosophers of the future have outgrown childishness and youth. On the contrary, their new ideas are new toys, and they are eternal children. (See *Zarathustra*, Part 1, "On the Three Metamorphoses".) This is important in part because it allows Nietzsche to avoid claiming that the new philosophers will just be martyrs to truth (see §25). It allows him to continue a theme of the celebration of youth, which is not mere youth or a youth that has not passed through maturity. We saw this theme in §31, and it will culminate in the ninth stanza of the "Aftersong" with which the book concludes. The "eternal child" is a figure of play and joy, of course, but is also one that is eternally growing up; the eternal child is always on its way towards its ideal.

§58

The religious life requires leisure, which is even akin to an aristocratic feeling that work disgraces [schändet]. It follows that the new culture of industry works directly against belief. This should remind us of §14 (and see *Genealogy*, Third Treatise, §18), and the presumptive reference to Hegel and Marx in the account of the slave revolution. This is also true of "industrious scholars", especially in universities. Even those who feel gratitude towards religion (one meaning Nietzsche has in mind here would seem to be the *amor fati* discussed above) nevertheless remain distant from true religious feeling.

The last few sentences of the passage work towards a scathing attack on the majority of scholars. Such a scholar feels higher, more advanced, than the religious person – but the former, the man of "modern ideas", is "a presumptuous little dwarf". Although, of course, Nietzsche generally has contempt for theism and especially Christianity, it does not follow that he has equal praise for those who thoughtlessly abandon religion. On the contrary – whether hard workers, major industrialists, or busy university professors – they are a type equally incapable of understanding the new ideal Nietzsche is putting forward. (A similar point is made in *Genealogy*, Preface 1.) Notice that this is not simply a moral or philosophical point – it is also an *economic and political* point. Modern conceptions of work, scholarship and even leisure act against the philosophy of the future. Nietzsche will dwell on the figure of the scholar again in Part 6; the picture will be more complicated there than this attack.

§59

This section concerns "superficial" [oberflächlich] persons, and how superficiality hides considerable wisdom. Note that the word is taken initially in its literal meaning: people exclusively concerned with surfaces, images and appearances. Those who are superficial may be so because it protects them from terrible truths – truths that are incompatible with the type of living being they are. There is a relation here to fear but, more importantly, a fear that has learned a way to live.

This is similar to Nietzsche's interpretation of the relation between Apollonian and Dionysian forms of art in *The Birth of Tragedy*, a much earlier book. The former (a Greek god, but interpreted by Nietzsche as standing for a broad type of art and of thinking) concerned itself with beautiful and clear images, shimmering, illusory and *known* to be illusory; the latter with a dangerous glimpse into the true, cruel and dispersed nature of reality. Tragedy is a unique art form in that it provides the spectator with Dionysian truth made bearable by the Apollonian beauty of its manner of presentation. *The Birth of Tragedy* is too often misinterpreted as claiming (i) that the Apollonian interferes with or hides away the truth; and (ii) that the genre of tragedy faded in significance because the Apollonian ideal "won out" over the Dionysian. We should be suspicious of the first claim because it appears to equate the true with the valuable, and the false or illusory with the dangerous or bad. We should be suspicious of the second because those who interpret Nietzsche in this way forget that, in the Apollonian, the illusion is *known to be an illusion*. Nietzsche's actual argument (in *The Birth of Tragedy*; he does to be sure change his mind later) is that tragedy "dies" when philosophers and artists misunderstand and confuse *both* the Apollonian and the Dionysian, and think of the beauty, clarity and order of the former *as equivalent to* the insight of the latter. The chief culprit in this transformation is Socrates, and one name he gives to the result is "scientific man". Nietzsche summarizes all this in *Beyond Good and Evil*, §80.

Here, in §59, we have the same structure, including the reference to art as essentially (but, we must not forget: *wisely*) falsifying, which means making *bearable* by making *beautiful*. For genuinely religious people, who are the highest ranking artistic beings, life must be completely falsified, for they have been "burnt" by some prior glimpse into the nature of life. Such a view is "wise" both because it contains this prior glimpse and because it preserves life without seeming to do so; however, it is also a "revenge" and thus a secondary, reactive act – not the primary, affirmative response of Nietzsche's "new ideal". The difference here is that Nietzsche posits a mode of life (the philosopher of the future, or the new ideal) that would be able to "bear" this infinitely cruel reality, able to affirm it, laughing; to that extent the relation between Apollo and Dionysus has changed fundamentally in his writing. This is why the mere rejection of the religious is so belittled by Nietzsche in the previous section: the religious contains unique and valuable insight. The issue is not the insight, but the response to it. Accordingly, too, this is yet another reason why the new ideal of that being who is able to affirm eternal recurrence is and must be discussed under the heading of the nature of religion.

Notice, near the beginning, the joke about "pure forms" – in artistic practice, this may refer to simple shapes and curves, or idealized images of people, animals and so forth. Within philosophy, however, the phrase takes us back to Plato's forms. In §14 we learned that Plato "nobly" turned away from *sensible* appearances, to intellectual forms. Nietzsche's joke is that such idealized intellectual forms or ideas, although to be sure not *sensible* (or perhaps we should say: not *obviously* sensible), are in fact just another version of superficiality.

§60

"To love man *for God's sake*" – Nietzsche praises this sentiment highly, as "most noble" [*vornehmste*]. Why? Is not the idea that only a God can redeem life or give value to life a basic theistic belief, and an act of revenge against life? Consider, though, the following passage: "What is great in man is that he is a bridge and not an end: what can be loved in man is that he is an *crossing over* [*übergang*] and a *going under* [*untergang*]" (Prologue §4 of Part 1 of *Thus Spoke Zarathustra*). Nietzsche there is discussing his infamous concept of the *Übermensch* ("overman" or some-times "superman"), which is an earlier version of this book's "new ideal" or "philosopher of the future". It is a concept of a form of life and thought that will or could (or perhaps is just desired to by the free spirit) super-sede current human existence. What "can be loved" about current human beings is first that they form a bridge to this ideal (they are a "crossing over" or "transition"). And, secondly, the extent to which they desire to "go under".

This last expression needs some discussion: on the one hand, it refers to the elaborate narrative beginning of Zarathustra, in which the prophet decides to leave his home in the mountains and "go down" among other people. The word "*untergang*" also means "sinking" (of a ship), "setting" (of a star), or more generally decline and destruction. So, what is also being indicated is that human beings as they are now, including Zarathustra, will make way for – risk or even sacrifice themselves for – a new mode of life. We have seen similar notions before, for example in §§26 and 41. The "making way", as we put it, could of course be a *personal overcoming* – that is, a basic change in one's mode of life and thought, such that one quite lit-erally ceases to be the person one was previously. (This should be thought through with regard to the synthetic account of "soul" or identity that Nietzsche has been using; see §§12, 54). Or, the "making way" could be the extinction of (or at least the removal from social, cultural and political power) a race in favour of a new race. In either case, notice that human beings as they are now are not simply irrelevant. Rather, they are the his-torical and/or biological "bridge" by means of which alone the new ideal can become real.

So, to love man for the sake of God is noble – the feeling has flown the highest so far and yet has most beautifully gone astray – because it very nearly captures Nietzsche's point. Remembering again that we are in the context of a treatment of a religious instinct without a theistic instinct, this point could be expressed: to love man for the sake of the god *that could become his immanent ideal*.

§61

This section and the next sum up, in a fairly straightforward manner, much of Nietzsche's complex attitude to the phenomenon of religion. It is worth pointing out that in this Part, as in most of the others, just as the first section is generally methodological, so the last few form a conclusion and transition. They may be summaries, or perhaps raise fundamental questions, but in any case rise to a climax, as if each part has the structure of a movement in a grander musical composition. (Thus also the idea of *entr'actes* in the title of the next Part.) The ruling classes make use of religion as an instrument of rule or (in the case of those who prefer not to rule directly) as an instrument allowing withdrawal from the "*necessary* dirt of all politics". Notice again that this is precisely the structure of the "mask", as we have been discussing it. Simultaneously, a mask distances one from those outside the mask while also being a specific mode of engagement within and operation upon that outside. To "rule", though, is not a self-serving tyranny (as it is often portrayed in caricatures of Nietzsche) but includes a "comprehensive responsibility" for the development of the human type.

Those individuals, classes and races who are ascending spiritually, from the "herd" towards rule, benefit from the forms of self-overcoming and self-cruelty in religion. Nietzsche thus says that "asceticism and puritanism" – although in many ways the most reactive and life-negating forms of religious life – are also important means for such spiritual ascent. Again, we see one of Nietzsche's basic historical principles at work, just as in the previous section: forms of life "lower" on the order of rank are necessary, as the path through which the free spirit and the philosopher of the future arise, and towards which they accordingly feel gratitude (*amor fati*).

For the "common man", religion is comfort: it beautifies and justifies the ordinary suffering and hardship of life. This suffering and hardship is "necessary" in several senses. First, in the sense of the historical principle mentioned above, they are necessary (although perhaps indirectly) for the growth of man. Secondly, necessary also in the sense that, in a common religion mode of thinking, suffering and hardship *in this world* are necessary and will be rewarded in the next; they are thus necessary for the "contentment" of which Nietzsche speaks. Thirdly, they are necessary because from the point of view of life such beings are "failures" (this is in the next section), whose very existence is to be "sick" and thus to suffer from themselves. Finally, necessary in that those who rule inevitably need those who are ruled – see the comments on "leisure" in §58. This last point is also closely related to a broadly economic point about the necessity of classes, an observation Nietzsche has been making since his early work (see *Birth of Tragedy* §18). Indeed, religion often even proposes a merely apparent inverted order of rank, according to which the common are beloved of God, while at the same time preaching contentment. We have seen many of these ideas previously, for example in §59, or §46 where it is analysed importantly in terms of "revenge".

§62

This section concerns, as he puts it, the "other side" of Nietzsche's analysis, which is what happens when religion refuses the role of being an instrument, and (according to the above mentioned inverted order of rank) wishes to be ruler and end.

The basic premise of the passage is that in the development of human beings, "failures" and the "sick" are the most common products. The appropriate conditions for the development of a higher human are difficult to determine, so that most often accidents occur and the higher human is destroyed or deformed in some way. "Successes" then are rare, and particularly rare as humans are the "*noch nicht festgestellte Tier*". This is an important phrase, especially in the history of existentialism, so let us try out a few translations. The "as yet undetermined animal" is most commonly employed, but uses "determine" outside its usual philosophical sense, and only captures part of the metaphor. "*Festgestellt*" is an adjective formed ultimately from the verb "*stellen*", meaning to stand something somewhere, or to arrange something. "*Fest*" is solidly or fixedly. "*Feststellen*" can mean to lock in place. So, we can try also "the animal that has not yet reached its final form", or "the as yet unstructured animal". Finally, there is an important pun on the other common usage of "*feststellen*", which is "observe" in the sense of both noticing and commenting on something. So, the phrase suggests "the as yet unremarked animal", perhaps meaning the animal that has not yet observed and expressed *itself*. The task falls to the free spirits and to the philosophers of the future properly to understand man and the possibilities of the human; and, as we know from above, this means to become that being whose *spiritual* existence is fully in accordance with itself.

"So", Nietzsche continues, "how do the two great religions relate to this surplus of unsuccessful cases?" This is a key question, both for Nietzsche's infamous analysis of the history of religions, and also for the problem of the affirmation of the new ideal. Nietzsche answers that they have sought to preserve, to sustain in existence, that which "ought to be destroyed". Notice here very clearly a *quasi*-evolutionary view: under the external pressure of environment, it is right that those less suited for survival should perish (i.e. it is natural or appropriate) so that the new, more suitable, may flourish. Religion would constitute a deliberate interference in this natural process, so as to artificially sustain in existence that which could not survive on its own. (A sort of human-focused version of Greenpeace, except that on Nietzsche's account the religions are a first-order interference in a natural development, rather than a second-order response to the destruction of habitats.) However, although it is frequently enough done, there are very good reasons for not bringing Nietzsche's thought too close to Darwinism of whatever variety. We have already seen one reason in §13: that what in evolutionary terms is considered "success" (survival) may be quite different from what, on Nietzsche's account of the will to power, should be so labelled. Indeed, as we can see in this and the previous section, success may mean the opposite. Especially if we think in terms of a successful adaptation to environment, it has been the least "successful" types (in Nietzsche's usage) that have most successfully adapted – that is, have found a way of dealing with and surviving hardship, scarcity, suffering. The adaptations that were developed were the great religions. At certain points, though, it *can* be helpful to see his problems as extensions of those raised by Darwin: we can illustrate this by turning to another possible Darwinian resonance here. Plants and animals evolve to a relatively stable configuration of physiology and environment; but with human beings alone there is also evolution in the spiritual realm (in terms of culture, for example). Thus human beings are indeed the "as yet unstructured" animal, because culture keeps changing. Some Darwinians were drawing these kinds of conclusions by the 1880s. However, it is more likely that the "as yet unstructured animal" should rather remind us of Nietzsche's morphology of development of the will to power, and also of the new ideal that might represent an adequate, transparent, self-structuring or self-remarking form of life.

Two additional comments should be made here. First, interference *per se* in the process of the development of human beings is not the problem, for the philosophers of the future will do the same. This is clear from the beginning of §61 and from the "calculations" of the conditions for higher men early in §62. There is nowhere, then, a purely natural state of development; if anything, to interfere is natural (part of the strategy of a particular form of life). Again, this is an important divergence from Darwinian thought. The question rather is the inspiration or ground for this interference: is it pity or the will to power? Is it sick or healthy? Is it reactive or active? Does it seek escape from, or love, existence?

Secondly, religion *in general* is not Nietzsche's target. He praises and thanks the "sovereign'" religions in §62. Furthermore, we have seen that Nietzsche is trying to reconceptualize the notion of religion in a non-theistic manner, as the will to a new ideal. This becomes increasingly clear as §62 progresses: for the talk of "religion" gradually disappears to be replaced merely by "Christianity". Despite the occasional mention of other world religions, Christianity is generally what Nietzsche has in mind in speaking critically (but also appreciatively) of historical religions. This is, of course, because he is writing from and often very explicitly about the European intellectual and cultural tradition, and Christianity is far and away the dominant religion in that tradition.

The remainder of §62 reinforces and details the result of preserving those who ought to perish. In brief, it encouraged the development of, and dominance of, weaker and "stunted" forms of humanity. (Compare the figure of the dwarf at the end of §58, and famously in *Zarathustra*, "The Vision and the Riddle".) An Epicurean – a mask that Nietzsche often likes to wear because it approximates most closely to the noble lightness of the new ideal and its *amor fati* – would have to laugh at this centuries-long, deliberate "birth defect" [*Missgeburt*]. An equally appropriate reaction – this time of someone carrying the "responsibility" Nietzsche mentions at the beginning of §61 – would be rage, pity and horror. The rage is at people who were not noble enough to merit being "artists" of the human material, and not far-sighted and disciplined enough to allow the weaker cases to perish, nevertheless trying to influence the development of the human type, and botching it. "Botching" is of course a value judgement, but one based upon the immanent ideal of human potential that has been revealed by eternal recurrence (§56). To encourage the weak or sick could be justified only by an account of the love of God (that is, by a value that comes from outside the world), or the forgiveness of sins or redemption in the afterlife (which cancels out or compensates for what is). Within the perspective of eternal recurrence, however, these transcendent values distort the values that life gives itself. My act, my sin or my suffering just is, and can never be otherwise (it is repeated to eternity).

With the end of Part 3, Nietzsche's "metaphysics", as we have called it, is pretty much complete. What remains is to ask is the question (perhaps one still more difficult and dangerous) of how the free spirits will prepare for the philosopher of the future – how morality, language, science, society, culture and politics must change. But first, we are offered a bit of (apparently) light relief.

5 "Epigrams and Entr'actes" (Part 4 §§63–185)

This whole Part represents a stylistic change from relatively continuous and sustained prose to "epigrams" or "aphorisms": short, sharp "sayings" [*Sprüche*]. This is not new; Nietzsche used a similar style in large parts of *Daybreak* and *The Gay Science*. Moreover, it is also common in Nietzsche's notebooks, showing that it is not simply an affectation for publication, but a mode of writing that felt natural to him, and perhaps even a technique of thinking. Nietzsche elsewhere writes: "Whoever writes in blood and aphorisms does not want to be read but to be learned by heart [*auswendig* – by memory, but related to '*wendig*', nimble or agile]. In the mountains the shortest way is from peak to peak; but for that one must have long legs" (*Zarathustra*, Part 1, "On Reading and Writing"). The notions of height, peak and agility here suggest a special kind of reader, interpretation and also thinking. Similarly, Nietzsche talks about a style that would have a "*minimum* in the extent and number of the signs, and the maximum thereby attained in the energy of the signs", a *noble* characteristic he has learned from Roman writing (*Twilight of the Idols*, "What I Owe to the Ancients", §1). Finally, the aphorism has a long and distinguished history in German (and, more broadly, European) letters – Pascal's *Pensées* is an obvious example. However, despite this tradition, it may be that Nietzsche is doing something distinctly different with this literary form as he struggles to find new styles suitable to the advancement of his new philosophy.

Nietzsche calls this Part "entr'actes" or "interludes" – generally something incidental and generally light or comic that occurs between the acts of a play, as a supposed refreshment for the audience. The most familiar example to us might be the clown scenes in Shakespeare's tragedies. (Speaking physiologically, Nietzsche's own failing health might account – if only in *his* mind – for the short, separated rhythms of these passages.) However, lest we think that Nietzsche does not intend Part 4 to be taken seriously, or that it *only* contains exaggerated rhetorical effects, the first section directly addresses seriousness.

For a philosopher who stresses subtlety and complexity as basic principles of proper thinking, we have seen Nietzsche be incredibly crude and simplistic, and these epigrams often *appear to be* still more so. Previously, we argued that this crudeness can be justified only in so far as it served one of several purposes. Perhaps Nietzsche is after a rhetorical effect – giving an entrenched metaphysical, moral or social prejudice a jolt by way of a deliberately hyperbolic expression. Or, perhaps, the approach with its simplistic manner of expression hides a double or triple meaning that allowed other, richer interpretations to branch off for the careful reader. Finally, equally significantly, often Nietzsche can be seen refining his thought in other sections, before or after, so that the over-simplistic nature of one passage is an appearance brought about by reading it on its own. So, the individual sections should be understood as part of an overall development and presentation of ideas, and not be taken in isolation.

All the above justifications are true of Part 4, too. This long collection of apparently discrete soundbites has several deliberately shocking or downright offensive moments. At least some of these should be seen as strategic "jolts", as we put it above. To take two early examples: whether or not §§69 and 127 contain any valid psychological observations, the manner of the expression is designed to shock. Even Nietzsche's punctuation shows us this, for both contain the long dash that forms the joke, taunt, or double-take that we discussed with respect to the Preface. But let us look again at §127. All one need do is recall the figure of truth as a woman and suddenly the aphorism means something quite different: it equates science with the dogmatists of the Preface and, in particular, to an ontological commitment of science to, in addition and behind appearance, there being *something that appears* (under the dress). What appeared as a misogynistic slight of women is (instead or at least also) a summary of a basic metaphysical point.

There is a kind of crudeness also in the apparently careless tumble of ideas and expressions, one after the other. The other Parts of the book often also have this appearance of being jumbled or cobbled together without thought for continuity. However, just as we have often seen a very careful and subtle interplay between sections in the other Parts, so too we will here. Here as elsewhere, the *effect* of spontaneity, with its apparent disorder and fits and starts, is a very deliberate one (it has much in common with the musical genre of the "impromptu"). Taken as a whole sequence, Part 4 can be seen as a complex web of thinking. It is as if Nietzsche is challenging us to be disciplined enough not to take individual passages out of context, but to rebuild the richer picture. There are several interrelated themes being developed here, each across several separated epigrams. The most obvious of these themes are: the affect of shame, especially in relation to knowledge; love and friendship; sexuality and sexual difference. Some of the aphorisms on the latter theme (and again in the passages at the end of Part 7) are less easy to reinterpret than was §127 above. One can agree with Nietzsche's basic point – that it is illegitimate, as an extension of political equality, to reduce sexual difference to some neutered or abstract equivalence, and not to take seriously the possibility of differently structured experiences – without having *also* to agree with the particular analyses he gives.

Here, we can only do part of this task of "rebuilding" the complex picture. We will look at the opening few epigrams, and show how they are linked and thus form a continuous meditation on a theme. Thereafter, however, because of the pressure of space, we will have to give in and focus on notable individual passages.

§§63–67

As in the other parts, the first section (though only a sentence) serves as a methodologically oriented introduction. Here, Nietzsche is speaking of someone who is "essentially" a teacher who takes all things seriously, including even himself, only in relation to his students. This may be a tautology at a first level of interpretation: for, if one is "essentially" (or "from the ground up") a teacher then of course the students are everything, and not, for example, anything self-serving.

Now, does this mean Nietzsche considers himself "essentially" a teacher? Certainly, this is a role (and also a mask) that he commonly enough discusses, as in "Schopenhauer as Educator" in *Untimely Meditations*. Zarathustra is also a teacher, and one who "goes under" – who risks or invites his own destruction – to deliver his teachings. This in turn should recall the idea, towards the end of Part 3, of both the free spirit and philosopher of the future having "responsibility" for the development of the human type. Taking "teacher" broadly or analogically in the above manner, we can now see its significance: it is a way of describing Nietzsche's central philosophical preoccupation with preparing the way for a new type of philosopher, indeed a new type of human being. The aphorism, however, also suggests that an essential teacher must also be a student; that to be a teacher means also to teach (advance, expand) "even himself".

These points are reinforced in the next section. Here Nietzsche criticizes the notion of "knowledge for its own sake [*um . . . willen*]". This belief would be something that prevents one being essentially a teacher: for the latter, knowledge exists so as to make a difference to the students. The former conception of knowledge is the last "snare" [*Fallstrick*] of morality for several reasons. First, because it assumes that knowledge is or can be innocent of moral perspectives; it thus allows moral perspectives to hide behind the screen of this supposed innocence. Secondly, because it asserts that knowledge *should* be useless, whereas Nietzsche intends that his new understanding of life as will to power should be put to use in the furthering of the development of human life. So, if genuine knowledge contains dangerous truths, then this "snare" serves to neutralize its significance in advance. Finally, because if we take the expression literally (as it is not normally done) as meaning knowledge itself has a "sake", has interests and is self-serving, then we are back to the original problem of Part 1: what is the value of the will to truth? As we have seen Nietzsche argue on many occasions, knowledge has value for life or, rather, for a particular mode of life.

But the German word *"Fallstrick"* comes to have another association when taken in conjunction with §§65 and 65a. These two sections are about knowledge, shame, sin and God. The metaphor of the Biblical Fall could never be far away. In the Biblical narrative, knowledge is ultimately knowledge of sin, and is consequently shameful; correspondingly, God is perfect and does not or cannot sin, and the Fall is a falling away of human beings from being the perfect image of God. In Nietzsche's version, though, shame is not a punishment for sin and knowledge, but its "attraction" or "stimulation" [*Reiz*]. Why? First, of course, it is not exactly shame but the *overcoming of* shame. This means "moral" advancement, for Nietzsche; it means no longer experiencing one's new mode of life negatively. In §40, we've already seen shame used in this odd way. Shame is the experience of knowledge or insight that is not for everyone, which must be hidden because it is of a different, higher "order of rank". Now, this may be experienced initially as something that must be hidden because it is valued negatively by a dominant moral system that I have internalized. To overcome shame, then, means to change the meaning *and the direction* of the affect.

In §66, this shame of a god is explicated as involving even being taken advantage of, lied to and so forth. Thus, suffering, broadly speaking, is seen as an often necessary and appropriate mask. Similarly, that a god is not allowed to sin (and thus is indirectly not allowed to feel shame) means that a god is not allowed to develop or advance – a god is kept in a perfect version of the herd or slave state. This strikes Nietzsche as just absurd and that is why he speaks of dishonesty: we lie to ourselves about the nature of the divine, projecting our own small, reactive virtues onto it. Accordingly, the irony of §67: if our god is only a perfect version of the common man and not elevated in rank – not, in other words, an *ideal* for us that incites us to growth – then it would indeed be a barbarism to love only one, for it would be against all "modern" democratic values. Other interpretations of this last section are possible; for example, one could begin by agreeing that the love of one God (monotheism) is indeed a barbarism in the literal sense of being foreign to the ancient Greek world. Then the irony comes only in the final sentence with the assertion that a non-elevated god has no unique right to our love. (In either case, the comparison with §172 is instructive.)

So, although at first sight the opening six sections do not "speak" to each other, and seem to deal with incidental notions, on reflection we can see them reiterating and developing quite central ideas introduced elsewhere. But doing so requires a forward and backwards movement, a reading attentive to second and third order signs, and a will to see development where there appears only discontinuity. Part 4, then, is not uninterpretable. But we can see part of the effect of Nietzsche's stylistic choice: the text demands a certain way of reading and thinking. Let us take seriously Nietzsche's statement that the long Third Treatise of *Genealogy* – which deals with a typology of ascetic ideals, and a historical account of their development – is intended as a model of the interpretation of an aphorism. Then the implication must be that *the kind of observing and thinking needed to interpret an aphorism is akin to the kind of observing and thinking needed to interpret history genealogically or, here, "morphologically"*. It is, therefore, and as the opening section already suggested, a type of training or education.

Although it would be useful to continue this relatively patient reading of all the epigrams in order, we need to move on. Therefore, we will look at just two further thematic "clusters".

§§73, 101 and 164

Nietzsche's alternative version of the divine is further explicated in these sections. These continue the ideas introduced in Part 3, of a religion without theism. That is, as we saw, a religion without God or gods as entities. Instead, Nietzsche proposes a religion that is the pursuit of an ideal of human possibility, defined above all in terms of its relation to the notion of eternal return.

"Whoever reaches his ideal, precisely thereby goes beyond it." This would appear to be an ontological claim – a claim about two different types of being or modes of life. There exist those humans who have ideals; the "free spirit" is particularly elevated by having as its ideal the type of being who could joyfully shout "da capo" to all existence. To embody one's ideal, however, is to surpass it in one of two ways. First, in the sense that one then must have another, further ideal; the first having been met is by that very fact no longer ideal. Or, secondly, one is the type of being that no longer needs ideals, or at least no longer has the need to posit something other than and outside itself by means of which it judges itself and towards which it departs from itself. This latter would be one description of the true "philosophers of the future". The philosopher of the future, that is, has a different relationship to the ideal, for the ideal can be described as the project of becoming that being which exists as truth *with respect to itself*. (One precedent for this ontological distinction is in Kant, who distinguishes between an "*intellectus ectypus*" and an "*intellectus archetypus*" in *The Critique of Judgement* §§76–77. This proposes a distinction between a type of being that is so constituted as to understand its world and itself by way of "images", and a being that does not have this limitation.)

"Today, a knower might easily feel like the becoming-an-animal of God." There is, of course, a joke here on the becoming-a-man of God in the person of Jesus Christ. The joke reminds us that, on Nietzsche's account, even the most spiritual aspect of human beings is rooted in the organic: in the body, instincts, desires – that is, in those aspects of us that are conventionally considered "animal". But equally significant is the implication of "knower" for Nietzsche. To know – here meaning to understand things according to the notion of will to power – is not so much an arriving at truth (although it may be that too), but an arriving at a point where the total transformation of one's being, from the most animal to the most spiritual, becomes an urgent ideal. (Think of the "longing" or "desire" with which Nietzsche begins §56.) In its structure, such a knower would have analogues with theological notions of God (again, see our discussion of §56), but *also* close analogues with the unmediated affective system of an animal.

Section 164 might come as a surprise to the reader of Nietzsche who has been struck by the sustained criticisms of Christianity. Significantly, Nietzsche distinguishes between the figure of Christ and the traditions of the religion founded in his name. This distinction is alluded to here and developed in scattered locations, but above all in a later book, *The Anti-Christ*. There, Nietzsche writes that the history of Christianity is an increasingly crude misunderstanding of an "original symbolism" (§37). Here, the issue is that, far from being the originator of a new moral code – morality thought of in terms of abstract and unconditionally binding laws of behaviour and of obedience to these laws – Jesus should be seen as inaugurating a completely different understanding of both morality and the divine. It is unclear, just from this section, what this would be, but here are two suggestions. First, perhaps he intends us to hear that the idea of reverence (and indirectly the *amor fati*) is intended, as Nietzsche articulates it in §260. Secondly, the relationship of son to father, rather than subject to ruler, is a relationship of *potential* equals. The father, then, is the temptation towards growth; the father is the new ideal.

§§77, 97, 108, 117, 154

Let us begin with §108. This is among Nietzsche's most famous aphorisms, but that does not mean it has been well understood. It would appear that

Nietzsche was saying that there are phenomena (things, events) and then, superimposed on these and often confused with them, there are moral interpretations of these phenomena. (Nietzsche makes a similar point in *Twilight of the Idols*, "The Improvers of Mankind", §1.) But, as we have seen over and over, the notion of appearance makes no sense, for Nietzsche, unless it is the appearance of the relation among the will to power of drives. That is, appearance is originally valued. Accordingly, the distinction between phenomena and interpretation is false. Significantly, also, "interpretation" is in the singular. We should read the passage as saying "There are absolutely no phenomena, moral or otherwise, there are *only* value-interpretations *as* phenomena, some of which are moral interpretations"; that is, phenomena being the world as it appears, to me (and to those sufficiently like me). So, Nietzsche's point here (and in the *Twilight of the Idols* passage referenced above) is not to distinguish morals from real facts, but to distinguish morals from *values*. Morals are a peculiar subset of values that relate systematically to a particular type of human life, and that require and encourage distinctive metaphysical errors. That is something we already discussed way back in §1.

Section 77 takes up the issue at this point: what makes someone sufficiently like me such that our moral (or rather value-) interpretations of phenomena are in agreement – or rather of the same order of rank – is not abstract principles (such as moral laws), but the instincts or desires that these principles represent or "bully". The point is made again in §117. One implication of such an analysis is a critique of the importance of general principles or laws. We have already seen this on many occasions, and indeed just above in §164. The point here is that the very notion of a principle, of the type that would bully or scold one's habits, is inextricable from the notion of democracy or Christianity, which sees only equality, at least in the eyes of God. Principles hide physiological differences between types. A shared ideal, in Nietzsche's sense, would not: for it is a spiritualized projection of an already shared physiology. It may have general significance and may be understood through abstract notions, but it is not itself thereby detached from human reality. It is "concrete", meaning that the ideal not only is but is truthfully represented as *within* the reality of a type or a historical epoch, rather than represented as outside or above.

Nietzsche now takes the implication one step further, asking the question "what is the value of the belief in general principles or unconditional laws?" Part of the answer is in §154: such a belief represents a degradation of health: "everything unconditional belongs to pathology". (By unconditional is meant that which is held to be absolute, without exceptions, without history; but also that which is understood to be necessary as an external *command* is necessary.) The notion of "pathology" should remind us of the "birth defects" and "stunted" growth discussed in §62. By contrast, the symptoms of health are "quibbles, infidelities, cheerful mistrust, love of mockery" – everything that is impure or deviates from the "straight and narrow". Of course, this deviation has to be understood as a mode of seriousness or responsibility, but one that can not be understood on the analogy of a moralist's devotion to the laws of duty. Again, this returns us to the idea of masks as always provisional or approximate modes of engagement. Finally, then, Nietzsche writes in §97: "What? A great man? I always only see an actor of his own ideal." It is easy to read this as a dismissal of many supposed "great men", and certainly in part it is (for example, see *The Gay Science*, §356). Similarly, he draws a distinction between *needing or striving for nobility* and nobility itself (§287). But of equal significance is this section as a dismissal of a certain way of understanding what great men are and how they are supposed to behave (see also §137). In particular, Nietzsche frequently demands that we distinguish between work and worker. It is not great works (or acting out great actions) that make a human great, and sometimes they are even quite misleading (§269, and see *Genealogy*, Third Treatise, §4). It is, rather, the man himself, his intention and especially what lies deeper than intention (cf. §32), that determines order of rank.

6 The Natural History of Morality: *The Development of Affects and Reactions* (Part 5 §§186–203)

In English, "Natural History" is a standard, but now somewhat old-fashioned, expression for the family of disciplines such as botany, zoology, ecology, and so on. These disciplines are not necessarily "historical" in the common meaning of that word. That is, they do not necessarily consider the past in their study of animal or plant life. This definition accords well with Nietzsche's discussion of "typology" in §186. Now, if Nietzsche meant only this much by his title, it would already be controversial, since by conjoining "natural" and "morality" he is negating one of the central principles of moral thinking for the previous 150 years. In Hume, there is a distinction between statements that claim that something "is" the case (statements of experience), and statements that claim something "ought" to be the case (moral statements). And, Hume insists, one cannot derive the one from the other. They are entirely different types of statements. Similarly, there is the Kantian distinction between theoretical and practical reason. Theoretical reason has nature in the broadest sense as its proper domain – that is, the type of objects concerning which it can legitimately reason; practical reason has an entirely different domain, that of free (and thus moral) acts. Again, the two domains are distinct, and the two types of reasoning must therefore be carefully distinguished. Nietzsche's title, however, claims that morality belongs within nature.

However, in German, *Naturgeschichte* also refers directly to study of the development or evolution of life forms, from the past to the present. At the end of the nineteenth century, the expression could not have but brought Darwinian theory to mind (although of course there were competing accounts of such development). Nietzsche's title tells us, then, that he is going to investigate morality in terms of its development over time, and perhaps even in terms of its evolution in a more specific, biological sense. This is, of course, also the spin he gave to the notion of "morphology" in §23: a science, let us say, of the forms of the development of forms. Such a proposal is still further provocative, as it is incompatible with any belief in universal or rational moral principles. A universal principle would not "develop" over time.

§186

Again, the first section is a methodological section – and this time very clearly so. Moral "sentiment" [*Empfindung*] is old, refined, complex, and the immodestly called "science" of morals is young and crude. A few sentences later we are given reasons for this discrepancy: moral philosophers have no taste or time for "description", their knowledge of actual moral behaviour is arbitrarily constricted to their own time and place, nor are they even interested in the past or other peoples. The basic problem of morality only appears *comparatively*, and for this reason moral philosophy has never even seen the problem of morality, which is the questionability of morality itself. Why only comparatively? Nietzsche does not precisely specify, but it is not difficult at this point to guess: moralities are systems or sets of values, and values are always values with respect to some other value or values. That is, moralities are always originally relational; they exist as an attempt to exert power over some other morality. So, when a moral philosopher looks into her own moral feelings, or just those of people near her, not only is she missing out on a vast quantity of moral data, but is unknowingly falsifying morality as a phenomenon from the ground up. She would be treating morality as a discrete and separable phenomenon, instead of as a moral interpretation of phenomena (see §108) and thus as always in relation. That is why Nietzsche says that in all moral "science" what was lacking was the "problem of morality".

Instead, moral philosophers have sought a "rational foundation" of morality. But rather than being a genuine penetration to the basic problem of morality, this attempt to find a foundation is just another datum among all the other feelings of value. "In a world whose essence is will to power", such an attempt at rational foundation, and the principles (like the one Schopenhauer states) at which it arrives, are "insipidly false". The mocking reference to Schopenhauer is significant for a number of reasons. First, much of Nietzsche's early career was heavily influenced by Schopenhauer. Nietzsche, then, is always on the lookout for an opportunity to distance himself and his later philosophy. Secondly, Schopenhauer is a famous pessimist, but it turns out that pessimism does not offer an avenue of escape from morality, as it appears to do, but is still caught in the misunderstanding typical of moral philosophers. Thirdly, similarly, in this distancing we can see the basic problem of morality: antagonisms of values, in this case the free spirit against Schopenhauer's "half Christian pessimism" (§56).

Nietzsche's alternative approach is more akin to the "natural history" of the title. He proposes a descriptive "typology" of the feelings and differences of value. This has clear analogies with the careful taxonomic systems of the biological sciences. Importantly, such systems are also relational: species are differentiated from out of a common genus by "specific differences", by which species X is marked out as *different from* species Y. Such a catalogue of types would therefore at least have the merit of not only permitting comparison but being based upon comparison, and thus allowing the genuine problem of morality to emerge. However, the sections that follow are not anything like a typology as, say, a botanist might understand it. At best, then, Nietzsche gives us an unsystematic fragment of such a typology. However, it might suffice for a glimpse of the "real problems of morality".

§187

There are at least three different questions one could ask of a moral proposition (such as Kant's famous "categorical imperative"). The first concerns its truth or validity; this is the main preoccupation of moral philosophers, but does not interest Nietzsche in the slightest. The second is "what is its value?" – that is to say, what is its interest? This, as we have seen, is a more Nietzschean question. But there is a third: "what does it say about the philosopher putting it forward?" We have seen this point before, in §§3 and 5, for example. Nietzsche summarizes this point by saying that a morality is "also just a sign language of the affects". The "also" is important. We have seen on several previous occasions that Nietzsche is, or comes close to being, a "reductionist": that is, claiming that all phenomena are derived from, and their significance can be reduced to, the affects – and, since an affect is a feeling for the direction and effectivity of the will to power of a drive, thus ultimately to the will to power (see in particular, §36). This is a strong claim, and the phrase "sign language" exacerbates it, since presumably a language can be "read" and thus the reduction to affects is not only possible in principle but can even be carried out by a skilled analyst.

Notice also, in the last of the examples Nietzsche gives of the service moralities do for their authors, a contrast between those moralists who would like to exert power over humans, and those of another type. This other type claims that what is worthy in them is their obedience. But, Nietzsche adds on their behalf, "and it *should* not be otherwise for you". That is, a moral claim is implicitly a universal claim and thus you too should obey. The joke is that in these last phrases is hidden a kind of command, just like the first type of moralist, even if for the latter the originator of the command is supposed to be outside them: in God perhaps, or in universal duty. All moralists seek to exercise power, though presenting themselves as either its originator or as merely an instrument.

§188, and discussion of nature

The notion of a morality as being a drive for power is made clearer in the opening sentence of this section. "Every morality . . . is a piece of tyranny", Nietzsche writes. Picking up on the idea of a language, from the end of the previous section, Nietzsche claims that every language has derived its "strength and freedom" from compulsion – in particular, from the compulsion of metre, rhyme and rhythm. Nietzsche is either referring to the formative power of poets working in a particular language, or more likely to the "natural" rhythms and rhymes of "everyday" speech. We should not forget that Nietzsche was a scholar of the history of languages, with a particular interest in Greek and how it was spoken. In any case, the analogy is clear (though, it later becomes obvious that Nietzsche intends more than an analogy). The compulsion of drives and their affects, their being shaped and channelled, is the reason why the "sign language" that is a moral system also has strength and freedom. The "discipline" [*Zucht*] and slavery amounts to a "cultivation" [*Züchtung*]. This pun, which Nietzsche makes near the end of the section, neatly encapsulates the idea.

The opening sentence contrasts this "tyranny" with "*laisser aller*" (letting go). This looks like a contrast between compulsion and freedom, and also (as Nietzsche says a few sentences later) between interference or meddling, on the one hand, and nature or "the natural" on the other. The claim Nietzsche is making is that both of these distinctions are false. True freedom only arises through compulsion, that is, through "tyranny"; accordingly, the concept of freedom as a "release" or lack of restriction is a false one. This notion we have come across before: see §§19 and 21 particularly. Moreover, though, this condition of compulsion is nothing other than "natural". *Laisser aller* is counter-natural, a type of interference. The clearest example so far is from §62 at the end of Part 2: the preservation by religion of weaker cases of human beings looks like a "letting be"; in fact, it is a ruthless interference in a natural process of development. Elaborating on both of these points occupies Nietzsche for the rest of this section.

The first argument concerns artistic practice. Nietzsche simply takes it as generally true and well known that constraints (however arbitrary, numerous and complex) are the precondition of artistic creativity. The laws of artistic making are incapable of conceptual formation not because they are vague but because they are so much more rigid and unequivocal than a concept. Elements of this idea had been mainstays of aesthetic theory for some time. Kant for example, in his influential aesthetics, contrasts the unfettered inspiration of genius with the lawfulness of taste. He argues that art can happen only by the combination of these two and that, if there is an irreconcilability, the former must yield to the latter. (See *The Critique of Judgement*, §50. From Kant, too, comes the idea that the "laws" of art are not conceptual in nature, although his reasoning is somewhat different to Nietzsche's.) Nietzsche's argument is that if in art – which some consider the most free of human activities – rigorous constraint is a precondition of freedom and greatness, then there is good reason to suspect this is the case more generally too.

Subsequent to this analysis, Nietzsche returns to a much broader set of claims. Obedience to arbitrary sets of rules, constant, unequivocal and pro-longed, always results in something "for whose sake it is worthwhile to live on earth". Nietzsche's examples of the arbitrary sets include the dogmas of the church, and the principles of Aristotelian thought. This idea, of a prod-uct or act that "justifies" existence and/or makes it "bearable", was a theme in §59. Religion makes suffering beautiful and thus justifies the suffering. Again, this is an idea that stems from Nietzsche's early book *The Birth of Tragedy*. Also, in §61, we saw the idea that strongly disciplined forms of life and thought – even where Nietzsche claims they are repugnant, reactive, destructive of much energy and strength, or even also promoting of weaker types – are necessary for the development of the human type.

The connection of this analysis with §59 is more than just an echo of an idea. Here, what is clear is that Nietzsche is talking of creations that are genuinely great or "divine". Section 59, though, speaks of "superficiality" and illusion. This is not as contradictory as it might appear. The assumption that what is great and divine could not be related to "superficiality" is another version of the assumption that the true is the good, which takes us back to the question in §1: "what is the value of the will to truth?" It is, as Nietzsche has told us many times, the falsification of the world that makes life possible. Importantly, he intends this basic idea to be applied not only to basic organic functions (for example, the crudeness of the senses in treating things that are similar as identical, is a form of sensory falsification that is a condition of the functions of nutrition, say, or reproduction), but also to spiritual matters: art, music, dance, poetry and religion. These are the things that, for the spirit weary of suffering and of the prevalence of the ugly, weak and craven, make it "worthwhile to live on earth" – notwithstanding that they trade in illusions, and even that we are perfectly aware that they do so.

There are two other apparent contradictions that we should deal with. First, that what in terms of its principles should be metaphysically nonsense and based ultimately on reactive drives (for example, the constraints on thought and action within Church doctrine) could *also* be the condition of the growth of the human type. This is an apparent contradiction because, as we have seen, this growth is towards a mode of being that embodies knowledge of the will to power, and affirms this being as such. There are two problems here: (i) explaining *how* this might happen; and (ii) showing that it is not a contradiction and thus is, at least, possible. The latter Nietzsche believes he has already done, in §2, by arguing that the faith in opposites is just another metaphysical dogma. Accordingly, he says explicitly in that passage, the growth of one thing out of what would seem its opposite is entirely possible and may even be a basic structure of natural events. The answer to the first problem has to do with the "arbitrary" [*willkürlich*] nature of the constraints, even their "stupidity". Life under rules, regardless of what the rules may be, is the necessary condition of the development of life, and again there need be no relation between the content of those rules and the direction in which life develops, or the beautiful artefacts that emerge. However, the fact that there need be no relation (the idea of arbitrary constraints) does not entail that to take advantage of, and subtly manipulate, conditions and thereby further the development of the human type, is impossible. Thus, for example, we have passages such as §62, wherein Nietzsche speaks of the "calculation" of the complex conditions for the emergence of "higher men"; or, again, in §61, in which religion (and other forms of compulsion) is used as a tool for the project of cultivation.

The second apparent contradiction concerns the broad, historical view Nietzsche takes of these phenomena. How can it be the case that the same mode of life and thought could be responsible for an enormous waste of spiritual strength (by, for example, favouring the survival of weaker types and perhaps positively choosing to crush the stronger), and yet also responsible for the growth of the human type and thus the emergence of "free spirits" and ultimately "philosophers of the future"? Certainly, there is no ambiguity about the fact that Nietzsche believes this to be the case. Nietzsche replies, in the parenthetical comment, "for here, as everywhere, 'Nature' reveals itself as it is, in its entirely wasteful and indifferent magnificence, scandalous but noble [*vornehm*]". The first point Nietzsche is making in this sentence is that a notion of "efficiency" is an anthropomorphism imposed upon nature. For example, a standard metaphysical principle used to be that nature "always took the shortest (possible) route". This was based upon the observation of such phenomena as water drainage. Water drains downhill, and if it curves this way or that, this is only because the curve is the shortest available way downhill. This is basic physical mechanics. However, the generalization of this principle to cover organic phenomena, life and matters of the human spirit, Nietzsche considers to be prompted by the idea of a designer or intelligence and, correspondingly, the idea of a perfect or rational universe. This analysis appears in §9, with the critique of the ancient Stoical idea of nature as rational.

The second point being made leads to a similar critique, against the notion that nature was not indifferent – that it had a purpose, that there was a reason for everything, or that God has a plan. At bottom, such a critique lies behind Nietzsche's attack on Darwinian evolution in §13: "survival" in a *purely* biological sense is too often (he believes) run together with a notion of "progress", "advancement", "ascent". As we have seen, on Nietzsche's analysis, in the human sphere that which has survived and spread is generally a regression, a "descent". More generally, Nietzsche has been arguing that the belief in the rationality of nature (in both the above senses) is a fundamental metaphysical error, but one that in various subtle ways still dominates the thought of his era. It shows up in the fondness of physical science for the notions of "law" and "cause and effect"; in evolutionary thought as we have just seen; in politics with the German nationalist notion of *"Volk"* (see for example §126); and above all in psychology with "soul atomism" and a Cartesian insistence on the transparency of consciousness. In short, the "stupidities" of the past, although destructive and wasteful (something profoundly difficult to affirm in the *amor fati*), are nevertheless part of the condition of that "tension of the spirit" (Preface) that Nietzsche believes will permit the development of an entirely new mode of human existence.

The final sentences of the section add something to Nietzsche's reply to both of these apparent contradictions. There is a moral imperative of nature, which is to obey "someone . . . or else" be physically or spiritually destroyed. But this imperative is addressed not to individuals, but rather to "peoples, races, ages, classes, but above all to the whole 'human' animal, to *the* human". What do individuals matter to nature, Nietzsche asks? Here, we compare the aphorism in §126. With respect to the processes of nature, an individual is only a nominal unity. This is part of Nietzsche's point in speaking of "soul atomism" in §12 and of its alternatives. The real units of nature are of a biologically, socially or politically larger scale. These are "real" because they are a form of life, rather than an arbitrarily isolated *instance of* a form of life.

Moreover, we should compare this whole line of thought with the end of Part 1, §23: "what do we [free spirits] matter?" he asks there. The production of "great" human individuals may be important as a means, but is subsidiary to the task of the cultivation of a new type of human. We can, then, understand the pursuit of the ideal by both free spirits and the philosophers of the future, both considered as *individuals*. It means to take up, both spiritually and corporeally, something like the perspective of nature. Thus, again, the idea of "going down", of risking or sacrificing oneself. Taking up this perspective is difficult. Aside from the risk, all our (previously or currently held) values are against it, all our metaphysical beliefs likewise – and this is not surprising, Nietzsche argues, since these values and beliefs exist precisely in order to preserve an already existing form of life. (This last point is explicitly stated by Nietzsche towards the end of this section.)

Nature, though, since it is profoundly indifferent, must also be indifferent to the ideals of Nietzsche's "free spirits". So, in that respect, it must be strictly impossible for any form of life to take on this perspective entirely. Life cannot by definition be thoroughly indifferent to itself; even the apparent indifference of ascetic self-denial is, Nietzsche argues in the third Treatise of *Genealogy*, in fact in the service of life. Perhaps the problem lies in ascribing a "perspective" to nature at all; "perspective" is a concept that attaches to a living being by virtue of the will to power of its dominant drives – precisely these drives characterize it as *this* mode of life, and also (partly by way of the fact that they *falsify* nature) make its life possible at all, or even sustain its existence. Nature is indeed characterized by the will to power, and (Nietzsche argues in §36) can be understood as proto-life, but perhaps is not an organized totality, is not *as such* alive. This is the point of the discussion of nature in §9. To be alive, Nietzsche claims there, means to will to be different from other beings and from nature as such. Only a god might be able to take up this "perspective" of nature; this is a clue to how the figure of Dionysus in §295 should be understood.

The problem of Nietzsche's new ideal, then, is the problem of becoming that being which exists as a set of values that are realigned to this conception of nature as will to power, while also of course remaining a form of life, and thus being intrinsically different from and even falsifying nature by being *this* system of organised drives. It is this problem that the notion of eternal recurrence and its affirmation is meant to solve. To be able to affirm eternal recurrence would mean to be able to take up a perspective in which the truth of one's being as realigned to the world as will to power is not incompatible with a simultaneous affirmation of oneself as a mode of life whose truths and values are always relational with respect to others. The nausea that Zarathustra experiences at the thought of the eternal return of the "small man" is an affect that must be overcome (*Zarathustra*, Part 3, "The Convalescent"), but overcoming it does not mean not to perceive smallness. Short of this new ideal, though, Nietzsche offers a number of intermediate "consolations": the love of illusory forms that, like the Apollonian in Nietzsche's early work, is at the same time fully aware of and colluding in the illusion; or, of course, laughter, irony and masks. All of these are states that avoid developing interpretations that are systematic, blind and reactive misunderstandings of the nature of life, and thus avoid *morals* that are, perversely, *against life* or, at least, against *health*.

§189

This section concerns "idleness" [*Müssiggang*] and its relation to industriousness (or other "powerful drives"). The point is a clever inversion of normal ways of thinking: a day of rest is not for bodily or spiritual refreshment, rather it is a hardship the purpose of which is to make the drives "hungry" again. There is a fine joke at the expense of (but also partly in praise of) the English. The section concludes with Nietzsche suggesting the above analysis might explain the "sublimation" of the sex drive into "love" under the pressure of Christian value judgements (cf. §168). Recall that, although we did not discuss it in any detail, the relationship between sex and love was a theme of Part 4. Nietzsche is suggesting both that Christian values put the strength of the sex drive to work in other ways, as the passion for God (see §50), and also that its sublimation into love in general is a kind of enforced constraint that serves to make the original drive stronger. Incidentally, although we have not had much to say on the issue, it has long been known that there is in Nietzsche a considerable anticipation of, and influence on, Freud. This use of sublimation – an important concept in psychoanalysis – is a key example.

§190

This section and the next have independent themes and analyses, but taken together offer an interesting account of Nietzsche's relation to the figures of Socrates and Plato. In §190, Nietzsche is speaking of the idea found in Plato that "badness" is a product only of ignorance. (The quotation by the way is not from Plato; it is Nietzsche summarizing with as little irony as he can bear.) This idea, Nietzsche claims, is in Plato's writings but really belongs to Socrates. In it, there is an equation of "good" with "useful" or "pleasant". This is a utilitarian morality (see also §174) that "reeks of the *rabble* [*Pöbel*]", for which Plato was "too noble".

Plato, Nietzsche claims, tried to read something "refined and noble" into this idea of his teacher, and "above all, [into] himself". This last phrase means that Plato saw himself as a refined and noble "reading" of Socrates. Such an idea obviously relates to Nietzsche's basic theme of the cultivation and transformation of the human – a theme that is by no means entirely alien to Socrates and Plato, neither of whom saw "knowledge" as the main purpose of philosophy, but only an instrument in the service of making people better. Accordingly, Plato "used" Socrates, transforming him into "all his own masks and multiplicities". This notion of mask is, by now, familiar: it is the methodological issue of a simultaneous engagement and detachment. The final lines make a complex joke of this: "Plato in front, Plato behind, and in the middle Chimera". A Chimera is a monster with the head of a lion, the body of a goat and the tail of a snake. Philosophers have long known that Plato's dialogues are anything but a transcription of Socrates' conversations; instead, that he uses Socrates to put forward his own philosophical ideas (thus, Plato in front and behind). But, working carefully to the middle, the heart of the matter, do we get back to the real Socrates? No, another composite. Either, then, this middle is yet another mask of Plato, or it is Socrates who is himself revealed as a composite monster because he is of the "rabble".

§191

This section concerns the relation between instinct and reason (which Nietzsche claims is broadly equivalent to the distinction between faith and knowledge) in moral judgements. Reason is ultimately utilitarian and oriented to ends; and this is why the Greek nobility, who were "men of instinct", were never able to explain to Socrates the reasons behind their judgements. But, Nietzsche adds, Socrates himself had the same difficulty, and the great ironist had to be ironic (and, what is more, *false*) even to himself, and persuade himself that for moral instincts there would also be good reasons to back them up. That is, Socrates tried to trick himself into believing that instinct and reason could be coordinated. Plato, lacking this "craftiness" [*Verschmitztheit*] just tried to prove that instinct and reason would converge on the "good". In Christianity, subsequently, instinct triumphed with reason in a subordinate role. But this instinct is apparently no longer that of the noble Athenians. It has been transformed into the dominance of "faith" and, Nietzsche baldly asserts, the "herd". True, Descartes celebrated reason, but he was "superficial", concerned only with surface effects – in other words, simply did not notice that what he called reason was bubbling up from an unhealthy instinct.

Now, on the face of it, this might seem to entail no less than three curious self-contradictions. First, and most obviously, everything here and elsewhere suggests Nietzsche is apparently approving (at least relatively) of the instinctual approach of noble Athenians, and yet a few lines later he equates instinct with the "herd". Secondly, why should the thesis of the *convergence* of reason and instinct towards the good be equated with the *triumph* of instinct? Thirdly, in §190, Plato is said to be a daring interpreter, keeping an ironic detachment from Socrates and thereby using him; that is, turning the figure of Socrates into his own "masks and multiplicities"; here, in just the next section, it is Socrates that is crafty, playing tricks, using irony while Plato is straightforward and innocent. The second and third of these may not be precisely "contradictions", but certainly suggest a much more complex picture than first appeared.

Let us go through these one at a time. First, then, Nietzsche does not consider instinct *as such* higher on the order of rank as compared to reason.

Instinct, after all, is a fundamental characterization of life; it is the extent to which its drives are automatic or unconscious. However, he does consider "healthy" or "noble" instincts higher than both plebeian instinct and an instrumental reason of the type described in these passages. We shall come back to such distinctions in more detail later (for example, in Part 7, "Our Virtues"). However, what is clear already is that a healthy or noble instinct is so in part at least because it does not arise out of reaction or revenge.

Secondly, the distinction between instinct and reason may have been extremely important for both Socrates and Plato – so much so that there are passages where they are almost asserted to be opposites. But for Nietzsche, as we have seen, reason is (or at least is in constant danger of being) simply a spiritualized expression of instincts. This was the point of §§3 and 6. So, it is not so much that instinct and reason *independently* correlate or converge, as rather that reason has become an instrument in the hands of the instinct of a particular mode of life, and thus no one should be surprised when they "converge". Instinct triumphs, Nietzsche is claiming, when reason becomes simply its instrument. (See, similarly, the idea of remaining "master" of the senses in §14.) From this it follows that to engage in rational debate with a philosopher (whether a moral philosopher or not) is to already concede too much; accordingly, Nietzsche believes he must be fleet of foot and employ a number of alternative methods of engagement. Is Nietzsche suggesting that, prior to Socrates and Plato, and utilitarian reason, there was a form of reasoning that was not simply spiritualized instinct? On the contrary, he is suggesting that prior to Socrates and Plato the instincts were healthy enough such that neither the concern over whether instinct correlates or converges with reason, nor even the need to oppose instinct and reason, arose in the first place. Perhaps, then, there is no method or form of philosophical reasoning capable of leaving instinct behind entirely. However, there are (or can be) modes of life the dominant instincts of which do not entail spiritualizations that comprise metaphysical falsifications of the world. The instinct of the philosopher of the future, the being that has "new ideal" as her ideal, would be spiritualized such that the world as will to power would not be an impossible or nonsensical thought.

Thirdly, this complex picture of Socrates and Plato should remind us of the complex relation to Kant that Nietzsche was developing, especially in Part 1. The *stylistic* problem is not that Nietzsche contradicts himself, but rather that he expresses his interpretations with such confidence on each occasion that we as readers tend to take them as "the last word". Even those statements prefaced by "perhaps", "suppose that" – what we have called the technique of hypotheticals – are expressed with this confidence. That is part of the desired effect of the technique. Similarly, as we discussed in §34, the effect of irony is created not by putting forward half a statement, or a weakened statement, but rather by statement and withdrawal. The *philosophical* problem is that, in accordance with his analysis of the soul for example, Nietzsche does not assume that historical philosophical figures or movements are unities, that they stand for one thing, or have one type of relation to culture or history. We can see an explicit example of this in the self-deception practised by Socrates. For others, it is an important aspect of the method of interpretation to assume that a philosopher *makes sense* or her writings "hang together". This is sometimes called the principle of generosity. Nietzsche, on the other hand, seems not only to claim that this principle *falsifies*, but that it may also be a kind of affront to a philosopher.

We should observe, however, that Nietzsche sometimes, but by no means always, associates a certain blindness or "will to stupidity" with the strong or noble (§107 is a particularly clear example), and "craftiness" or "cunning" with modes of reaction, weakness, and sometimes with the plebeian or "slave" class (see §25, but then also compare §§39, 40).

§192

Most of this section is a recapitulation of an already familiar theme: the necessity of falsification, although Nietzsche does not here add "for life" as usual. The senses are not sharp and quick enough to see, read, hear or notice everything – the senses must be supplemented by "invention". (We should notice here the reference to the artist – both the one who lies, and the one who lies wisely, beautifully and in accord with the very nature of appearances.) This is especially true for the perception of things that are not already very familiar to us, for in the simplest processes of sensation the "affects dominate". That is to say, the affects – the having-a-direction and an object of drives, and their relations to other drives – determine whether sense "pays attention" to something, and for how long. And, in particular, Nietzsche seems to be talking of such affects as "fear" of the unknown, and desire for what is familiar and comfortable, both of which might motivate sensory attention. Such a claim also backs up the claims about the relation of reason and instinct above: if reasoning in general is in thrall to instinct (and, it follows, to the affects), then it is not surprising that *empirical reasoning* – that is to say, our first-order thinking about perception and the objects of perception – should be so too. Moreover, it is not just that the reasoning about empirical data is dominated; so too is the data itself.

The above analysis is introduced by a statement about the early development of sciences. *Because* of the falsification of sense, the early stages of a science are characterized by rash hypothesis and "dumb good will to 'believe'". Subtle observation can only come later. Although a general point, here this is most obviously intended as a commentary on the development of a "science of morals", and thus expands upon the observations made in the first few sentences of §186. The coarse, earlier attempts at understanding how morality functions were necessary as a familiarization, such that later attempts (Nietzsche's) could be more subtle. Nevertheless, this is also a kind of self-criticism: Nietzsche too makes rash hypotheses, and describes the noble person as sometimes possessing a will to stupidity (see discussion above in §192). In other words, the early stages of even the philosophy of the future, as a matter of methodology as well as in terms of a necessary course of development, will possess its own form of crudeness and baseless self-confidence. Notice that neither crudeness nor subtlety are the same as rationality, in the traditional philosophical sense; subtlety and taste replace such rationality. The last few sentences confirm this. I observe another's thought – or what I think is their thought – expressed in their face so clearly – or what I think of as both clear and subtle – that it could not actually be "observed", but must be created by me. That I am nevertheless able to communicate with someone must mean that I *already understand* their thought, because we share a mode of human life and the other's thoughts are spiritualized drives and instincts of this life (see §286). I arrive at this understanding in advance not by a rational process of observation, communication and argumentation, but by organic growth.

§193

This curious section continues the theme of the entrapment of reason and conscious thought by the unconscious. Previously, Nietzsche has worked through the "triumph" of the instincts, and the influence of the affects upon immediate sensibility. Here, it is dreaming. Within the modern philosophical tradition, dreams are taken to be parasitical upon waking life, and the imagination is not taken to be a genuinely creative faculty. Descartes is the most obvious example, arguing that dreams are never productive of new forms, but merely rearrange or recombine forms from waking life. Nietzsche does not perhaps wish to invert this relation entirely, but certainly wants to emphasize the influence of dreams on wakefulness, altering our waking thought.

   His example is telling: flying, with complete independence of gravity and of the symbolic meanings of gravity (resistance, being "dragged down", humiliation, being tied to earth, tiredness, etc.). This alters, Nietzsche claims, our waking concept of "happiness" [*Glück*]. Significantly, this is both an important "everyday" word and feeling and also an important philosophical concept. (Recall that in §190 Nietzsche discusses the rabble's equation of "good" and "pleasant"; shortly, in §198, he will return to "happiness".) We must not forget that "*traum*" in German, like "dream" in English, also means "wish" or "desire". So, this section is not only about the psychology of dreams and their impact upon waking thought. It is also an allegory of philosophical ideal. The figure of Zarathustra is frequently tormented by the "spirit of gravity", who counsels caution, predicts calamity, twists ideas into caricatures. He is the voice of the extent to which Zarathustra has not yet overcome all the "tests" or trials, and has not fully realigned himself to the notion of will to power. The dream here – in which one "inhabits" a Zarathustra who has overcome his spirit of gravity – is a portrait of how the new ideal will transform the *philosophical* conception of happiness. Accordingly, compare, "I am an enemy of the spirit of gravity, that is the bird's way" (*Zarathustra*, Part 3, "On the Spirit of Gravity"). This whole passage, then, should be read alongside §56 and its depiction of the new ideal's response to eternal recurrence.

§194

This section is about the nature and meaning of "possession". What is considered good differentiates types of humans; even more clearly differentiating, however, are their various meanings of possession. Nietzsche gives four examples of types of possession. First, the possession, on the side of the man, in heterosexual love. Some men are "satisfied" with sexual gratification. Others are more suspicious of possible illusion in mere sex and want to know their partners are truly devoted; the test is whether she has given up something important to be with him. A third, final type, wants to ensure the woman is not deceived about him in giving herself to him; if she were, then it wouldn't be he who truly possesses her. Accordingly, he wants to be loved for everything he is, and reveals himself to the depths.

The problem of interpreting this passage begins here. For Nietzsche immediately and without further comment gives three other examples that are *presumably* meant to be in parallel. However, in the other examples, there are not *three* sub-types given, only two or even one. Identifying the analogies among all four examples is tricky.

The second example is political possession by a ruler or one with power. The first instance employs all the "higher arts of a Cagliostro and Catiline". Cagliostro was an ambiguous figure in the eighteenth century: mystic, forger, swindler, renowned physician. Catiline was a populist politician in ancient Rome who led an unsuccessful revolution against the Senate. The point presumably is that these men gained power through deception; but they also coaxed considerable sacrifices from their supporters thereby. So this "type" looks as though it matches the middle type of possession best, but this is unclear. The problem is that nowhere in the first example (of sexual love) do we find a counterpart to gaining possession through deception. (On the contrary, there the *man* is the suspicious one, who may want to ensure the woman is not deceiving him.) The other, a politician who chooses to drop the mask and let himself be known by his people, is unambiguously in the third category. Notice that being known by others requires, first, knowledge of self.

The last two examples only offer one sub-type each. First, someone who offers charity but also employs a clumsy "ruse" [*Arglist*]. The ruse ensures that those who are helped feel that just *this* person's help was needed, and thus feel grateful and faithful. Then, in the last few sentences, the final example of parents who possess their children, to the extent of indoctrinating them into all their own values and ideas. And, Nietzsche continues breathlessly, as with the father so with the teacher, class, priest or prince. Notice that I have put the case of the parents in the last category. For here the parent (or rather, *the father*) is determined to possess by making the child just like him, by not allowing differentiation to happen. The child will know the father to the depths, at least to the extent that the child will become him. Nietzsche is playing a game with his readers. He is offering them a puzzle, without a clear solution, and the section finishes with "*Woraus folgt . . .*", "From this it follows . . .". We have seen this trailing off device before, signalling perhaps that there is an implication that Nietzsche wants us to draw for ourselves. But what is it? That, as sons and daughters, students and subjects, we are *all* possessed by others, in an unbroken cycle of possession.

Love	Politics	Charity	Parenthood
sexual gratification			
demand for sacrifices	ruler encourages sacrifice	charity "ruse"	
self-knowledge and revelation	ruler removes the mask		child subject to father's values.

With this trailing off, is Nietzsche also leading in to his next section – that is, is the next section meant to expound on what "follows"? An ellipsis also ends §202 and there follows a clear thematic link to §203. However, many other sections also conclude with the ellipsis, without such an obvious link. So, the mere presence of the punctuation will not decide the issue. Instead, we must look to the next section to see whether its content bears the hypothesis out.

§195

If we are searching for a thematic link that will justify the claim that this section is the answer to the puzzle of the end of §194, then it can only be the quote that Nietzsche attributes to Tacitus: the Jews are a people "born for slavery" (see Cicero, *The Consular Provinces*, 10). For Romans such as Tacitus and Cicero, the Jews were a particularly contemptible and uncivilized people, and so being "born for slavery" means being entirely unfit for rule. But whatever else he is, Nietzsche is not a racist of *that* type. Instead, he is indicating a *structural* and ultimately *self-imposed* reason for this innate enslavement. The previous section gives us this reason. The Jews are a people born for slavery because they automatically enslave themselves by virtue of the possession of, and moral indoctrination of, children by parents (and teachers, priests, princes, etc.). Children were raised as slaves, even before they were factually enslaved by, for example, Rome.

So it would appear that §195 does serve as a continuation, across the ellipsis, of the thought of §194. However, there is no mention of Jewishness whatsoever in the previous section. Instead, this particular mode of possession of children by parents (and other authority figures) is "involuntary"; no mother doubts, no father questions. The "slave revolt" in morality that, according to Nietzsche, *happened to begin* with the Jewish people, is *now no longer* a Jewish issue at all. Instead, it is the "natural" mode of existence of all modern people. These days, the implication goes, we are all born slaves. Or, to adopt the language of the title of this part, the species "born slaves", once it developed, successfully rendered extinct (or virtually so) any competing fauna. This point is made explicitly in §199.

What then of this "slave revolt"? The Jewish people accomplished a "miraculous" feat of the inversion of values, inaugurating a slave revolt in values that culminated in the advent of historical Christianity. (See our discussion of §46 for more elaboration.) Notice we do not say culminated in the figure of Christ himself – that is a much more difficult and complex issue as we have seen (cf. our discussion of §164 above and §269 below). Notice the explicitly given "thanks" for the "charm" that resulted; we now know that this "thanks" is ironic but never entirely so. According to *amor fati* and its affirmation in eternal return, the new ideal will have the profoundest gratitude for whatever has delivered the world *as it is*, whether or not, according to a new set of values, it has *also* been an unparalleled disaster. But there is another reason for this "thanks": as inspiration for, and a model of, a new "revaluation" of values.

The characteristics of this inverted morality are that to be rich (literally but especially metaphorically) is to be godless and evil; to be poor is holy and a "friend". These we discussed already in the context of §46, as an act of revenge against Roman masters. In addition, according to this inversion, to be of the "world" is an insult. This is particularly significant for Nietzsche, and virtually serves as a symbol of his treatment of the phenomenon of the slave revolt. What is of the world (the sensuous, for example – but, in general, life) is denigrated; all value, all good, all ultimate origins and destinations, are placed outside the world. Interestingly, this is one of the very few aspects of historical Judaism that Tacitus gets approximately correct in his *History*: the God is transcendent to the world, without image, without change [*History* book V].

Let us back up a little from this "natural history" and think about history as such. Nietzsche is, between the lines if you will, proposing a grand account of history and of the logic of history here. Moreover, on this account history is not determined by human freedom, but determined by human *nature*. There are historical epochs of decadence involving a crisis of the instincts, and there are the responses that human life makes to this decadence. These responses of life are not a "plan" or a "reason" within nature, but rather unfoldings under particular circumstances of the basic structure of life, will to power. One such period commenced with Socrates in Greece and culminated in the triumph of Christianity in Rome (for a particularly clear version of this narrative see *Twilight of the Idols*, "The Problem of Socrates"; it is, though, broadly the same narrative as the "slave revolt" we have seen here, in *Beyond*). Another such period began in the eighteenth century, when Christian morality began to implode and the "magnificent tension" of the spirit reached a point of explosion (signalled by, for example, the French Revolution and democracy, the rise of Marxism and the advent of nihilism). This historical epoch has now culminated in – Nietzsche himself, "the last disciple of Dionysus" (§295) (or, perhaps, only slightly more modestly, culminated in Nietzsche's creation, Zarathustra), the point being that the current historical moment offers a once in two millennia opportunity to address oneself to a spiritual crisis through the creation of new values. And this time, Nietzsche is determined, the "cure" for decadence and a crisis of the instincts will not be a disguised form of the very same illness, but a form of life and thought that is realigned to the basic nature of life.

§196

"Countless dark bodies are to be *inferred* [*erschliessen*] near to the sun – these we will never come to see." What are we to make of this "parable among ourselves"? The reference is to (fanciful) astronomy: if there were planets in orbits still closer in than Mercury, how could they ever be detected, since they will always be lost (as Mercury itself often is) in the Sun's glare? (It is worth bearing in mind that one of the controversies between Galileo and the Jesuits was the nature of sunspots and whether they were, in fact, planets.)

Given the context, it will be helpful to think back to §2. Opposites are not incompatible (here, symbolically, the dark bodies and the blinding light of the sun), as metaphysical prejudice would have it. And "perhaps" it is even the case that the value of good things has developed out of the "wicked". That is why this is a "parable" among ourselves, since, for the others, there is just the sun and its light – darkness cannot be "near" light, but far away as the mere absence of light. The "book of the stars" [*Sternenschrift*] is a language written entirely in light. However, it is a language of signs and parables (in which "much is left concealed [*verschweigen*]") only for the "psychologist of morals", like Nietzsche. The passage, in this particular context, refers to the slave revolt as the hidden origin of contemporary European values. More generally, it refers to the unseen (and considered impossible) inter-relation of values and their apparent opposites.

There remain two questions, though. First, why "never come to see"; secondly, what it means to "infer". Let us begin by supposing that the primary meaning Nietzsche has in mind is that these "dark bodies" stand for the original inversion of values on the ground of a spirit of revenge. Since, if Nietzsche is correct, this event took place more than 2000 years ago, its nature can only be inferred and not seen, in the same way as any historical event has to be reconstructed from records and traces. (Significantly, "*erschliessen*", although usually and plausibly translated as "inferred", can also mean to "reconstruct".) While this might be part of an answer, it does not explain why the parable is written in the present tense, and also does not account for why it should be that those bodies are any darker than any other event from the past.

We need one more philosophical reference. Nietzsche is by no means the first philosophical or cosmological writer to use light or the sun in a symbolic fashion. We should think of the beginning of Genesis, or the "natural light of reason" in Descartes (among others). Most probably, though, Nietzsche has Plato in mind and the various analogies making use of the sun in the *Republic*, the most famous of which is the "allegory of the cave". The sun makes things visible to our sight just as the form of the good makes intelligible things "visible" to our intellect (*Republic*, VI, 508). Then, shortly thereafter, Plato describes the philosopher leaving the cave, where all things are seen merely as shadows, and emerging into the light (VII, 514a ff). The light is again the pure intellectual forms of things which the philosopher, once accustomed to the light, can gaze into. The basic point of the move from dark to the light is to describe, allegorically, "enlightenment"; and to show that it has an endpoint, a final stage. On Nietzsche's analysis, the sun is identified with the basic concepts and structures of philosophical thought, and accordingly philosophical thought could not subject itself to further illumination. That which illuminates could only itself be understood as precisely that which illuminates, and could not be further illuminated (Plato would not disagree, so far). But what if the basic concepts and structures of philosophical thought are *effects*, that have arisen historically through the predominance of a particular mode of human life and the instincts, drives and the system of affects that comprise the nature of that mode (the dark bodies)?

It follows that the "dark bodies" could never be seen, because the very nature of what it means to see something is defined by light, by the sun. That is, philosophy *as such* could never directly "observe" its own constitution. (There is in this an important parallel with Kant's account of the limits of theoretical reflection; there is also an implicit critique of the phenomenological unfolding of absolute self-consciousness in Hegel.) Such "dark bodies" could only be indirectly inferred. Understanding the nature of such indirect inferences is one of the important tasks Nietzsche has set himself in this book. The very word "inference" already signals the difficulty of the task, something Nietzsche has been telling us since the first two sections of the book: for, the concept "inference" is a concept *within* philosophical thought, rather than one that lies outside (or behind) it. This is why Nietzsche has been careful never to define his method as simply opposed to or entirely other than philosophical technique; instead, he must use (and use *in earnest*) philosophical analysis as one among many masks (e.g. §§16, 19), each one provisional and temporary.

§197

The "men of prey" – men like Cesare Borgia, the ruthless military and political leader who was, it is often argued, the "Prince" of Machiavelli's book, and who struggled to free his Italian power base from the influence of the Pope – should not be understood as mentally ill, defective specimens of the human species, nor as spiritually tormented by their own conduct. Instead, they are the healthiest of tropical growths. Notice in this idea of "tropical" is an obvious, and perhaps unexpected, contrast with the Northern type discussed in Part 8, and also in the infamous notion of the "blond beast" (*Genealogy*, First Treatise, §11), which is also associated especially if not exclusively with Northern Europe. The tropical metaphor returns in §258. This may be a case of Nietzsche mixing his metaphors, but it may also signal a complex distinction among "barbarian" types.

Here, at least, Nietzsche finds the analysis of such types relatively uninteresting – for him, they are simply straightforward beings. More interesting are the moralists who have such hatred, and fear, of the "tropics". Why should this be? Nietzsche does not provide an answer in this section, but our analysis of §196 might give a clue. The pure expression of the will to power of drives that these tropical monsters are is not *essentially different from or opposite to* the morality of the "temperate zones". The "men of prey", then, are living reminders of the dark source of conventional moral codes, or else of the act of revenge out of which these codes emerged. Such men are hated and feared accordingly. Section 198 will elaborate upon this idea, and indeed much of the rest of Part 5 is a treatment of the relation of fear and morality. All of which does not, of course, mean that Nietzsche wants everyone to be a Cesare Borgia, or that he represents the ideal of noble man. He is a type; and Nietzsche uses the term "*Untier*" – "monster" – without any obvious irony.

§198

This breathlessly written section says explicitly what was only hinted at in the previous section: that moralities are attempts to contain "dangerous" affects. They are "baroque" (that is, convoluted, intricate) and also unreasonable because universal in form, generalizing where generalization is not possible. The impossibility of universalization is a frequent theme in Nietzsche; it is particularly pertinent here because, as has been stressed several times in the previous few lines, we are speaking of the passions and tendencies of *individuals* or at least of distinct types of human life. They are "good sense" [*Klugheit*] – in so far as the release of these affects or drives would be precisely "dangerous"; but also "stupidity" [*Dummheit*] in so far as they are based upon, and lead to further, misunderstandings and fears of the affects. Moreover, moralities are a symptom, and ultimately also a further cause, of a kind of illness within life itself. They exude the smell of "nooks and crannies" [*Winkelgeruch*]. This smell only becomes "seductive" when it is over-spiced and "of another world" and thus itself "dangerous". (The reference here is obscure, but might refer to exoticism [note the reference to Hafiz at the end of the passage], or perhaps less restrained varieties of the passion for God.)

Nietzsche then runs briskly and satirically through a number of famous moral systems, claiming that they all represent this same phenomenon: Stoicism, Spinozism, Aristotelianism, and aesthetic or religious moralities. In "religion" the affects regain rights as citizens, Nietzsche jokes, provided – he breaks off, but we can complete the thought: provided God is the monarch and love of God the law. And, finally, morality as defence against dangerous drives includes even the letting loose the reins of the affects, provided only one is so elderly that it hardly matters any more. Note that Nietzsche is himself "generalizing" – although because he is speaking of types of moral system, instead of the system of affects that belongs to an individual, some degree of generalization may be appropriate.

§199

This section explicitly draws the conclusions of §§194–5: today, there are only slaves, only the herd. The natural historical reasons for this (here in the sense of the development of a type across time) are that (i) there have always been "herds", people who broadly speaking are in a position of having or wanting to obey, and such people are necessarily more numerous; (ii) the instinct for obedience (that is to say, the defining drive of this type as expressed by the reactive affect of needing to obey) is "inherited best". This latter is presumably a biological reference. Nietzsche's nineteenth-century understanding of how genetics works, of how traits are inherited, is unsurprisingly rather creaky. In particular, he believes that characteristics acquired by an individual (e.g. habits) can be inherited. It has long been known that this is not true *biologically*, but that it might be true as a matter of social conditioning. Such a concept of inheritance, as social or psychological conditioning rather than genetics, is much more defensible. The social conditioning thesis is in fact used by Nietzsche at the end of §194: and the reference to parents and teachers there is repeated here. In any case, we have seen on many occasions analyses of certain value systems that conclude that these values serve to favour or preserve the weaker types, here identified with the instinct of obedience (§42, for example). One way or the other, then, through one or more of the means of inheritance suggested above, the preponderance of the instinct for obedience is encouraged.

The upshot of this development is that it might happen that the "herd" has flourished to such an extent that the commanding type is extinct. Or, at least, that the illness is spreading and the commanding type develops a "bad conscience", and refuses to acknowledge itself as in fact commanding, preferring instead to imagine the commands coming from outside it (from tradition, the will of the people, law, constitutions, God, etc.). This, Nietzsche claims, is precisely the situation in Europe "today". At the same time, according to the system of values that was instituted through the slave revolt, the instinct of obedience, and all related characteristics such as "benevolence", "moderation", "pity" and so forth, are elevated so as to be identified with virtue as such. Nevertheless, the (now very rare) appearance of a commander with no bad conscience is seen as a relief and "higher happiness" by such a people.

§200

This section offers a counterpoint to the previous one. "Late cultures", Nietzsche says, are often characterized by a kind of interbreeding of classes and types, the product of which (again, this could be understood as biological or social or both) are people who embody opposite drives, who are continually at war with themselves. Expressions like this – "late" cultures, civilizations, ages – are common in Nietzsche; he is referring broadly to historical periods in which the dominant form of human life is nearing the end of its slow degeneration and within which the forces are building for some type of revolution. There are two possible responses to being such a mixed type: one can long for rest or peace – and, Nietzsche suggests, many moral systems including the Christian have this as one objective. Or, one can experience this internal conflict as "one *more* stimulus and incentive to life", and develop skill and finesse at this war. This second response results in those "magical, incomprehensible and unfathomable ones" such as Caesar or da Vinci.

This raises the question of whether, according to Nietzsche's analysis, his present-day Europe is such a late and "disintegrating" culture. He does not say so here, but he will in §208. However, there is good reason already for thinking it must be so. For in the previous section, the natural commanders are struck with a "bad conscience" which is precisely the partial inheritance of the instinct for obedience. In other words, they are "mixed" types. So, this section is a description of (one way, at least) in which the cultural (and biological) situation that Europe has reached might be overcome, how the necessary types might emerge in order to effect Nietzsche's "revaluation of all values". This is an extremely important new idea. It suggests that the overcoming of the European malaise (e.g. of nihilism) can and must arise from a pan-European source. That is, not from some conception of racial purity or an atavism of the barbarian (this is how Nietzsche is too often interpreted), but precisely through the democratic mixture *which is also in itself part of the problem.*

§201

This section concerns the "morality of neighbourly love". This notion, a cornerstone of Christian morality, turns out to be an illusion. It is merely an abbreviated or truncated version of a morality of the welfare *of the whole* which, in turn, is related to the preservation of the whole (the community, the state, the people) from what threatens them. According to Nietzsche's analysis, neighbourly love is always secondary to neighbourly fear. In the first instance, this means fear of that which is outside the community, and which encourages for a time the development of strong and dangerous drives that could serve to protect the community. Our neighbour resides outside the "us", and might threaten our destruction. Then, once established, this fear turns on those protective qualities (drives) themselves – the neighbour who is feared is the strong and rapacious type "within" the community. At first, presumably, this means those types who emerge in such a way as to present the "dangerous" qualities. Eventually, though, this develops into fear of such qualities *in oneself.* Fear thus motivates the crafting of a moral code that favours weakness and submission. By the end, there is no education that leads to general severity, and every severity (Nietzsche's example is the punishment of criminals) therefore becomes an object of fear. So much is the morality of the herd based upon fear that, if conditions were one day arrived at where all danger (within and without) was eliminated, then such morality would be abolished because no longer necessary. "Progress" is the name Europe gives to the attempt to reach that day.

This whole section is cast under the shadow of its beginning: "As long as . . . there could not yet be . . .". Ultimately, this means: "As long as the current European situation *vis-à-vis* morality continues . . . there could not yet be . . .". This raises the prospect of an end to this situation, and also the prospect of a new situation in which there *can* be – "neighbourly love". Although Nietzsche does not explicitly turn his analysis around in this way, it would appear to be the implication of the structure of §201. Thus, the surprising question is raised, whether one way of characterizing the moral and political consequence of Nietzsche's "philosophers of the future" is in terms of some kind of *genuine* "neighbourly love", one not founded directly or indirectly upon fear. As we shall see, Nietzsche's book turns increasingly to the *future* social and political implications of his new ideal. During the course of this, Nietzsche will indeed be developing a new characterization of friendship and love, and these notions will have significant social and political implications.

§202, and discussion of notion of pity (or "compassion")

This section begins with an apology of sorts. Nietzsche admits it must be difficult and even offensive to hear humans spoken of as animals in "herds". But this is where his insights lead; it would be dishonest to speak in any other terms. Where people value *en masse*, and feel down to their core (and again *en masse*) that they already have the answer to the question Socrates claimed not to, and which the serpent in the Garden of Eden promised to teach (i.e. the nature of Good and Evil), this collective evaluation is a clear symptom of the instinct of the herd animal. This, though, is but one type of morality, among others. Especially, Nietzsche emphasizes, among *higher others*. This means not just that another morality would value itself as higher (for all moralities do that). Rather, it means a moral system that is consistent with – rather than reacting against, denying or consistently misunderstanding – the basic nature of life. This is potentially confusing since Nietzsche does not very often refer to the values of his new ideal as a morality; much more often, morality is a particular subclass of values as such.

Significantly, this Christian/Democratic moral system that Nietzsche is criticizing has one other *formal* feature that may mark it out from other moral systems: it identifies itself with *morality as such* and accordingly refuses even the possibility, much less the reality, of other such systems. Again, confusingly, the presumptive universality of this moral system is often considered by Nietzsche as the mark of morality as such (see e.g. §187). There are internal debates within this system, to be sure: Nietzsche's examples are anarchists, socialists and democrats. But these are only internal, for there never even arises a questioning concerning the basic principles of this morality – or even the manner in which it defines what a morality is, or values its existence (cf. §186). They are united by their instinctive hostility to any conception of society other than herd; by opposition to any special claims or rights; by mistrust of punishment as justice; but above all in the "religion of pity". Pity translates *Mitleid*, which is rendered frequently as "compassion". The latter is etymologically more accurate. It captures first the basic sense of the German word as "suffering with". Also, with the root "passion", it captures the double sense of "suffer" – to feel pain and to be passive – as in the "passion of Christ" to which Nietzsche here alludes. Most English versions of the New Testament translate 1.Peter 3.8 using the word "compassion", which Luther rendered as *Mitleid*. On the other hand, in English, "compassion" sounds too dignified or rarefied. Moreover, given the importance of fear in this Part also, we should be reminded of Aristotle's definition of tragedy in terms of "pity and fear"; the Greek *"eleos"* is almost always translated as "pity". Nietzsche consistently uses *"Mitleid"* to represent this concept, from *The Birth of Tragedy*, §22 to *Beyond* §§229 and 239. "Compassion", then, would miss this important reference to Aristotle. Here, we will use "pity" mostly, although in this case as in so many the reader should keep in mind what is lost as well as what is gained in such choices.

The idea of a "religion of pity" seems particularly significant for Nietzsche: not only is it said to be a key feature of modern European morality, but it is likewise a key feature of the remnants of religion in nineteenth-century Europe. That is, a "religion of pity" captures the way in which an atheist, for example, surreptitiously retains a direct connection to Christianity through the continuing commitment to morality. We have seen Nietzsche treat of the notion of pity before (e.g. §30, and in the "tests" of §41), and these analyses continue throughout the rest of this book. Nietzsche's analysis of pity is extraordinarily rich and complex, and therefore also difficult to reconstruct from the brief sections of a book like *Beyond Good and Evil*. (A key external passage is *Zarathustra*, Part 2, "On the Pitying".) There have been and will be other angles to the treatment of the notion of pity, but here let us mention four essential aspects of the analysis. First, Nietzsche objects to the notion that pity is a *fundamental* moral concept (cf. §201), as in many versions of Christianity. For Nietzsche, on the contrary, if pity has a place it is in fact as a derivative affect, one that follows rather than leads one's valuations. For example, pity is a perfectly valuable affect to feel *on the basis of* an affect of the difference of order of rank (cf. §§225, 293).

Secondly, pity always *demeans*. This may simply be because it is a show of power; or because the affect stems from a lack of self-respect on the part of the one who pities (e.g. §222); or, in other cases, by asserting the equivalence in rank of pitying and pitied, or indeed of everyone (§29) – that is, of asserting a universal "community" of suffering, as Nietzsche puts it here. In the current section, additionally, we can see that pity ignores orders of rank and other differences in the idea of pity for "whatever feels". In all of these cases, there is an abandonment of the height of evaluations that one may have attained through the realignment of these valuations to the will to power. An example of the implications of this is given later, in §205, where Nietzsche talks about the relationship between self-respect and "leadership" in knowledge.

Thirdly, pity represents an intolerance of, and an attempt to eliminate, suffering. This is perfectly clear here at the end of §202. That is, it relates to the basic utility-focus of dominant European moralities. On Nietzsche's analysis, a morality that seeks to eliminate suffering thereby also eliminates precisely those conditions under which alone the growth of the human type is possible. Accordingly, here at the end of this section, he uses the words "height" and "Redeemer" with heavy irony. This goes to the heart of the problem for Nietzsche. Pity, then, is a key part of the disastrous interference by Christianity in the development of human kind, which has resulted in a herd-like Europe. It may even be an appropriate disguise for those whose moral instincts drive them to interfere by eliminating higher types (§206) – perhaps genuinely thinking these higher types are in moral torment (§197).

Finally, to pity any *individual*, even and especially "higher men" whose elevation (or perhaps lack of sufficient elevation) brings them suffering, is to wilfully misunderstand the "extravagant cruelty" of nature (this is a theme of the last book of *Zarathustra* and of the end of *Beyond Good and Evil*). In such pity there remain traces of both a moral condemnation of nature itself – and nothing could be more absurd (this is implied in the discussion of Stoicism in §9) – and a moral (indeed, democratic) commitment to the value of the individual *per se* which in turn entails soul atomism (cf. §12). It is such pity that the analyses of *amor fati* and especially the eternal recurrence are intended to identify and overcome. Pity for the human *as such*, however, might be a noble affect, in so far as the very possibilities of the human are diminished, crushed or misunderstood precisely by pity in the ordinary sense (see §225, and also the next section, 203, in which Nietzsche clearly draws a distinction between two senses of "degeneration": the individual and the human as such).

§203

The previous section ends with the idea of "faith in the community of pity". Faith, that is, that the universalization of the morality of pity will redeem and offer hope of the end of suffering. This section begins "We, who have a different faith". Initially, and intermittently throughout, Nietzsche carries on with the theme of the previous sections: "we" see democracy not only as a debased politics but as a debased form of humanity. But much of this section is a kind of rallying cry to a new faith: the faith that would comprise pursuing and valuing the "new ideal". Nietzsche is not being entirely ironic in calling this "faith"; there is, after all, something messianic about the new philosophers to come. Moreover, we have already discussed the new ideal as an alternate form of religion without theism.

This faith is not faith "in" something (unless it is the possibilities of the human) but rather a faith "towards" something: towards the new ideal, or the philosophers of the future. These are the human type who will set in motion the "revaluation" of values that Nietzsche has been speaking of for some time. They will be "strong" and "original" [*ursprünglich*], and through them the "revaluation" will be initiated and gather momentum. By the former concept, strength, is meant having drives (or "will") consistently able to affirm their own nature as will to power (to be able to countenance the thought of eternal recurrence) and accordingly able to overcome the "tests" of pity, fear and so forth. By the latter, originality, Nietzsche signals the inventiveness required for the task: in German the word means, literally, to be the first source of. The new values are not borrowed from outside, not received on tablets from God. Rather, they are expressions in terms of relational values of drives and instincts that have been realigned to the will to power. Accordingly, the creation of such values is an act of originality. Similarly, Nietzsche speaks later of exploiting existing conditions; so this originality might also refer to the resourcefulness or cunning that this would require. The faith, then, is towards humans of the future who "in the present commence the compulsion and tie the knots [*den Zwang und Knoten anknüpfen*] that will compel [*zwingen*] the will of millennia into *new* channels [*Bahnen*]". (In addition to providing a convenient pun, the "knots" are an allusion to the fates of Greek mythology.)

Finally, this must be faith towards future philosophers who can teach humanity that its future is not only dependent upon but identical to its will. This in the sense that, for a being realigned to the will to power, the values expressed by its will (the moral direction of its drives) must be values that also affirm the nature of that will (of all will) as will to power. Accordingly, these philosophers of the future will prepare to undertake the vast and risky attempt [*-Versuche*] of "breeding and cultivation" [*Zucht und Züchtung* – recall also the connection of these words to "discipline"]. This "attempt" will put an end to the chance and nonsense that has passed for "history" thus far. By this is meant a number of things. First, as we have seen, the development of great and truly noble humans has previously been left to chance; as sometimes has their degeneration. The defining moments of history, then, do not form a narrative (and no hand or even finger of God – no plan or purpose of God – was involved), but are instead characterized by tragic accident. Secondly, what attempts there have been to organize the development of the human type are based upon nonsense – that is, not only moralities of lesser worth, but that are also irretrievably linked to metaphysical prejudice about the nature of life, knowledge, or truth. Accordingly these attempts yielded only dwarf or herd animals. Thirdly, important historical moments can be interpreted as "blind" reactions by life itself, such as to an impending collapse of the instincts for life (this example is the narrative of Socrates discussed above under §195); and because "blind", therefore "chance". What it could not mean is that the rule of future philosophers will bring to an end the rule of chance: the notion of risk above, and the "dark thoughts and storms" Nietzsche speaks of later make that clear. Such a possibility would be to misunderstand the extravagance and cruelty of nature and the impossibility, indeed undesirability, of "taming" it.

What preoccupies Nietzsche and the free spirits are the risks and challenges involved in a series of tasks that comprise the "preparation" mentioned above, which would produce "leaders". The first task is ensuring that the conditions are in place for such production. By this Nietzsche means: (i) the cultural, economic and political climate in general so as to ensure appropriate social/psychological inheritance, and (ii) the breeding conditions, the gathering together of appropriate genetic material, to ensure appropriate physiological inheritance. To modern ears, this sounds dangerously like eugenics. Nietzsche's counterpoint to that would be, presumably, that it is a Christian/Democratic moral system that devalues such eugenics and more importantly, that it does so precisely to prevent the conditions for the development of new types of human being – because of its commitment to its own mode of life, because of the virtue of pity, and because of its constitutional fear of these new types. This moral system is also "eugenics", therefore; indeed, it is a kind of *genocide*. Notice that of the conditions some will have to be created, others exploited (this should remind us of the manner in which religion can be used, §61).

The second preparatory task is education: to anticipate and provide the means by which a being would understand itself according to the will to power, and be compelled to will itself as such. The talk of "discipline" is relevant here, as well as the earlier discussions of the relationships of leisure and labour, of "tests", and of severe moral training (such as Puritanism, for example). We should also compare the narratives and examples in §194. The third is the "revaluation of values", the hammer of which would steel the spirit for its heavy responsibilities. This means to discover and overcome (which is more or less equivalent to "revalue") all affects not yet realigned to the doctrine of will to power. The blacksmith metaphors here (hammer, steel, bronze) correspond to the idea of breaking near the end of the section.

The risks of the whole project correspond to the above three tasks: to the first, the risk that no leader emerges at all; to the second, that what we called education fails; to the third, that the being "degenerates", that is, falls prey to one or another of its residual affects. These are, Nietzsche says, anxieties without comparison. Again, that the risks should correspond to each of the tasks signals that the new historical world Nietzsche envisages is still within or at the mercy of an indifferent nature. The last thirty lines of the section are, broadly speaking, repetition.

7 We Scholars: Science as the "Hammer" of Philosophy (Part 6 §§204–13)

The title is *"Wir Gelehrten"*, "We Scholars". What must not be missed is the relation to *"Lehrer"*, meaning teacher, as in the first section of Part 4. So we have the double idea of scholarship. First, as assiduous and objective enquiry, akin to or equivalent to science; indeed, in §204 Nietzsche uses the term *"Wissenshaft"* (science, but not exclusively natural science – thus, again, an objective, "scientific" enquiry) apparently equivalently. And, secondly, teaching or education. The second part of this meaning already anticipates one of Nietzsche's key points in this Part: being a scholar is not an end in itself, nor for that matter is the scholar's production of knowledge. The aim, rather, is to make something possible through scholarship as mode of a teaching.

§204

There has been, Nietzsche claims, a harmful change in the relative ranks assigned to philosophy and science [*Wissenshaft*]. As noted above, this term refers to activities well beyond the scope of the natural sciences (which is the "natural" usage of "science" in English), to include the human sciences (e.g. psychology, sociology, linguistics) and other disciplines that see themselves as objective and methodologically precise, such as history. Thus, the distinction between the terms "scientist" and "scholar" (as in the title of this Part) is by no means as marked in German as in English. Nietzsche is referring to philosophy's gradual replacement as the chief mode of approaching and knowing. There are, however, two risks associated with even raising this issue of relative rank. First, that it all might be a question of sour grapes, so to speak. Nietzsche, as we know, was once a university professor in one of these sciences – philology – but he and the expectations of both university and discipline found themselves variously at odds. We should view in this light the quotation from Balzac, and the discussion a few lines later of the "memory" of various naive slights of philosophy by science (and, he adds, especially philology, his old colleagues). Secondly, there is the risk that we might speak blindly *against* science, like "women and artists", because it seems to peek into embarrassing questions (see §127 and our comments on it above). Only "experience" [*Erfahrung*] allows one to address such "higher" questions of rank. Nietzsche asks, teasingly, whether "experience" must mean "bad [*schlimm* – or 'wicked'] experiences" – this could refer to the idea of "sour grapes" above, or even the embarrassing questions, but more likely to (i) the kind of dangerous and difficult insights about the nature of life and knowledge that Nietzsche has been describing since the beginning, and (ii) the fact that, from the point of view of contemporary morality, the free spirit and philosopher of the future will sometimes appear "wicked" (cf. §§23 and 205). The question of the necessity of experience for the development of a philosopher is a major preoccupation of this Part.

In Nietzsche's addressing the harm entailed by the elevation of science above philosophy, the solution could not be a simple subordination of one inside the other. After all, the first Part of the book was a sustained attack on a number of metaphysical ideas that Nietzsche clearly believes are still at work within *both* disciplines. Rather, the issue will be how a new, future philosophy might put the virtues of science to work, exploiting them for its ideals.

The elevation of science has a number of aspects. First, and most importantly, Nietzsche sees it as part of the triumph of democratic ideals, of the overthrow of any masters. In the case of science, these masters included theology and philosophy. The sciences want to play the master; indeed, they want to play the philosopher. Secondly, the sciences encourage specialization, and a specialist, from his own particular "nook", resists thought that tries to be "synthetic" – that is, that tries to reach across particular disciplines in order to say something that could not be said with one alone. This idea of the "synthetic" becomes increasingly important in the rest of the book. However, the way that Nietzsche employs this idea here should also remind us both of the use to which the concept of synthesis was put in the account of eternal recurrence, and (in the sense of using a particular manner of thinking or speaking for a purpose not contained or containable in that manner) of the notion of "mask". Thirdly, the industriousness characteristic of the sciences feels slighted by the "otium" and nobility of philosophical thoughts. This point clearly reflects the kinds of anxieties and resentments that, on Nietzsche's analysis, led to the slave revolt in morality.

Fourthly, he speaks of the utilitarian point of view of the sciences, which sees philosophy as useless, just a set of old and refuted systems. Incidentally, there is no reason to suspect that here Nietzsche intends "utility" to refer narrowly to the ethical utilitarianism of Bentham and Mill; rather, Nietzsche intends the term more broadly, as any sense that the role or value of science is to serve the Christian/Democratic ideals of humanity. So, what is meant is a utility for morality and its ideals, rather than just for a utilitarian morality. Fifthly, the elevation is also grounded in a fear of mysticism and a corresponding tightening of the supposed limits of knowledge. Sixthly, there may be a lack of respect for an individual philosophy generalized to all philosophers. Seventhly, finally and, Nietzsche claims, most frequently, this elevation of science stems from a cutting oneself off from one philosopher without also cutting oneself off from the critiques he gave of still earlier figures – and a resulting "irritation" with all philosophy. His example is Schopenhauer's savage (and Nietzsche thinks naive) attacks on Hegel, which caused a whole generation of German thought to turn away from those subtleties of historical analysis that were precisely what distinguished Hegel.

Since these arrogant attacks on philosophy are from Nietzsche's memory, they most likely refer to particular aspects of his biography. We mentioned above the experience of working inside the discipline of philology at Basel, and of course Nietzsche himself had a significant early investment in Schopenhauer, later repudiated, and it could be that he sees himself as only now emerging from the after-effects of that repudiation. But we will here not investigate further the biographical connections. Rather, the important general aspects of the account are clear: that the elevation of science above philosophy is closely tied to Christian/Democratic moral values; and that a scholar's biography has a lasting and largely hidden effect on what she believes to be her objective and scientific reason – which is just the claim Nietzsche made about philosophers in §6.

There are, however, other reasons for the suspicion of philosophy today that have to do with philosophy *itself*, and specifically with the poverty of the most recent generation of philosophers. Particular bile is reserved for positivism and the conception of philosophy as merely epistemology. No philosophers of his own day, Nietzsche says, are of the stature of Heraclitus, Plato, Empedocles. These are all early Greek examples – and this presumably reflects a genuine belief that philosophical activity has been lacking something (or more likely that it has been declining along with the stature of the human) for two millennia. To take two obvious examples much nearer Nietzsche's period, despite the considerable and noble greatness of Kant and Hegel in other departments (such as being synthetic thinkers, and critical; see §210), even they do not stack up as value-*creating* philosophers. This does not mean either that Nietzsche simply agrees with any of these Greek figures, or even admires much of their philosophy, but rather that they represent a synthetic and also a value-creating type. (On this, see the Second Preface of *Philosophy in the Tragic Age of the Greeks*.) When he looks at philosophers around him, Nietzsche sees only specialists and scholars, who have been brought back under the dominance of science and now are tokens of the resentfulness of the "unbelief" in philosophy. Just as the diminution of humanity as a whole might properly inspire pity, so might the diminution of philosophy – in so far, that is, as philosophy might be important for reversing the former.

§205

The philosopher should be "synthetic" and (among other tools) employ and bring together the techniques and results of science generally. If so, however, then the enormous edifice of science poses a threat. Faced with the now vast depth and breadth of its data and theories, will the philosopher grow weary, become a specialist, become a dilettante or amateur and lose self-respect, or just arrive too late, but in any case fail to attain that height from which she can survey and "look *down*"? This last expression means, as always, not some height of abstraction, still less of refined snobbery, but rather the "height" of the valuations realigned to the will to power, the only genuine (as opposed to self-deceiving or "nonsense") height. The notion of "self-respect" two sentences later reinforces this. Losing self-respect or self-confidence must be a sign that a lower or diminished set of affects, and thus drives, has interrupted the process of realignment. Moreover, the philosopher faces an apparent contradiction in practice. She demands a "yes or no" about life, but is naturally cautious and reluctant to believe in her right or duty to render this judgement. That is, as we shall see later, it is philosophy's ultimate job not just to analyse but to create values; and yet many of the necessary subordinate virtues of philosophical thought (scholarship, scepticism, criticism are three that Nietzsche works through in the next few sections) make her cautious about precisely this "job". We have seen the wisdom of this caution often before: for example, the naive youthfulness of yes and no in §31, or the many discussions of the dangers of "unconditional" thought. Only the most disturbing and destructive experiences can lead her to a sense of this right and responsibility.

All of these dangers have derailed philosophers so frequently that the "rabble" now think of philosophers as always mystical, desensitized, and "drunk with God" – in other words, "prudently" not of this world at all. On the contrary, Nietzsche asserts, the genuine philosopher must be engaged, and thus precisely not live prudently, must risk herself constantly in playing the "wicked game". This is clearly another version of the idea of "going down" or "going under" first announced at the beginning of *Zarathustra*. It is also the idea that, although the noble and wise "love masks", a mask is as much a mode of engagement as it is of separation. The "wicked game" refers to a life of engagement with – negotiating with, critiquing, using, being tempted by – values other than one's own. "*Schlimm*" can also mean "bad" or even "ugly", and this should remind us of the discussion of the "necessary dirt" of politics in §61. These lines help us to understand what has been meant by the disturbing and destructive experiences of the philosopher. It is not merely that the philosopher must be engaged in order to learn about, or transform, the existing conditions of the human. Rather, this engagement is also part of the development of the philosopher as such.

Notice also the second mention of "Cagliostro" as an archetype of a man whose power or influence was founded upon deception (see also §194). The type is here called a "great actor" or "pied piper". This is a course open to the one without self-respect; one *pretends as if* one has achieved a measure of the nobility of spirit, or insights into the hidden ground of knowledge. One wears masks from out of the desire to hide self-contempt, rather than from out of a self-confident use of available discourses and roles.

§206

The scholar is not a genius [*Genie*]. Like a respectable "old maid" (meaning old "virgin", neither experienced *of* a man or *as* a woman) they know neither begetting nor giving birth (see also §248). Nietzsche is here making a correlation between the creative acts of a genius, and the "value creating" acts of the philosophers of the future described in §211. The concept of "genius" is obviously an important one for aesthetics in the late eighteenth and nineteenth centuries, but is employed less often than one might expect in Nietzsche's work. Nor is the scholar noble – he does not dominate and is not self-sufficient. Rather, he is a herd animal, with an emphasis on the reciprocal dependency on his equals. Notice the reference, a few lines later, to the "inner *mistrust*" sedimented in the hearts of herd men. This is a reference back to the discussion of "fear" in §201. Similarly, again a few lines later, "He is friendly, though only as one who lets himself go but not *flow*". That is, there remains a reserve, a lack of trust, genuine friendship or even love. With reciprocal dependency comes the impossibility of genuine trust. Implicit here is a critique of the whole range of political theories that try to understand the origin of the social or political order by way of a "social contract". (We shall return to this theme as Nietzsche's book continues to move towards explicitly political ideas.) The scholar's worst fault is that his instinct for mediocrity drives him to seek the destruction of the exceptional.

§207

Nietzsche has now spent several sections savaging the recent subordination of philosophy under science (or even the inclusion of philosophy within science), and thus also the subordination of philosophy to the values and virtues of scholars. This section continues this, but also turns to the question of the value of this scholarly type *for* philosophy, as Nietzsche understands it. We are often grateful, Nietzsche observes, for an "objective spirit". It is a blessed relief from subjectivity and "*Ipsissimosität*". This last is a made up word, meaning "my own-most-ness". Nietzsche is having a brief jab at, first of all, philosophers like Descartes who begin with the "I", resulting in the kinds of ideas and analyses he criticizes in Part 1; but also at a widespread nineteenth-century obsession with inner feelings, self-analysis, biography and so forth. But this gratitude for the objective spirit has limits. Evidently Nietzsche does not, then, mean "gratitude" in the sense of the *amor fati*, but rather in a more everyday sense of the word. There is something requiring our caution about this objectivity and "depersonalization". Certainly it is not, itself, a goal or end in itself. Rather, the objective spirit (once she has outgrown pessimism, that is) is a precious instrument [*kostbarste Werkzeuge*], but only an instrument. In particular, she is a delicate apparatus of *mirrors*. We should note that, in *Twilight of the Idols*, Nietzsche rather complicates the distinction between the two senses of gratitude: "we make it a point of honour to be *affirmer*s. More and more, our eyes have opened to that economy which needs and knows how to utilize . . . which finds an advantage . . . What advantage? But we ourselves, we immoralists, are the answer." ("Morality as Anti-Nature", §6.) In this passage, the cunning that exploits (see §203) is not different from the *amor fati* understood as gratitude for that which conditions us. And this we should have expected, for from the perspective of eternal recurrence there would certainly be no sense in the distinction.

Nietzsche then spends some time developing an elaborate analogy with the mirror. This is hardly a new analogy, since the idea of science as a "mirror of nature" is a classic figure of the scientific revolution; moreover, thinking about knowledge in terms of mirrors goes back at least to Plato. But Nietzsche is thinking less of knowledge, than of *the type of the knower*, as a mirror. The objective spirit is *himself* mirror-like, subordinating himself and "spreading himself gently" before any phenomenon. Accordingly, self-knowledge is lacking; he cannot be objective *about himself*, about the particular person that he is, because he is skilled only at "general matters". Moreover, the capacity to love (and also to hate) is absent; in the case of the objective scholar, love is a fake. We have seen some of the reasons for this in §201 and §206; additionally, though, Nietzsche claims it is a dispositional impossibility to be both objective and person-less and *also* to be capable of genuine affirmation or negation. Nietzsche ends the section with a related and crude joke: "It follows also that he is nothing for women, *in parenthesi*." We should immediately think back to the first lines of the Preface: nothing for women would, in that context, mean useless for truth. The joke is that "*in parenthesi*" is meant as both "incidentally" or "by the way", but also literally as a sexual image: a parenthesis is a subordinate or unimportant "insertion" into a sentence.

Nietzsche repeats often enough that the objective spirit is a tool or instrument, and should be valued and protected as such, but is not either beginning or end. Above all, he is not a "complementary man in whom the *rest* of existence is justified [*rechtfertig*]". This striking expression is important. "*Complementar*" is an unusual word in German (*Komplett* is more often used), derived from Latin, meaning "completing" or still more literally "filling up". "*Rechtfertig*" means "justified", but is made up of two roots: "*recht*" meaning "right" or "just", and "*fertig*" meaning, again, complete or finished. So, we might loosely translate this passage as: "not a man who completes existence by completely justifying it as it is". Expressed in this way, we can see the integration of this idea with the ideas we discussed under the heading of the eternal return, back in Part 3 (§56).

However, it is not stated clearly *why* this instrument is precious and to be valued. Three reasons suggest themselves. First, as the beginning of the passage states, such objectivity is a refreshing change from interminable self-analysis; it thus constitutes a step towards the philosopher of the future by criticizing and also embodying as a form of life a counter-concept to the metaphysical notions of the "I", "soul", "thought", and "will". Secondly, the knowledge gained by such scholars is inevitably nuanced, subtle, conditioned and complex; accordingly, although it is simply incapable of the yes and no of the philosopher of the future, it provides the latter with material and tools. It thereby also avoids the instinct for the unconditional characteristic of the herd (see for example §46); and, again, avoids the unconditional not as just an intellectual act without further foundation, but as a matter of instincts, in a form of living. Thirdly, as was suggested in §205 and will be again in §211, Nietzsche hypothesizes that the philosopher of the future must pass through, wear the masks of, a number of component positions – most of them falling under the title of Part 6: "We Scholars". In other words, the notion that this type is not to be considered a "goal" must be understood in two senses: that its values are not the values of a mode of life realigned to the will to power; but also, that it is a transitional state *within* the development of the philosopher.

§208

This is a curious section that begins with the relation between philosophy and scepticism and ends with a prophecy of global conflict or near conflict between Europe and Russia.

If a philosopher of the future is not a sceptic then – is he a pessimist or nihilist? By scepticism (as a movement in Classical Greek philosophy) is meant the incapacity of our knowledge to determine the truth or falsehood of a number of theoretical claims. Belief in such claims is to be suspended; and the result is a way of life called "*ataraxia*", characterized by tranquillity in the face of such undecidability. Nietzsche parodies this with the talk of tranquillisers, sedatives [*Schlaf- und Beruhigungsmittel*] and opiates, a positive abhorrence of decision or action. More recently, scepticism tends to designate any philosophical position that in some way denies the possibility of one type of, or all, knowledge. If a philosopher is not a sceptic, then it could be that he has found some positive knowledge, or that he has found some *negation of knowledge*. This negation is the suspicion that grows around the philosopher – that he is a pessimist or nihilist – who does not just say "no" but "*does* no". It leads Nietzsche to a fine joke, the idea of "Russian *nihiline*" (a made-up name for an explosive, after the model of nitroglycerine or trinitrotoluene, with an allusion to political nihilism in Russia, a label commonly levelled also at Russian writers such as Dostoevsky).

The passage continues with a lengthy discussion of the modern sceptical type, as a common version of the objective spirit and thus of the scholar in general. Nietzsche claims that scepticism is a symptom of a disease of the will – and he relates this disease to the sudden mixing of classes. The unplanned mixture of conflicting and confusing drives and thus values leads to the inertia and reciprocal dependency characteristic of scepticism. This passage should be compared with §200. Notice the explicit linking of class and race. Class is obviously an important word in socialist thought, of which Nietzsche is always wary. Nietzsche's point is that, at least in most cases, class is not an artificial product of contingent economic circumstances (as it is for most Marxists), but rather the "natural" grouping of human beings of a similar type. Or, if it *once* was an artificial product, the class has now developed a distinct physiological profile through the mechanisms of preferential breeding that are part of broadly Christian/ Democratic morals.

Nietzsche then turns to the geographic distribution of such scepticism which he sees as centred on France. The opposite tendency, the "will to will", is stronger in Germany and still more in England, Spain, Corsica (the birthplace of Napoleon). But the will today is by far strongest in Russia (Nietzsche thus makes further capital out of the nihiline joke earlier). How, though, will it discharge? To release this tension Russia would have to be fractured, or become democratic (the "newspaper over breakfast" is another fine joke in this section – recall the gunpowder and printing press joke in the Preface). But Nietzsche rather hopes that Russia will continue to be a threat, and that Europeans will have to respond by acquiring "a single will", precisely through the development of the philosophers of the future as a new ruling "caste". This is the compulsion to move from the petty politics of European fragmentation to a "great politics".

§209

The political theme is linked back to the discussion of the attributes of the new philosophers. The coming "warlike age" may be favourable for the development of a different kind of scepticism. Nietzsche discusses this by means of a "parable", a speculative account of a moment in German history, namely the rise of the figure of Frederick the Great. Instead of being weakened by the "leach" of scepticism, Frederick developed a harsher and more dangerous scepticism: a scepticism that does not believe but appropriates or takes possession anyway, does not "lose itself" [*verliert sich*]. (This phrase also means to fade or die away, and is an allusion to the scepticism that exhausts itself as nihilism.) This, then, is a sceptic who does not *thereby* lose the capacity to will, to make decisions, and does not cease to be a person.

There follows a brief discussion of the manifestations of this new scepticism in subsequent German culture, particularly in the "great German philologists and critical historians" who were "also artists of destruction and decay". Nietzsche is referring to a mode of thought oriented towards understanding the history and language of thought, an important current of intellectual life in Germany in the eighteenth and early nineteenth centuries, and one that had an obvious influence on, for example, Hegel. They were artists of destruction, in Nietzsche's view, perhaps because they pursued their intellectual endeavours without any ahistorical or universal basis for so doing; they did not believe, but *carried on regardless*. Moreover, in their historical researches, Nietzsche apparently regards them as practising a kind of artful destruction of any such ahistorical basis (e.g. conceptions of human nature, historical progress, naive notions of the nature of language). A new conception of the German spirit emerges, despite all romanticism, one that notably overcomes an earlier conception of the German character as gentle and weak.

We should not pass on without noting in "critical" and especially "dogmatic slumbers" the reference to Kant. The next section will pick up these references; and recall that Nietzsche names "our task" as "wakefulness itself" in the Preface. Kant, the great critical philosopher, was (he claimed) "waked from his dogmatic slumbers" by Hume the sceptic (presumably in the older, weaker sense). Perhaps Nietzsche means that he was awoken to a higher scepticism (interestingly, Kant was famously named the "all destroyer" by metaphysical opponents, and this ties in nicely with the metaphors Nietzsche has just been using). In return, through scepticism

Europe was likewise woken from its slumber in old dogmas, *including* the curious type of dogma that is the older form of scepticism itself.

§210

Just as the scholar and especially the objective spirit is only an instrument in the hands of the philosopher of the future, so this new warlike and destructive scepticism is at most only an aspect of her character, not the whole. Other aspects would have to include being a "critic" and also being a person "of experiments". As a critic "in body and soul", she will experiment or make "attempts" in a new, broader more dangerous sense, certainly further than the propriety of a democratic century. Certainly, the great attempt to breed a new race of philosophers would go much further. However, these experiments will be not merely "bolder" but experiments in a new sense. What does this mean? Experiments, conceived of in the manner of experimental natural science, will be objective, scholarly, and in the service of knowledge. Experiments in this new sense will not be so seemingly neutral, but rather oriented towards the notion of will to power; they will not be so in thrall, albeit surreptitiously, to metaphysical nonsense and prejudice; and they must sometimes even be in the service of the falsehoods that make *the appearance of* knowledge possible. One example of an experiment in writing would be the hyperbolic hypotheses that Nietzsche employs. We have been drawing attention to these since the first sentence of the Preface. The purpose of these "experiments" is not to assert or prove a truth, but to intervene dramatically within a self-complacent sphere of "truths", in order to pursue the tasks Nietzsche described at the end of the previous Part.

What, though, is meant by "critics" or criticism? In Kant's sense, it is the task of dividing according to principles; for example, in the *Critique of Pure Reason*, dividing the proper sphere of rational activity from its speculative, dialectical activity. The former serves knowledge of nature; the latter leaves reason adrift and troubled by unanswerable questions. Nietzsche emphasizes, later in the passage, the virtues of discipline, methodology and rigour – all notions that Kant too stresses. An earlier, more general usage means "to subject something to an enquiry so as to determine its self-consistency or validity; and its historical genesis or dependency-relations to other phenomena, ideas or events". To be a critic in "body and soul" would mean that such an approach is not just a method to be adopted, or an intellectual programme of study, but a mode of life, a basic drive or instinct (similarly, recall the "teacher from the ground up" at the beginning of Part 4). Criticism being a basic drive annuls the distinction between the self, its knowledge, and the object of that knowledge or study. Moreover, it does so in a much more fundamental way than in Nietzsche's account of the "objective spirit", the pure scientist, who remains a person but without access to his personhood, without "hands to grasp his needs". For this reason, it is not surprising that the experiments undertaken by such a critic will be of a different type. The name "critic" has been taken up, Nietzsche remarks at the end of the section, as virtually a synonym for philosophy. But a true critic is not a critic in *that* sense (because she is a critic in body and soul) and, further, is not yet a philosopher.

The philosopher of the future will be part critic, but in such a way as to overcome the differences between the new sense of scepticism, on the one hand, and criticism on the other. These revolve around the extent to which the critic is still a type of dogmatist – concerning method, for example, or the necessity of elevation or pleasure that is associated with truth. Accordingly, even a true or great critic (such as Kant) is not yet a "whole" philosopher. The reason for this incompleteness is provided in the next section.

§211

Part 6 began with Nietzsche disturbed by the elevation of the scientific scholar above the philosopher; part of any understanding of the proper relation between these two must involve distinguishing them. The distinction is not simply between two types or two activities, because the philosopher as part of his education may have to pass through the whole range of human scholarly (or, still more broadly, spiritual) types and activities. It is essential to be able to "gaze with many eyes" – a continuation of the theme of the philosopher as synthetic. But he does not come to a stop on any of these "steps"; none of them is, nor do their values represent, an "end" in itself. Moreover, the philosopher may continue to occupy one or the other mode of enquiry, methodology, language, set of values – as a mask, that is as a particular, calculated mode of engagement. They become parts of him, in so far as he understands, can employ at will, and even *be* that type when it is called upon. He accumulates instrumental operations; he becomes (to borrow a modern phrase) "tooled up". So too with earlier stages, such as the free spirit (as Nietzsche calls himself and his best reader): we have seen Nietzsche wear these masks, and speak of them, on many occasions.

These are all "preconditions" [*Vorbedingungen*] of the true purpose. We must not pass over this idea of precondition: these stages, masks, instruments are *absolutely necessary* for the very existence of the mode of life of a philosopher. (Nietzsche is here borrowing again, if loosely, from Hegel the idea of the historical "evolution" of philosophical consciousness, see *The Phenomenology of Spirit*, particularly the sections leading up to §80.) Thus the gratitude that should be felt to one's history and culture, but also, of course, to *oneself*, as an integral part of the whole channel of fate (as we called it earlier in speaking of the eternal recurrence in §56) by means of which the philosopher completes and redeems all existence.

The various modes of scholarship are necessary conditions of the true task [*Aufgabe*], but not *sufficient*. For the true task is to "*create values*". Scholars, critics and so forth have the task (a great and wonderful one) of assembling and understanding the whole of inherited values. This means to "overpower" [*überwältigen*] the past, in its dispersion or chaos, in its long and manifold development, in its complexity and inconsistency, and in its seeping unseen into judgements and even into our very mode of life. But this task concerns values that were once created. The scientific scholar is a "hammer" in the hand of the philosopher (notice again that blacksmith metaphor, like the end of Part 5); but he does not himself create.

Near the end of the passage, Nietzsche expands upon this by way of three slogans. For the philosopher of the future, their "knowing" is creating [*Schaffen*], their creating is a law-giving [*Gesetzgebung*], their will to truth is the will to power. Knowledge, then, does not represent the world – stand before in such a way that the ideal of this standing is to be a mirror – but rather fashions it. The formula is closely akin to a standard formula for God's creative act: the divine intelligence is productive, not reproductive (see the discussion of §§73, 101 and 164 in Part 4 above). But the philosopher of the future does not create value-neutral things in themselves (atoms, substances; as if there ever were such neutral things), but rather through the creation of new values produces new appearances, which are the products of value (cf. §34). Similarly, the ideal for the philosopher is no longer something *represented as ahead and outside* him; he exists as the project of his own ideal. The philosopher's sense of the future has changed; it is a stretching forward of this ideal of continual self-overcoming, the ideal's unending but also unswerving development as the future. If the critic overpowers the past, the philosopher overpowers the future by "internalizing" in this manner their ideal and their sense of task. Accordingly, in the next section, Nietzsche speaks of the philosopher as "*necessarily* a person of tomorrow" (and cf. §73).

This creative act is law-giving: that is, produces *codes of values* for others to follow or in whose image others will be remade, and ultimate goals that will organize the new history of man. Thus, this act revolutionizes, and thereby inaugurates a history, indeed a new relation to history, and ultimately a new type of human being. In so far as this revolution requires the rejection (on grounds we are now familiar with) of pre-existing laws or codes, and moreover a rejection in body and soul, then the *right* to be a law-giver is equivalent to the *capacity* so to do. This does not mean that "might makes right", although it is often confused with that idea by interpreters. First of all, Nietzsche's conception of power or strength is quite different from the simple idea of political dominance in "might makes right". Secondly, this is law *giving* as a *creative* act; the capacity to *impose* law is at best a secondary phenomenon. Again, we must not miss the theological overtone: God's creation cannot be judged by any law but the law of God evidenced within creation, for there are no other laws.

Finally, the "will to truth" is a phrase that takes us right back to the opening sections of the book. The will to truth, we have seen, has surprising masters. This will is to preserve a mode of life by interpreting (or indeed "falsifying") the world as a place that not only permits but positively reflects its values. For the will to truth to be the will to power could only mean for the values that the former serve to be "realigned", as we have put it, to the will to power. It is truthful in so far as Nietzsche (in his more scientific or scholarly moments) asserts that the world is will to power and nothing besides. But *this* truth is secondary, it is only another "hammer". Much more important is that here is a being whose mode of life not only does not have to turn away from or negate life, but is itself a celebration of the essence of life, whose existence completes and justifies existence. (How, though, is this "justification" to be distinguished from the justification through the beauty of mere surfaces, and especially the justification of the suffering of the slave? We'll look at this problem in §222.)

§212

The relation of the philosopher to the future and the past necessarily puts her in contradiction to her contemporary environment. She is the "bad conscience" of her time. This is not only because the ideal is different from the ideal of today, but also because (as we discussed above) the ideal as "internalized" is structured differently; it relates differently to past and future. This involves the vivisection of contemporary ideals. Notice in this Part how common this theme of cutting open or dissecting has become, particularly associated with the idea of critique. This cutting open exposes the extent to which contemporary virtues have been "outlived" [*überlebt*]. This word means literally "over lived" and thus "antiquated" – this relates to oft-used expressions such as "late culture". However, the word also involves a pun on "outlived" in the sense of "survived", which is important because it signals the link to the continuing underlying surge of life – the health of life has survived the disease. Nietzsche's point, at least in part, is that this virtue is an out of date mode of life and in itself possibly also a threat to life.

Faced with specialization, the philosopher would locate the "greatness of humans" in "wide range, multiplicity and wholeness in the multiple"; in the capacity to take on and extend responsibility [*Verantwortlichkeit*]. This continues the important theme of the philosopher as "synthetic". In

Nietzsche's understanding of the world as will to power, specialization – adopting a narrow set of values and accordingly a narrow set of responsibilities – is a metaphysically illegitimate and also dangerously diminishing isolation of the self from the totality of its world, or from the many interconnected varieties of experience. Part of the realignment to the will to power is to recognize the imperative of comprehensiveness, of full "participation" in the many modes of experience or existence, of being therefore "complementary" to all existence. To be sure, this may involve apparent self-contradiction between various posited values, or the serial adoption of various masks. But, as we saw above, in so far as none of these is in itself a goal, the "wholeness" comes from the subordination (as instruments) to the task of the philosopher.

Nothing is more "of its time" than the weakening of the will – contemporary morality, that is, provides an ideal of weakness and indecision, or of small, local and specialized decisions. The "capacity" for "long term commitments [*Entschliessungen*]" must also be accounted among the meaning of "greatness". Long term relates to the notion of "range" above; the comprehensiveness of the philosopher will include not just modes of life and valuation, but also overpowering the future such that it is not seen as something detached from will and decision (see §§19 and 21). To be sure, in an era such as Socrates', with its no longer noble nobility, what was necessary or what signified "greatness" was the ironic approach that used the plebian/democratic notion of equality to puncture moral illusions. But today, longer after the slave revolt, greatness means being "noble". And this in turn comprises a mode of life that emphasizes precisely the difference from others, thus loneliness, independence and the assertion of inequality. This is what is involved in being the "bad conscience" of one's time. There is the suggestion here that the genuine philosopher – as a being whose ideal is the *project* of continual self-overcoming, who must find the strength to shout "*da capo*" at every new moment – is always such a "bad conscience". That is, the philosopher will always be untimely. As we have noted before, the theme of "too early" or "too late" is a common one in this book, right up to its final sections and the poem with which it concludes. Moreover, Nietzsche's next book (*Genealogy*) begins with a meditation on being too late.

§213

In the previous section, we noted that the comprehensiveness of the philosopher might lead to apparent contradictions in values and associated behaviours. Here, Nietzsche addresses just this question: what the philosopher is cannot be learnt (that is, one cannot be told, nor can it be derived from principles) but must be experienced. Since the majority of people are constitutionally unable to have the relevant experiences (in particular, are unable to experience their will to power as action and affirmation), they cannot know and must speak nonsense. There has been a theme throughout the book of the necessity of experience. It is not that Nietzsche is an empiricist in any *ordinary* sense. (As if anticipating such a misunderstanding, we get a brief attack on empiricists later in the section.) Rather, one reason for this emphasis on experience is that the possibilities of philosophical or rational language and thought are intrinsically limited by the very principles that make them possible (e.g. grammar, logic, abstract concept formation, the imperative of the possibility of communication with others). Accordingly, if any thought is to "reach" such a new ideal, it can only be through the immediate "experience" of the affect (for the thought is essentially a spiritualized affect). Of course, even our most fundamental experiences are interpretations, Nietzsche argues; so there are no guarantees, no sure methods. (Please see "On Truth and Lie in an Extra-Moral Sense", a posthumously published text, which gives a fuller discussion of the relation between the limits of language and the experience of the immediate and particular.)

So what, then, can Nietzsche *do* as an author? Two things, perhaps. First, he can speak to those who indeed have these experiences – those whose type is already "higher" in the relevant sense – but who may have had difficulty understanding, articulating and acting on behalf of their experiences. Thus, he addresses "we free spirits", "we good Europeans", and so forth. To them, Nietzsche can offer an analysis, a new (though of course never entirely satisfactory) way of thinking, and a task. Secondly, a part of Nietzsche's method from the beginning has been the rhetorical tricks, the "hyperbolic interventions" as we called them, the rapid shifts of masks – in general, his idiosyncratic style. From the beginning we suggested that part of the purpose of this style was to try to shock or jolt readers into a glimpse of a different set of values or associated mode of life. The idea of "glimpse" is used significantly in §56, a passage that must be considered central for other reasons too. (And see the "sensing" at the end of the Preface and in §24.) Nietzsche will try every trick in the book to *make us see*. This, significantly, is also part of the traditional game of other modes of style, for example the poetic (it is, for example, part of how Aristotle understands the significance of style in tragic poetry). It is significant that this book ends with a poem; this is not an add-on or afterthought, but it is in poetic writing that Nietzsche sees the possibility of finding a style of writing that genuinely matches the projects of realignment and revaluation of values. (In addition, see the comments on tempo in §§26–7, and indeed the "presto" in this section, the discussion of "rhythm" in *The Gay Science*, §84, or finally the remarks on the project of style in "Attempt at Self-Criticism" in *The Birth of Tragedy*.) We will return at length to the problem of style in §296.

Nietzsche pursues an example of this requirement of experience. Thinkers and scholars understand "necessity" as a kind of "painstaking compulsion" and thought as "slow". Consequently, the very notion of a rigorous and necessary thinking with the *presto* tempo seems impossible. It must be experienced. Does Nietzsche believe he is providing this experience? Few would deny the *presto*; the rigour is what most readers struggle to "experience". So, Nietzsche's style of writing is an attempt to represent and ultimately provide a glimpse of a different way of thinking. However, the major significance of this passage lies elsewhere. Nietzsche is working through the possibility of the conjunction of the notions "necessity" and "*presto*" – or rather, in the latter, the notion of a dance free from the spirit of gravity (dance and gravity being, as we have seen, two of Nietzsche's most favoured images). The claim is that freedom (not in the moral sense, but in Nietzsche's sense, meaning strength and creativity) is in part a product of compulsion; we have seen this already in §188. Associated, then, with the order of rank of souls is an order of rank of *problems*. Thus the question "what is a philosopher?", or the problem of working towards the ideal of such a philosopher, are simply impossible objects of thought for anyone not already "predestined". Accordingly, above, when we said that Nietzsche's stylistic tricks might "jolt" us into a glimpse of a new way of thinking, even this possibility is not for everyone; it is only possible if we are "predestined".

This predestination means that, although a philosopher must also be educated, ultimately he must be "born" or rather "cultivated" at least partly in the sense of "bred". This, Nietzsche believes, is a process that takes generations. This is because the constituent parts or virtues of the philosopher – in this Part we have spoken of the various varieties of scholarship – have to be individually nurtured before the synthetic "range" of the philosophy can occur. The philosopher may, at times, be a "mechanic" or "empiricist", but is only a "guest" in that country of the spirit (§44). But to *be* an empiricist would mean to be a type of being that cannot understand what it would mean to be a "guest" there. Nietzsche then provides a partial list of such virtues, most of which are by now familiar. New, and perhaps unexpected, is the virtue of "the genial protection and defence of anything misunderstood and slandered, whether it is god or devil". The point is a subtly modified version of the traditional Christian virtue of sheltering the outcasts. There are at least two modifications: first, that the suspension of moral judgement, or even the assumption of inner goodness, that is characteristic of Christian charity is entirely sidelined: "whether god or devil". Secondly, that the outcasts in question are those "misunderstood and slandered", generally *by* the Christian perspective. This last point becomes an important theme in the next Part: the honesty (even to the point of cruelty) of the philosopher.

So, both in education (passing along and up the various steps of, for example, scholarship; see §211), and in terms of "breeding" or "cultivation", the development of the philosopher requires a careful identification, manipulation and organization of conditions. Previously, this "task" was left to chance, or to positively harmful nonsense and prejudice. This whole discussion serves to elaborate upon the task and responsibility introduced in §203, the end of Part 5.

Just as the end of Part 5 introduced the purpose of Part 6, so this last section of 6 introduces, with its discussion of individual virtues, Part 7: "Our Virtues".

8 Our Virtues: Honesty and the "Democratic Mixing" of Peoples, Classes, Genders (Part 7 §§214–39)

The title of Part 6, "We Scholars" might, in retrospect, be seen as ambiguous. Does the "we" refer to the "free spirits", and thus the study is of the free spirit in so far as she is also or in part a scholar? This is a natural reading, and one certainly borne out by the text, especially at its end. However, it could also mean "we modern Europeans", and the analysis of the scholar is an analysis of the moral predicament we find ourselves in. In that case, it would be a study of how the scholar is a symptom of just that predicament. This too is borne out by the text, in its earlier sections. The two interpretations are not incompatible: even the philosopher of the future must in some sense be "of his time" in order to function as its "bad conscience". He must be engaged in and against it, in the sense of overcoming its sedimentation within him, in the sense of using its constraints and roles (e.g. religion or scholarship) for other purposes, and in the sense of a revaluation of its core values as part of the continuing social or political task of cultivation.

Part 7 is entitled "Our Virtues", and the same ambiguity arises. The very first part begins by interpreting the "our" as meaning "free spirits". But, since it opens with a question mark it is not surprising that the Part soon turns also to the virtues (and vices) of the modern European culture of today, in general. The compatibility of these two readings appears to be more difficult than above, however, unless we are able to understand even virtues as "masks". Nietzsche will tackle just this issue quite early on. Before we start, though, what is meant by "virtues" [*Tugenden*]? Briefly, this is a term from moral philosophy. A virtue is a disposition I have, anything that I do frequently and well, in so far as it is seen to lead me to being a good person (e.g. charity). Thus, vice is the opposite: anything "bad" that I do frequently or compulsively (e.g. sloth).

§214

It is probable [*wahrscheinlich*] that we "Europeans of the day after tomorrow" have virtues. But they will, first of all, be different from those of our "grandfathers". This is because, second, these virtues must have learned to get along with our (new) inclinations [*Hängen*] and desires [*Bedürfnissen*], with our curiosity, multiplicity and sugared cruelty. ("Sugared cruelty" takes us back to the "genial protection and defence" in §213 and our analysis of that in terms of "honesty".) Notice that it is the inclinations and desires that are in control, so to speak; they define who we are and at what we aim. The virtues must reflect that. This is a reversal of the traditional way of thinking about virtues. As we indicated above, most often virtues were understood as inclinations that have been trained in order to form a part of my being a good person.

But why only "probably"? Nietzsche answers this a few lines later. The search for one's virtues – requiring a belief that one indeed has virtues, or a "good conscience" – is a moral "pigtail" that our grandfathers wore too. So, although we are "of the day after tomorrow" in many ways, we are in this one still within our today and yesterday. (Thus the ambiguity of the title of this Part, discussed above.) But, Nietzsche promises or warns us, things will soon be different. This means, presumably, that the philosophers of the future will dispense with "good conscience", and not because they have a bad conscience – rather, none at all. By "conscience" is meant an immediate or unreasoned moral feeling; thus the expression something "pricks my conscience". Conscience is thus a guide to the discovery of the morally good or bad. To have a good conscience would mean to have the unreasoned feeling that one is behaving morally – that one's habitual behaviour is characterized by virtue and not by vice. However, what Nietzsche emphasizes is that conscience can be "trained" (§98, 208). That is, it can be made into an instrument for deceiving us about morality or at least about the *value of* morality.

§215

It was surprisingly recently, only in the nineteenth century, that astronomy discovered that some "double stars" (two stars that appear very close together) are actually in orbit one around the other. This then makes possible the fantastic scenario Nietzsche envisages. A planet orbits two different stars, of two different colours, and is thus illuminated sometimes by one or the other and sometimes even by both. This is a parable of how "we modern men" embody different and even incompatible moralities, how the modern soul is "multiple". We need to make three observations: first of all, notice the quick switch from "we Europeans of the day after tomorrow" in the previous section to "we modern men" (that is, *all* we modern men). This confirms our hypothesis above concerning the ambiguity of the title of this Part. Moreover, the obviousness and briskness of the switch suggests that Nietzsche wants to make of this ambiguity a theme – that is, to pursue the question of how people of tomorrow *must also be* people of today. Secondly, this image of the double star refers us back to the problem of the mixture of races, classes and types in this "democratic" age, and the dangers and possibilities inherent there. This, indeed, becomes a preoccupation of this Part of his book.

Thirdly, the phrase "starry skies", although not exactly the same wording, should bring to mind one of the most famous passages from Kant. In the conclusion to the *Critique of Practical Reason*, Kant writes "Two things fill the mind with ever new and increasing wonder and awe . . . : the starry heavens above me and the moral law within" [V: 162]. For Kant, this meant that although each of the two spheres of reason had wonder and awe in common, they were otherwise quite distinct. The sphere of nature had no authority over the sphere of morality. The significance of Nietzsche's reference now becomes clear: the sphere of morality is just another natural phenomenon, to be understood in its "complex mechanics". There is no moral law within; instead, there is a natural development of moral types. We should compare the magnificent passage in §230, where Nietzsche argues that we must "translate humanity back into nature".

§§216–17

The section drips irony in its analysis of the way in which a key Christian virtue has turned out, psychologically. Do we love our enemies? Sure; and more, we even despise them! But, we do so without showing it, because morality as a "pose" offends our taste. We no longer regard someone highly who makes a show of their morality – so we judge without noise. But not, Nietzsche's irony tells us, out of the virtue of modesty but rather out of cunning, or perhaps shame. This, Nietzsche says, is progress, just like the abandonment of the pose of religious fervour (and with it anti-religious sentiment). But, what Nietzsche does not say he wants us to deduce: the morality (and the religion) is still there. It occupies our politics, our philosophy, our science, our psychology. That it does not come to the surface is "progress", again, only ironically.

Section 217 is a continuation. Someone who is ostentatious with his morality or even his subtlety in making moral judgements is bringing what is ordinarily hidden to the surface, exposing himself. If he makes a mistake in our sight, if his virtue of judgement turns out to be weak, or a fake, then he cannot forgive us. We must be slandered to discredit our testimony and ultimately our judgement of the mistake. We must be made out, that is, to have a vice worse than his failed virtue. This is a game of power and of revenge. Virtue, even the virtue of meekness, say, (and finally, even the principle of democratic equality) is a show of the will to power. The last sentence is a double joke. First, appropriately, it is a joke on "Blessed are the meek, for they shall inherit the earth"; second, it is a joke on the virtue of forgiveness – which in reality, Nietzsche tells us, is just forgetfulness.

§218

Psychologists in France are fascinated by the stupidities of the middle class, Nietzsche claims. Just as if – Nietzsche trails off. But the last sentence of the section suggests that he would have continued: just as if they did not share both that stupidity and class. But, this is so "tedious" [*langweilig*]. This apparent aside announces a theme of the tedious or boring; we shall return to this. Much more entertaining – a spectacle to suit the gods – is the craftiness [*Verschlagenheit*] of the mediocre against higher spirits. That is, instead of observing the norm *per se*, observe the norm in its fight against the exception, in its resentment and revenge. This spectacle is more entertaining; it is also more revealing – Nietzsche here continues the theme of the necessity of "going down" that we first saw in §26. The "craftiness" is unconscious, instinctual – and *therefore* greater as an intelligence. Nietzsche has already suggested that the purpose of "intelligence" in general is the pursuit of the aims of the organism or its type – for example, he has identified reason with utility. Instinctual intelligence is the purest expression of this purpose. It has, after all, succeeded admirably. Importantly, *it is the same middle class* (perhaps among others) that is both intelligent in the sense of crafty, *and also* stupid; indeed, crafty by means of stupidity. This intelligence is perfectly compatible with stupidity of various kinds, if by stupidity we mean *either* the fact that instinct simplifies or falsifies the world in order to control it better, *or* stupidity in the domain of thoughts, expressions, ideas, beliefs. This relation is made explicit in, for example, §§188 and 198.

§219

The analysis of revenge is a continuation from §218. Moral judgements are the favourite mode of revenge by the "spiritually limited". All moral judgements seem to be modes of gaining power (this was our interpretation of Nietzsche in §217); here, he adds that they are directed especially against the "exception", those of a less limited spirituality. The moral judgement serves to "lower" or make equal the higher. This is, by now, a fairly familiar notion. But, what Nietzsche calls high spirituality is the final product of moral qualities, a synthesis of moral states. This statement takes us back to the broad idea of the "range" and "synthetic" nature of the philosopher of the future; but more specifically, it repeats the analysis of both breeding and education at the end of §213.

Nietzsche writes that this synthetic spiritualization of virtues knows how to impose upon itself a task, that "of preserving the order of rank in the world among things themselves – and not only among humans". This last sentence is a curious statement, and its meaning and implications can be interpreted a number of ways. First, it could be a statement of a kind of reductionism in Nietzsche, which we saw previously in §36: all moralities and virtues are expressions of the order of rank, and the order of rank itself is rooted in the will to power as nature of reality, organic or inorganic. The order of rank simply is; the task is to become that being who can affirm it as such. This interpretation is reinforced by the echo of Kant's famous "things in themselves", by which is meant the things that appear to us sensibly, but considered separately from all the conditions of sensibility. We know from §34 among others that Nietzsche finds Kant's notion absurd, and yet it might here be useful to signal that even human beings are only effects or appearances. Secondly, it could be a modified version of the virtue of "genial protection" stated at the end of §213: it is not just humans who can be "slandered", but also things, and thus they too need to be "preserved". The fact that the previous sentences seem to be repeating ideas from the same parts of §213 lends weight to this reading. It is the world itself that is slandered by the religions of the other-worldly; and the new ideal will be a redemption of existence. Of course, the two interpretations are not incompatible, and it is possible that Nietzsche meant both.

§220

Differences in the order of rank are determined, among other things, by what is found to be of concern or "interest". What then appears to the common person as "disinterestedness" may in fact be an interest he does not or cannot share. "Disinterestedness" is an important concept in the history of aesthetics, but also morality, and has been given a "mystical" status by some philosophers. According to these accounts, to judge an aesthetic object properly means to judge it without reference to my personal inclinations or moral beliefs. Analogously, to judge a moral object – or, to follow Nietzsche's text more carefully, to act morally towards something – would mean to judge or act objectively, without employing any non-universal value claims. Similarly, it is precisely this disinterestedness that we would expect today, from judges in a democracy, whether they sit in court rooms, or on the panels of literary prizes.

But, Nietzsche argues, if an act appears disinterested to an observer it may be only because the observer is incapable of feeling the interest that the one acting feels. Assuming – again, we see Nietzsche's gambit or joke of breaking off. He might have continued: assuming the observer and agent are of different orders of rank. Thus, the general claim is that disinterestedness is a red herring; there are no such acts. All acts are acts by drives in their will to power, including even love and self-sacrifice. But, Nietzsche adds, this is dull and truth "yawns". Supposing truth is a woman (Preface), one cannot win a woman by boring her. But why again this theme of boredom? Three reasons suggest themselves. First of all, because general claims about all actions or all drives ignore what is genuinely important, what needs our attention and indeed demands our interest: the *differences* in values expressed by the differences in drives. Thus, secondly, what is particularly interesting in this sphere is the cunning act of revenge by the "common" or "herd" (§218). The third reason will become clear in the next section.

§221

This passage is an instructive rebuke by Nietzsche to himself. Most of the passage is, presumably, in the voice of a moral pedant. I say presumably, because in the original there are no quotation marks, only the "Thus [says] my moralistic pedant" near the end, which appears to mark the end of the pedant's rant.

What the pedant says is a version of what Nietzsche would like to say, but one that goes off the rails at some point. "Self-denial" in one born for command would not be a virtue but a wastage of virtue; unconditional morality is a temptation to the injury of the higher; morals must be compelled to bow before the order of rank – all this expresses ideas we have seen before, in slightly different versions, but in Nietzsche's own voice. But the conclusion subtly changes: "until they are finally in agreement with one another that it is *immoral* to say 'what is right for one is fair for the other'". There is a contradiction in this statement that makes it "laughable". The contradictory assertion amounts to: it is right for all *not* to assert what is right for all. This is teaching moralities how not to be moral precisely by being moral. We could express a similar absurdity as "we should all agree not to be democratic". One should not be too right, Nietzsche admits. If his analysis is pushed this far then it becomes a universalism of its own, forgetting its metaphysical basis in a notion of perspective and appearance, and forgetting its duty to preserve the order of rank.

But, the rebuke goes a touch deeper than this. For all the previous pronouncements (about self-denial and so forth) are also expressed in universal form. These are, as they stand, falsification in the same sense that our basic awareness of the world falsifies it by reducing similarities to identities. This is the third reason why reason "yawns" in the previous section; and even why we are close to doing her violence. In so far as philosophical texts make such universal claims, they will be falsifications of their objects of inquiry; but, in so far as they do not make *something like* such claims, they will be failing in their duties (for example, the duty to protect what is misunderstood or slandered). The problem might be language: there is no form of words, in any language, capable of expressing *perspectival universality*. This is not surprising, since it has never been in the interests of language users to do so.

The best Nietzsche can do is speak about "taste". This is because "taste" involves a similar apparent paradox. On the one hand, we seem happy to admit that taste is not universal, and everyone has their own taste; on the other though, we are genuinely offended if someone dislikes a meal or a piece of music that we love. In making the judgement, we hope and expect agreement from others. This *presumptive* universality is how taste functions as a social phenomenon. (This analysis of taste goes back to Kant's *Critique of Judgement*; it is yet another way in which Nietzsche is forced into articulating his philosophy using Kantian concepts.) Nietzsche is using this observation to begin to carve out for himself a language of philosophical analysis that does not immediately falsify the metaphysics of perspective. He does not, it must be said, get very far in this new language; rather, he has frequent, simple recourse to the notion of taste almost as a kind of code for "I do not, of course, mean 'universality' in a logical or metaphysical sense". More common is the strategic use of irony, as indeed he does here by creating the pedantic alter ego.

§222

Here Nietzsche returns to the important theme of pity. The religion of pity dominates (though not necessarily in the overt form of a religion: more likely a political, social or moral system), but through all the noise of the preaching of pity the psychologist should hear "self-contempt'". This self-contempt is either a symptom or a cause of a hundred-year long uglification of Europe. The human of modern ideas suffers [*leidet*] of himself; and his vanity wants it that he "suffers-with" [*mit leidet*] others, that is, has pity [*Mitleid*]. The virtue of pity is actually a vice: vanity. We have seen the problem of vanity before, in §217; and see our discussion of pity above under §202.

Why, though, is the modern person "unhappy with himself"? There are many reasons for Nietzsche, but the most important is also the reason behind the reactive revenge of the slave revolt. The "slave" only understands the condition of enslavement, of being subject to someone or something (a master, a moral rule, God, etc.); but this condition is necessarily equivalent to not being equal to, or up to the task of, the master. I am less than the master or God, I am not up to the demands that my moral rule makes on me. This condition of suffering can be relieved by the inversion of values that makes of it a kind of virtue (again, blessed are the meek), and which rewrites the virtues of the masters (excepting God) as vices. But, despite this, the suffering remains; indeed, the new beliefs intensify it and make it more cruel. I am now not *meek enough*. The inversion of values is not accompanied by a *complete* inversion of the nature of the underlying living organism. And this is not surprising, since life itself is will to power and thus could not exist within a pure form of this new moral system. Accordingly, there is a kind of deep self-deception and self-contradiction involved in the herd morality: they live, but their morality is anti-life. That is to say, their mode of life is redeemed – and indeed made possible – not through *fundamentally* changing it to align with their new values (for in this case that would mean death), but through misunderstanding it. In other words, morality functions *against* life, but the moral being yet lives; it is therefore a diseased form of life that expresses itself in such values. This point is made with particular clarity in *Genealogy*, Third Treatise, §13. One particular implication of this wider observation that is pertinent here, and involving a similar type of self-contradiction, is that their pity and vanity are predicated upon self-contempt.

§223

The mixed humans [*Mischmensch*] of Europe require many costumes – this is a metaphor for the beliefs of previous ages that are "tried on" by contemporary groups, for example, romantic, classical, nationalist. It is also a metaphor for the struggle for dominance of mixed instincts. Presumably, the costume wearers are quite unaware of the fact that they are wearing merely a costume; this is given away only by its poor fit, that these beliefs and their variety seem anachronistic, arbitrary, and thus comic. The variety of costumes reflects but also disguises the variety of modes of life that are within each one of these mixed people. This section is clearly continuing the theme of "restlessness" that began in §200. One product of this need for costumes is that costumes come to be studied – Nietzsche is referring to such disciplines such as historical studies of morals, politics, religions, tastes or character. This study has two consequences: it makes still more and finer costumes available for a truly grand carnival; and it may be where contemporary Europe finds its own field of "invention" [*Erfindung*], as parodists. Again, perhaps, as *unknowing* parodists, but very funny for all that, Nietzsche claims. The costume is different from the mask at least partly because of the lack of irony: the mask-wearer is aware, in some sense, that the reasons for wearing the mask are not equivalent to the mask. Or, in brief, she is aware that the mask is a mask. The resulting carnival of costume-wearers is laughable because it is so *serious*. Nevertheless, the parodic effect, whether intentional or not, is very important to the free spirit: where else would the typology of moral values find and observe its materials?

§224

This section continues the thought in §223. There is at least one related consequence of the democratic mixing of class and race discussed above: an unparalleled historical sense. By this Nietzsche means a talent for knowing the order of rank of values by which a people has lived, and also the relations between the "authority of values" and the "authority of effective forces". By this last part of the definition, Nietzsche would appear to be referring to the manner in which manifest values and their order of rank are founded upon underlying forces (e.g. basic drives and their will to power). We have this historical sense because the European of today is, in her very physiology, composed of many "pasts". This is an advantage, providing insight into all parts of European history. But not only insight: also our *taste* – what we find fascinating or pleasurable. As with the "costumes" discussed in the previous section, this taste is broad, indiscriminate. Nietzsche's example is Shakespeare, who was frequently enough in the eighteenth century criticized for a lack of classical form and discipline and, correspondingly, in the nineteenth century equally often praised for the remarkable mixture of styles, voices, genres.

But this is also, by the same token, not noble. That which is noble – precisely because of its lack of dependency, its self-sufficiency – finds the foreign not to its taste, even to the point of nausea. So, the taste of the historical sense finds itself biased against the mature or "ripe" art of any culture, its particular height or perfection. More generally, Nietzsche continues with rising rhetorical enthusiasm, our taste finds it difficult to understand or appreciate those moments of human life when a great force stands still just before the limitless, when it overflows with delight and takes a firm and self-determined stand on "still shuddering ground". In these moments, a culture, a mode of living, achieves its height and fixes itself there; it arrives at an enduring and unparalleled expression of its values. Our contemporary European, plebeian, taste is for the unlimited, unmeasured, and its dangers. This is because we modern Europeans are characterized by self-loathing and a structural dissatisfaction, as we saw above, and thus in flight from ourselves. Among other ideas, this analysis accords with the metaphysical idea of freedom as lack of constraint, whereas we have seen Nietzsche on several occasions argue that freedom exists only by suffering *within* rigorous constraint. It is not surprising, then, that precisely this theme is taken up in the next section.

One important allusion Nietzsche is making here is to the enthusiastic taste for the sublime in the arts, which dates roughly from the second half of the eighteenth century (although it was by no means absent prior to this). The sublime is an object or experience that overwhelms us with size or power. It is contrasted with the beautiful in ways very close to the concepts Nietzsche is employing here: the sublime is the formless, the beautiful is the formed; it is the unlimited against the bounded; wildness against control or perfection. Significantly, however, it is normally argued within aesthetics that even the sublime must be perceived, not *entered into*. That is to say, the observer remains apart and merely looking on. So, here, the noble culture stands *before* the boundless, rather than letting go the reins. It is almost as if Nietzsche is suggesting that noble beauty consists of taking a stand in the face of the sublime. This notion of beauty is found frequently in *Zarathustra*, and especially in Part 2, "On Those Who are Sublime". There Nietzsche writes: "If he grew tired of his sublimity, this sublime one, only then would his beauty commence; and only then will I taste him and find him tasteful". The sublime one is an ascetic and a hero who has not yet learned to laugh. He is consumed by the *seriousness* of self-denial, desires it as something outside himself and thus is not, Nietzsche suggests, a complete being. The ascetic hero's completion or ideal may not be transcendent to the world, but it is transcendent to *himself*; whereas laughter (and especially laughter *at oneself*) is "*this-worldly* consolation" ("Attempt at Self-Criticism", *Birth of Tragedy*). The notion of measure we saw above is found there too (as it again is in *Genealogy*, Third Treatise, §22).

We should be careful to distinguish this idea of noble beauty from the "beautification" of existence typical of superficial interpretations of existence. The former is the beauty of what is, the complete, brought to perfection; the latter the beauty of the garments that cover up shame, scars and exoteric desire. "When power becomes gracious and descends into the visible – such descent I call beauty" (*Zarathustra*, *ibid*.). This noble beauty is elaborated in remarkably similar terms in *The Gay Science* §339, but there with respect to the concept "life is a woman". Thus, the relation of the sublime and beauty is linked with Nietzsche's elaborate metaphorical use of the figure of woman. We will return to this link in our discussion of §§231–9 below.

§225

To measure value in terms of pleasure and pain – broadly speaking, the "utility" Nietzsche has spoken of often – is a naïveté. It should be "looked down" upon with pity by anyone conscious of artistic formative powers. In our treatment of §202, we discovered pity can be an appropriate reaction of a higher spirit when confronted, as here, with a situation leading directly to the diminishment of humanity. This pity, then, is different from the pity for the distressed or the sick; it is pity for the advancement of humanity that might be possible if only the damage done by this ordinary form of pity could be avoided. Suffering, Nietzsche asserts, has been the condition of all advancements.

Nietzsche elaborates upon the point through the contrast between creature [*Geschöpf*] – chaos, fragmentation, abundance and clay – and creator [*Schöpfer*] – the hammering of the divine blacksmith. In humans, he argues, we find both of these. A human being can be creator *of itself* but only under the condition that it *works on itself*. Accordingly, it will suffer *of itself*. (And not, as in §222, the suffering of oneself that is a necessary consciousness of *not being up to* the level of something.) Indeed, one only stops suffering in this sense when one has realigned one's drives and values to the will to power, assuming that is ever *fully* possible – that is to say, employing the metaphor here, when the creature (life and its instincts or drives) no longer wants to resist the hammering (the revaluation of all values or the creation of value); when it *joins the creator*. It is this being that "our" (Nietzsche now speaking as a free spirit, and not as one of his contemporary Europeans) pity is for; a pity for the philosopher of the future in her struggle to emerge.

§226

A brief section continues the theme of constraint and suffering as a condition. We "immoralists" are beings of duty too, although fools will say otherwise. This immoral world of subtle commanding and obeying concerns us [*uns angeht*]. Nietzsche's point is that to be an "immoralist" does not mean not to have values and not to be bound to ideals. It does not mean to be unconcerned, or to eschew love or hate; nor does it mean that one's concern, love or hate are arbitrary, whimsical, or purely "subjective". Rather, it is the world's character as "subtle commanding and obeying" and our analysis thereof, that drives this "concern". As we shall see in the next section, the duty of the "immoralist" is based directly upon his "honesty" about himself and about his world.

§227

Honesty [*Redlichkeit*], Nietzsche "supposes", will be a virtue of free spirits, perhaps the only one that genuinely belongs to them. Notice the contrast with the "dank and dark" seriousness of his day, which is quite unconscious of the carnival it is (§223), and which should therefore be mocked. "Honesty" means, as it has done since the beginning of the book, an analysis and exposure of morality in its dependency upon psychological and physiological conditions of a mode of life, and also its determining relation with metaphysical nonsense of all types. But more, "honesty" also means for Nietzsche a form of life that is realigned to will to power. (This is particularly clear in the brief discussion of lying in §260.) This honesty must, because of its independence of moral systems, appear like mockery and malice but, as we have just seen, will have its duties and ideals.

And should honesty grow weary, and reason "yawn" as in §220, we free spirits must reinvigorate or reinforce it with what appears to be its opposite: devilry. Do we know what this leading spirit wants to be called? Nietzsche will, in the sections that follow (and already in §225), come to associate honesty (a virtuous name) with "cruelty" [*Grausamkeit*]. There is at least one important point hidden here behind Nietzsche's irreverent writing: a reference to the synthetic integration of virtues and dispositions in the philosopher of the future. The free spirit does not in the end know herself, but must feel the necessity of this integration and assume its possibility. In so far as this synthesis is a characterization of the ideal of the free spirit, she must allow or indeed force her "virtues" and her "devilry" to function together, to reinforce one another, and be integrated in pursuit of her "duties". In any case, life is too short to allow our honesty to become a *boring* virtue. You would have to believe in eternal life to – Nietzsche breaks off but in this case the completion is not very cryptic: to require of yourself a boring virtue. (The joke is at the expense of Kant's "Postulates" in *The Critique of Practical Reason*. The argument there is that a *belief* in – as opposed to an assertion of the fact of – immortality is entailed by one's awareness of oneself as a still-imperfect moral being. The argument here is that virtue is so boring one would have to belief in immortality as a consolation.) The next section forms a clear continuation.

§228

All moral philosophy is boring, especially its advocates. But this has utility; people should think as little as possible about morality, and not begin to believe it might be *interesting*. The point is that those who do not instinctively feel compelled to interrogate morality – those who are not free spirits – should not even think about morality; perhaps then the slave revolt in morality can be reversed through inattention. Nietzsche then spins an elaborate joke: the true utility of utilitarians is, by being as dull as possible, to prevent any such interest. There follows a speculative analysis of English utilitarianism. It is characterized by cant (empty discourse) disguised as science, by the bad conscience of the Puritan trying to be scientific, and by nationalism for particularly English virtues and values. This nationalism disguises itself as universalism, and claims that "the general welfare" is or should be the ideal for all. But this is no ideal, it is an emetic. More than a joke, Nietzsche is referring back to the kind of nausea discussed in the context of the overall diminishment of humanity (see the end of §203). We should also think of §56 and the new ideal who does not just learn to "get along" with what is – i.e. to not be nauseated by the thought of the eternal return of all things – but positively to affirm it. Thus, here, the emetic is to be *encouraged*.

§229

"[A]lmost everything we call 'higher culture' is based upon the spiritualization and deepening of *cruelty* [*Grausamkeit*]." The "wild, cruel animal" is a complex figure. It is a reference in part to the masters who were undone by the slave revolt; but also to certain instincts or drives that one might want to repress, reinterpret, or encourage, in particular the instinct for self-mastery; and finally to the conditions of nature within which the weak or sick tend to perish. So, this "animal" was not killed off, after all, but came to have a modified form. We should be reminded of the notion of spiritual self-dominance in §46, and similarly §61. The modified form is the imposition upon oneself of harsh moral demands (ancient asceticism and more recent Puritanism were Nietzsche's earlier examples, and reappear here). Cruelty, then, does not originate only or even principally in the suffering of another, but rather in the suffering of oneself. The seeker after knowledge is cruel against own inclinations, his fundamental will to superficiality (see next section). He is an "artist of cruelty", and thereby the agent of "higher culture". Thus, the honesty in §227 is compelled by the thirst for cruelty; it is itself a "transfigured" cruelty.

§230

Nietzsche in the previous section used the expression "the fundamental will [*Grundwillen*] of the spirit". This is an expression he had not used before, although the notion it conveys is familiar. The analysis has to do with the power of the spirit to appropriate what is foreign to it [*Fremdes sich anzueignen*]. It is always easier to interpret what is given as the same as what is already known – to reduce the foreign to the familiar. The fundamental will of the spirit, then, is a will to be "master" within one's domain, for one's feeling of power to increase. And this requires that everything be simplified to the familiar and nothing be foreign. The analysis covers organic growth – the absorption by life of what is around it into its body – as well as the spiritualized growth that is knowledge. This appropriation takes several forms. First, it might take the form of an assimilation of the foreign into itself. Secondly, it might be a "decision in favour of ignorance" (the analogy of the stomach here should remind us of the earlier metaphors of emetic and nausea). Thirdly, finally, it might take the form of the deception of masks, with which the spirit engages with its world apparently on the world's terms (but expressing its multiplicity, the range of its familiarity, and thus feeling its power) and simultaneously with which it hides and protects itself.

This basic will to deception or superficiality is, again, a requirement of life itself. Notice also the connection of this to the analysis in the previous sections of the difference between noble and plebeian "tastes". The noble taste rejects the foreign; but it does so not as a reaction or fear of that which is foreign, but out of a sense of self-sufficiency. The plebeian is drawn to the foreign, wears many costumes, has its historical sense, and so forth. Indeed, the plebeian may even be in danger of losing itself to the foreign, of not having a self at all. But this being drawn to the foreign occurs through the democratic instinct: that is, through a wider belief that everything is or should be equal or equivalent (under moral law, under God). What is *truly* foreign to it (e.g. the cruel animal of the previous section) is feared and its destruction sought. So, it too is a form of assimilation.

Only the genuine seeker after knowledge resists this fundamental will. Honesty, refusing to falsify *naively*, is thus equivalent to cruelty. For the seeker for knowledge must oppose, constrain, or even modify its own fundamental will. This, too, is the reason that the philosophical path Nietzsche proposes is dangerous: for it must ultimately oppose (if only ever in part) precisely the conditions that make life possible in the first place. As we have noted before, the cruel task of the philosopher then is to bring about – to become – a mode of life the fundamental will of which is at least not always or *essentially* at odds with its honest interpretation of the nature of its world. A part of this task must be to "translate the human back into nature". This means to understand the "soul" – that which, it was previously assumed, makes human beings "higher" or "more" than animal – as no more than a spiritualized mode of the basic operations of all life. An example of this would be analysing the fundamental will of this soul in terms of basic organic processes.

But, then, why have knowledge as a task? That is, if knowledge opposes life and is dangerous in the above sense, why pursue it? More clearly still: does this task involve a deep self-contradiction? The being who is capable of translating the human back into nature could only do so by becoming, in a sense, unnatural: "strange and mad" as Nietzsche puts it at the end of §230. Of course, Nietzsche has never said that the fundamental will of the spirit is the *only* will. After all, §229 just finished illustrating the enjoyment of cruelty to oneself well outside the domain of knowledge. Moreover, the opposition of knowledge to life is relative to the form of life in question. The task of the philosopher could never be just to know differently, but to be differently – *through* knowledge, perhaps, to alter the basic structure of her drives or values. Another answer to these questions is stated in the first sentence of the next section: "learning changes us". The subtle shift from "knowledge" [*Erkentniss*] to "learning" [*Lernen*] is important. First of all, this is because the latter is a process rather than a state. But, more importantly, because learning is about how one responds to the "foreign", it concerns knowledge that is not already known and which is different from the expected, or which comes from outside one's own "domain". The very concept of "learning" thus repeats the contrast between the "fundamental will" and the "will to know".

§§231–9, and discussion of Nietzsche on women

So, yes, learning changes us, and like nourishment does not merely sustain. But this is followed immediately by an apparently opposite claim. There is also, "deep down", something unteachable, something "stupid", a "spiritual *fatum*" (meaning "fate" but here also a pun on "*factum*", fact), a decision that has already been made and a question that has already been asked. Thus, some things cannot be learned *in a new way*, but only learned *about oneself*. Although "deep", it does not necessarily follow that these stupidities are all-important; that is, it does not follow that this stupidity makes incidental or superficial the claim that "learning changes us". It *might* be that "learning changes us" is indeed a response to the problem of the previous section – who is the human being who can have knowledge without killing herself with the cruelty of it? – and that the deep stupidities are relatively few and unimportant.

For Nietzsche, at least, one of these unteachable stupidities concerns the nature of women. This forms the topic of the last sections of this Part. These are some of the most notorious in Nietzsche's work, expressing on the surface at least a retrograde understanding of women. Now, we can read all this in several ways, and clearly all are meant. First, and most obviously, what Nietzsche has to say about women is a product of some deep stupidity in *him*, a misogynistic prejudice (in the literal sense of pre-judgements, judgements already made in advance) of his own. Section 234 then becomes an apology of sorts for the statements made thereafter. In a sense, they are not even about women; they are about Nietzsche himself. Secondly, what follows expresses what is unteachable, about women, in *men* – in other words, a prejudice shared by all male humans by virtue of their gender. (See, for example, "we men . . ." towards the end of §232.) Again, this serves as an apology, and an assertion that what follows concerns the self-understanding of men. Thirdly, the same assertion, but about women: by virtue of their gender, certain traits are inescapable, and in particular certain modern ideas about women are falsifications.

Even these three interpretations, however, do not cover the complexities of Nietzsche's position. There are also historical factors being analysed (e.g.

the changes in the conception of women), and the broadly racial (the "oriental" of §238, but also "nobility" in §236). There are also seven rhyming "little epigrams", and a couple of analogies or parables, to add stylistic and rhetorical complexity (and even make tempting the idea that this whole passage is an elaborate joke). Although the passage is clearly *at least in part* a firm restatement of fairly traditionalist prejudices about women, as we shall see it is also an exploration of the relation between the drives or instincts that preserve life and those that advance it. This is in keeping with how the figure of woman (and accordingly, at least in part, the figure of man) is used in other writings. *Zarathustra*, in particular, returns again and again to the figure of woman: wisdom is a woman, eternity is a woman, life is a woman, among others. These are games, roles and, simplest of all, metaphors for sex, desire, ideals. Often, it is relatively easy to distinguish Nietzsche's use of woman as *trope* from straightforward biological or psychological commentary; but sometimes it is not (witness §127 and §144, for example, in addition to several of the sections under comment here). More interestingly, and more commonly, to *distinguish* in this way would be to miss something.

The basic *surface* argument is that "modern ideas" about the equality of women are simply expressions of the democratic notion of equality. They stem from the same ignoble values and misunderstandings of the nature of life. Just as within the human species there are different modes of life and different sets of values (e.g. plebeian, aristocratic, scholarly, etc.), so there are different genders and these two are different modes of life. Importantly, Nietzsche is not *necessarily* asserting that women and men are not equal in the sense that one gender is the natural and general master of the other. Although in fact he does make this claim (in §238), it does not follow from what we called the "basic argument". Instead, what does follow is that the sexes are different in inescapable ways; they are physiologically different, and this physiology manifests itself in what we have been calling the mode of life: that is, dominant drives and the manner in which they are spiritualized as values. It also follows, to return to the titular theme of this Part, that each sex will have its own virtues and vices. In the sections that follow, Nietzsche argues that the vices of modern women stem from their mistaken and indeed misguided attempt to leave their natural virtues behind in the name of progress and equality. This surface argument is, again, meant both straightforwardly as a thesis about what is "unteachable" either about women or about how men conceive of women, and is the "vehicle" for a sustained and complex metaphor.

The selections commence with the problem of knowledge, thus carrying on with the theme of §§230–1. With the intention of becoming independent (of men, presumably, but this might also be a reference to the independence of the noble or free-spirited), a woman wishes to know and express "woman as such" in a scientific sense. What is this "knowledge"? It might be a trying on of "finery", a new costume. If not, it must be an attempt to inspire fear and gain dominance. But it is not in the interest of "truth", Nietzsche asserts – for "what matters truth to a woman?". The "great art" of women is "lying", and thereby the arts of appearances, beauty, superficiality. This has to be understood correctly: let us not forget the "wisdom" of superficiality in so far as it justifies suffering and makes life possible. The basic talent of women lies in the falsification, thus beautification and finally justification of existence. (And it is here that men can seek relief from enlightenment and self-cruelty.) Women, Nietzsche is saying, are natural artists, in body and in spirit. Thus, the claim is not that women are incapable of knowledge, but rather that this sex is incapable of a will to truth, since that will (as we just saw) involves the cruelty to the wise will to "falsification". To ignore her nature and pursue knowledge is, Nietzsche says, "comic" (§233).

This analysis raises another interpretive possibility. The "art" that Nietzsche is assigning to women is of course the "fundamental will" of *all* spirits (§230). Moreover, the "cruelty" that he assigns to men is ascribed also (albeit with irony) to a "Wagnerienne" in §229. So, the simplicity and purity of Nietzsche's assertions here are undermined by earlier passages. Perhaps what is at stake is only in part, and perhaps as a disguise, a description of the virtues and vices of men and women as gendered individuals. (This would be the "surface" argument, as we called it above.) Perhaps this is a passage of experimental philosophical writing that attempts to use our prejudices about men and women as the "vehicle" of a "deep" metaphor, the purpose of which is to describe the nature of and relationship between the fundamental will and the will to knowledge – between "masculine" and "feminine" instincts, say – and also between previous moral systems and the new ideal Nietzsche is putting forward. "Let us think this over for ourselves", Nietzsche tells us with a wink, at the end of §238. So, we appear to have a sustained "surface" argument – calling it "surface" does not necessarily entail that Nietzsche did not intend his "truths" about women (or again, about the beliefs men have about women) to be taken seriously – and this "surface" serves to explicate and explore a wider issue about the nature of the will and of instinct.

Let us start by thinking over the "what matters truth to a woman?" The book began with the famous speculation that "truth is a woman". At the time, this seemed a way of insulting dogmatic thinkers for their lack of subtlety and skill in seduction. And so it is. But if the figure of woman, even in the Preface, is taken (in the "deep" argument) to stand for the feminine instinct – that is, for the will to preserve life by falsifying it and its world – then we get a new result. "Truth is a woman" becomes an elegantly precise statement of one of the basic themes of Nietzsche's book: that what we take or have taken for truth is prejudice, metaphysical nonsense, superficiality (though in itself also wise, beautiful, necessary). It would also follow that exposing this would require a quite other approach to philosophical enquiry, and indeed a quite other type of philosopher.

Evidence for this experiment can be found especially in the last two sections of the part. Section 238 refers to "he" who is a shallow thinker, too "short" for the fundamental questions of life, incapable of harshness and strictness. In short, *too feminine* properly to understand the "abysmal antagonism" between the sexes, but also between the will to the preservation and the will to the advancement of life. Someone who can understand this will take on an "oriental manner", just as the Greeks did, and treat women as a possession, predetermined for and fulfilled by servitude. The relation between this extreme but very particular claim, on the one hand, and the whole problem of the seeker after knowledge and the ideal of the philosopher of the future, on the other, seems tenuous. If it is read, however, as referring to the "service" rendered life by the feminine instincts (whether these are in a man or a woman) and their relation to the problem of the advancement of life – then the link becomes clear.

Similarly, a further aspect of this experiment can be seen in §234. Although this section has an awkward feel about it, it is actually quite a sophisticated attempt to bring an enormous number of themes together. As cook, woman is responsible for sustenance; but, as Nietzsche already claimed in §231, nutrition can also change us. If women were thoughtful, capable of learning, they should know this already. Instead, bad cooking has delayed the development of the human type. The feminine art "sustains" life, making it possible, but does not amount to knowledge or learning, which could change life. So, the delays and damage are also a reference to the interference by herd morality in the human type, its sustaining in existence the sick, its destruction of higher types. Finally, of course, we have seen repeatedly in this Part the notions of nausea, emetics, or digestion. Women's cooking (in both literal and metaphorical senses) is nauseating to a higher, nobler spirit.

To complete the picture, we need to jump forward to §248 where Nietzsche describes a kind of masculine and feminine version of genius, two different but entirely complementary modes of creativity. In anticipation, we should notice two things about that passage. First of all, it arises quite explicitly in the context of nationalism and Nietzsche's characterization of the key features of various European peoples. Moreover, it arises in the context of a discussion of a pan-European political sense, which could be achieved not by the exclusion of peoples but through the welcoming of each particular genius. So, notions of masculine and feminine here at the end of Part 7 (in the "deep" argument) merge seamlessly into a political and historical analysis. Secondly, the gendered ideas of genius and creativity in

§248 also need to be understood within the additional context of Nietzsche's views on the aesthetic modes of the sublime and beauty. In §224, we distinguished between beauty in the sense of the wise though superficial falsification of existence, on the one hand, and beauty in a different sense of coming to stand as perfected form in the face of the boundless. The former is associated with the feminine will. However, the masculine will would seem associated with a sublime urge to create that is hardly different from destruction. (See, for example, "On those who are sublime" in *Thus Spoke Zarathustra*.) Just as Nietzsche elsewhere emphasizes complementarity, so in the *Zarathustra* passage and in §224, noble beauty is *neither masculine or feminine*, nor simply a unification or merger of them, but a moment of perfectly poised antagonism, "on still trembling ground" – what Nietzsche also calls "love". This moment, and the noble beauty that is thereby made possible, is described in *The Gay Science* §339. There, not surprisingly, the fact that such moments are rare is ascribed to the fact that "life is a woman" – hiding her secrets, the feminine will.

The last section of Part 7 resumes the discussion of §232, namely women in Nietzsche's contemporary Europe. The reasoning is slightly unexpected: the new respect for the "weaker sex" has not made it stronger, but has weakened it. The influence of women, Nietzsche asserts, has steadily lessened since the French Revolution. Instead of "progress", by turning to culture and education instead of the strength of will and their natural virtues, women are "going backwards". A woman who forgets her fear of men also abandons her "most womanly instincts"; she forgets her genuine weapons and strengths in favour of illusory ones. That is, she loses sight herself of the authentic ground of respect for women, her "predatory animal and cunning suppleness", impossible to train, and her "scope". In §236 (and again at the end of §237), Dante and Goethe see the "eternal feminine" as the route to higher spirituality. Nietzsche sees this (i.e. both the unalterable nature of women and the feminine instinct) quite differently: as the *most natural*. The feminine instinct, in particular, corresponds to the fundamental will of the spirit, life itself. As we saw in our discussion of §234, this is by no means founded upon fear – life is made possible, it is sustained; and life, like a woman, can be noble – although in its diminished state it may arrive at a reactive fear.

This diminished state is described by Nietzsche, at the very end of the Part as the unenchanting [*Entzauberung*], the becoming-boring [*Verlangweiligung*], of women. This relates to what elsewhere is called the "taming" of the human. The result of this taming is, as we have seen in this Part, mediocrity moralizing about mediocrity, studying mediocrity, and "striving" for an ideal of mediocrity – all, Nietzsche insists, very boring. This theme of boredom, to be sure, reflects Nietzsche's tastes; but it is also an elaborate and sustained metaphor for the flattening down of the human, the diminishment of its possibilities (cf. §241). Metaphysically, will is only possible in relation to will. Thus, where the human has been flattened down and made equal, the will becomes listless, everyone is just *so tired*, nihilism looms. (This analysis is continued and extended in *Genealogy*, starting in Third Treatise, §17.) So, the becoming boring of woman stands for the becoming boring of the human in so far as the *struggle* of will against will (sometimes against itself) and above all between what we have called the feminine and masculine wills – and thus also the possibility of a truly noble beauty or creation – becomes impossible.

This change in the status of women is intelligible if man has lost that which inspires fear – "when the *man* in men is no longer wanted or cultivated [*grossgezüchtet*]" – indeed, such men as are described later in the section as "scholarly asses of the male sex". As we have seen Nietzsche state over and over, his contemporary Europe is the result of a centuries-long diminishment of the human, a virtual extinction of the noble or higher form of life and thus of those instincts or drives we are here calling "masculine". This was discussed much more explicitly in §201, including the use there of the concept "progress". It is now clear that this diminishment is also a defeminization [*Entweiblichung*]. There is a correspondence between this idea and our modern taste for the sublime in §224. The modern European, because *both* demasculinized and defeminized, has only one mode of creativity: unending carnival or, equivalently, fleeing from its self-loathing into the unmeasured. Just as the diminishment of the human in Europe was explicated in part through the historical, democratic mixing of races and classes, so here the failure to understand the difference between men and women is ascribed to a form of life that is a democratic mixture of genders, and is neither male nor female. In particular, it is ascribed to scholarly asses (who are "nothing to women") and to the "woman as such", one of whose exemplars is Madame de Staël, who was earlier called a "masculinized woman". Thus, what is here discussed as the progress of women stands for (is a symptom of but also a metaphor for) the dangers of the ultimate triumph of herd morality. What happens to a morality based upon fear when there is nothing more to be feared? *Nothing more for an essentially reactive will to react to*? Such a triumph would mean the destruction of that morality and with it, perhaps, the destruction of the human.

The end of the section recalls the myth of Europa, a mortal princess who was seduced and carried away to Crete by Zeus, in the form of a bull. The name is the presumed source of the name of the Continent. Nietzsche is addressing himself, by way of this myth, to Europe. This is the clearest hint yet that Nietzsche is speaking about European humanity in general by way of the "surface" argument about the nature of women. Europe is carried away, this time, not by a god, but by a "modern idea".

9 Peoples and Fatherlands: Towards the Political Task of Philosophy in Europe (Part 8 §§240–56)

Nietzsche wants us, his readers, to hear the title in a particular way. *"Völker und Vaterländer"* would have had two immediate connotations. Much more than "people" in English, *"Volk"* is a German nationalist's word, and thus might be taken to refer to the right or destiny of German unification. This is still more evident in *"Vaterland"*. Clearly, then, Nietzsche is evoking a particular type of nationalism that, with good reason, he saw all around him. But, of course, in the title of Part 8, these words are *plural*. The whole point, the whole ideal, of German (or any other nationalism) is that "people" should be *one*, and the nation *united*. Simply by using the plural, Nietzsche is evoking nationalism but then also pulling the rug from under it, at least by suggesting nationalism is itself not something national, but *shared* with other peoples. There are two implications. First, that this Part will be dealing with the variety of and differences between different peoples and nations. Secondly, though not yet obvious, Nietzsche is or wants to be a *European*. Every nationalism is a kind of insanity, for Nietzsche. First of all, it is the apparent insanity of a rejection of those "modern ideas" that threaten to carry away Europa (see end of previous Part) – thus, the notion of the "good European" that we shall encounter at the beginning of §241, who allows himself a brief lapse into nationalism. However, although nationalism appears to be a genuine step away from "modern ideas", this is the first of several misunderstandings.

This Part is yet another experiment on Nietzsche's part. It attempts to yoke together two notions that appear, at first and for a long time, quite disparate: art, especially music, on the one hand; and politics, on the other. Nietzsche is employing an analysis of music (and associated ideas, such as the "music" of speech or writing) both on its own terms, but above all to elucidate his thoughts on the political present and future of Europe. There are two straightforward reasons for this yoking together. First, music certainly may have political themes or consequences, and very often did in the nineteenth century. Wagner's music in particular was often associated with forms of nationalism. This reason Nietzsche deliberately ignores as superficial. Secondly, music is the clue to the nature of nations and races, and thus of how they have contributed to the future of Europe and can continue to do so. This second reason is where Nietzsche focuses his attention.

Part 8 is particularly dense in references to (mostly) nineteenth-century composers, novelists, political leaders and intellectuals. We shall, unfortunately, not be able to explore these references in any detail; instead, we shall be focusing on broader themes.

§240

This Part begins and ends with Richard Wagner, Germany's most famous opera composer of the mid- and late-nineteenth century. Section 240 describes at length the overture to *Die Meistersinger von Nürnberg*. It is important for us to notice several ideas. First, Nietzsche describes this music as a broad and formless "mixture" of "flavours and forces, seasons and regions". The notion of being wide-ranging is, as we have seen, an important concept within Nietzsche's analysis of his "new ideal". But, at the same time, a mixture of races, classes and types is a characteristic of the democratic weakening and loss of identity in Europe. Other than in §200, we have been left to think of these two ideas as in conflict. Nietzsche's political vision will gradually bring these ideas together. Secondly, he also observes a multifaceted current of "contentment" [*Behagen*]. Although it is not clear here, it is worth asking if this "contentment" is to be related back in any way to the idea of self-sufficiency of the noble.

Thirdly, the music has nothing of the south, of sun and dance. This introduces a theme that assumes a particular importance in this Part, of certain physiological and thus also spiritual differences between southern and northern European peoples and countries. Fourthly, we must not miss the complex temporality of Nietzsche's description. The section begins with "I heard, once again for the first time . . ." (*Meistersinger* was composed roughly two decades before Nietzsche is writing, but regularly performed). The section ends with the idea that the Germans have a yesterday and a tomorrow, but no today. The relation between these two is clear: not to have a "today" is to be without a stable temporal location within which that which is experienced in the present could be repeated in the present. Thus, hearing the overture will always be "for the first time". This "not having a today" might mean not having a clear and stable identity, being in continual transition – and, indeed, in §244 this will be made explicit. Instead, the Germans have a vast and imposing past (the two centuries of music, for example, near the beginning of the section), and a specific (here unnamed) future. They are a people on the way. Without even mentioning it, the first section of this Part already punctures one pretension of German nationalism: that there *is* a *Volk*, clear, well-defined and pure.

§241

Good Europeans have brief moments of nationalism, but it does not take them long to get over it and return to "reason". Nietzsche then presents a kind of parable. He stages a dialogue between two old "patriots" who are both partly deaf, assume everyone else must be partly deaf too, and therefore shout. The first speaker attacks contemporary German politics and the figure of Bismark for having strength but lacking the thought that makes great. Bismark forced a certain politics on a people (the Germans) who distrusted its emptiness, and who were forced to put aside their previous virtues of being bystanders and cosmopolitans. This, he asks, is great? The second replies: of course, or he wouldn't have been able to do it. It may be insane; maybe all great things are insane. And the first retorts: insane and strong merely, not great.

Nietzsche imagines himself listening, unperturbed. How soon it will be that one stronger will become master over the strong, he thinks; and likewise that for every spiritual "flattening" of a people, another becomes deep. (This metaphor of "flattening" is used, with reference to German culture and politics, again in *Twilight of the Idols*, "What the Germans Lack", §3.) Although the precise meaning of these two points is not yet clear, we can speculate that the "stronger one" is the philosopher of the future, that being whose thought is integral to her "strength"; and that the "other people" made deep might be the new ruling "caste" – not specifically German but rather European – that Nietzsche mentioned in §208 and will shortly discuss again.

§242

Behind the democratization of Europe is an immense physiological process, the mixing of classes and peoples. This is not a new idea; it was already important in Parts 6 and 7. In particular, this process comprises a becoming similar through a detachment from the conditions of their original growth; and the arrival of a "supra-national" and nomadic type, able to adapt anywhere. The "tempo" of this physiological change might be slowed by nationalism, but it might also thereby gain in "vehemence and profundity". Notice that this has neatly taken over the idea at the end of the previous

section: nationalism involves a flattening, and this might slow the physiological change but also deepen it.

The process of democratization (perhaps only in so far as it is deepened
by episodes of nationalism?) will lead to results quite other than the ideals
of democrats. It will lead to "exceptional human beings", to "tyrants", in all
senses of the word. To be sure, Nietzsche adds, the creation of herd animals
does not lead to strength – rather the opposite, to weakness of will – but
within this environment one who is strong will have to develop unprecedented strength. This is due to lack of prejudice in education (prejudice,
presumably, for or against peoples, classes, types – but it might also mean
lack of prejudice in the sense of selecting the best and brightest pupils), and
also to a "multiplicity in practice, art and masks" (because of the mixing
and migration of peoples; we should compare this with the notion of
"wholeness in the multiple" in §212). In other words, because of the lack of
discipline or *constraint* – which Nietzsche has emphasized over and over is
the condition of advancement and achievement – if someone is to develop
strength of will under these conditions, she would indeed have to be
extraordinary simply in order to exist, in order to have arrived at herself,
so to speak.

§243

The sun and solar system have a relative galactic motion towards a point
located in the constellation Hercules. This had been known since the late
eighteenth century. Nietzsche's point is a simple metaphor: just as the sun
is heading towards a paradigm of strength, so (the good European hopes)
are human beings.

§§244–7

The next four sections are analyses of the German type. As Nietzsche's
treatments of women in the previous Part appear quite crude, so too do
his discussions of national types (the English and French are next). How
could they be otherwise? Nietzsche, in a sense, is producing a rhetorical
simplification for at least two purposes. First of all, because he wishes to
employ for his own reasons the discourse of nationalism, in the same way
we have already seen him employ the discourses of physics, history, psychology, and so forth. That is, as a mask that is not merely surface, and with
an irony to which no proper sphere of discourse belongs. Secondly, this
simplification serves as a counter-balance to a naive understanding of the
Christian/democratic movements in Europe which speak of equality as if
it were a *given* rather than an *achievement*.

Nietzsche begins this treatment in §244 with the notion of "profundity", picking up on the problem of depth we have seen just above. An earlier understanding of the German personality considered it "profound"; things seem to have changed. But this profundity should be looked at again anyway. The German people, Nietzsche claims, are actually an already very mixed set of races, surprising and eluding definition, with a mixed taste that amounts to none at all. They *are not*, they only "become" (thus have no "today", as in the opening section). For these reasons, their nature involves contradictions, such as "good-natured and spiteful" or, more significantly, the "ponderousness" of the scholar combined with an "inner and agile tightrope dance" [*innewendigen Seiltänzerei*]. The final trait in this section is deception. German openness and frankness turns out to be a disguise; profundity is too, and a useful one.

Section 245 turns to German music, and although the following two sections talk about prose, the constant theme is the *musicality* of prose. In both cases, the issue is to explore the way in which tastes and styles of music or prose serve as symptoms of the changing nature of the people. Section 245 traces the development of music from Mozart (whose work Nietzsche always sees as a swan-song) through Beethoven (a great but transitional figure between the mellow past and the coming future). In the analysis of Beethoven we can hear the yesterday and tomorrow but no today of the first section of this Part. It is not just that stylistically Beethoven formed a transition between "classical" and "romantic" styles; rather, that he and his age were "transitional" through and through. But transitional to *what*? The music after Beethoven was not noble enough to have a validity outside crowded theatres; that is, it spoke to the emerging democratic masses. The last composer Nietzsche discusses is Schumann, in whom German music ceased to be the voice of Europe and descended to mere nationalism. The only Wagner opera mentioned in this section is an early work; and Nietzsche in §240 clearly saw *Meistersinger* (1867) still as a transitional piece, having a tomorrow but no today. So, is this nationalism that Nietzsche sees in Schumann the next *genuine* phase of German music, and thus also of German culture – or is it *still* a kind of transition?

Sections 246 and 247 make a natural pairing, having in common Nietzsche's lament for the state of prose writing and reading in Germany. Writers produce books that do not dance. Readers simply do not have the ear, and do not even feel their duty to hear, subtleties of style and rhythm, nor to hear their significance to meaning. We should look back to §§27 and 28 and the idea of a tempo of thought and of translation there; and recall also the partly deaf patriots in §241 above. Even, and precisely, the best German musicians write badly (this is likely a reference to Wagner). Just as *Meistersinger* is cumbersome and does not dance (§240), so German prose has no ear for rhythm and tempo. This has led to two very different masters of prose being confused. Nietzsche doesn't name these two, although in the next section he speaks of Luther and his Bible as the best German book "up to now"; suggesting that Nietzsche himself, in the present, may be the second master. (A similar comparison of Luther and Nietzsche's own *Zarathustra* is made in a letter to Rohde in February 1884 (*Selected Letters*: 221); though there Goethe is suggested as a third possibility.) The mistake is not only to fail to see the differences in style, but also to fail to see the significance of these for meaning and thus treat *Zarathustra* as another bible. That would be to treat *Zarathustra*, and by extension Nietzsche's other works, as testaments to the divine, or tables of values and laws. Implicitly, he is asking his reader: "are you a good enough reader to appreciate – to *hear* – my writing and what it signifies?"

Nietzsche next looks to the ancient world. Here, writing and reading *to oneself* was done audibly; thus, there was no great change required for speaking *publicly*. That is, the physiological act of speaking out loud relates directly, for ancient writers, to writing and "inward" thought. Whereas, the argument appears to be, these two dimensions are disconnected in recent German writing and reading; thus the problem of deafness in §246. Accordingly, this ancient "public" is meant to contrast with the theatre crowds of §245. The word "period" sets in motion a complex set of metaphors. A "period" refers, first of all, to a complex, doubled-up rhythmic structure in classical prosody. It was a "physiological unit", related to breath control. We moderns, Nietzsche scoffs, are "short of breath in every sense". This "in every sense" alerts us to the fact that Nietzsche is not speaking just about lung capacity. The joke is that "spirit" means "breath", so to be short of breath is to be diminished in spirit. We should be reminded, first of all, of the dogmatists who were breathing their last, in the opening sentences of the Preface. Something (the philosophers of the future) is coming, rediscovering and taking the good air. Secondly, the term "period" means more than a specific poetic unit – it also means a period or stretch of time, an era. Those ancient lungs were part of a genuine historical and cultural period – also, as we know, for Nietzsche an era will be characterized by a certain physiology. Notice also that the period is a *double* rhythmic form, returning twice in the same breath. It is thus unlike Nietzsche's hearing of *Meistersinger* which was heard "again, for the first time", because there is no "today" within which its repetition could be located. Accordingly, we have no right to the "great period" – no right, that is, to *either* a style for which we are physiologically and spiritually ill-equipped, or to claim that ours is a "great" historical period – it is not a "period" at all. Nietzsche, however, is attempting to create a style of writing that is "modern" *not* in the sense of being for his contemporaries with their small lungs – rather, modern in the sense that it looks to be a part of the conditions of the philosopher of the future. It would be a mistake to see

Nietzsche as simply regressing to the styles of Roman public speaking; that is one rhetorical mask that he employs, among others (he also employs the styles of, for example, Luther's translation of the Bible, or of Homer). Rather, the reference to Rome here simply provides an example of what it would mean for a style to fit, and indeed to *encourage*, a certain mode of life.

All this should be no surprise. Nietzsche has reminded us over and over that the basic characteristics of a people (race, class, type or whatever) are physiological, including their use of language. So, this physiology should show itself in language use in general – its ability to cope with or understand the use of certain styles, tempos, rhythms. However, we would do Nietzsche a disservice if we thought of language use simply as a symptom – and thus a kind of separable representation of something, rather than being a part of the "disease" (or the health). This is made clear by the end of §247. There is only one type of public and more or less artistic rhetoric in Germany, who have a "conscience" in their ears, though often a bad one: preachers. ("Conscience" here refers back to "duty" above.) Accordingly, Luther's translation of the Bible is the masterpiece of German writing, that "grows into German hearts". In short, the use of language (or music) is not just an effect of physiological health or deterioration; it can also be its cause. Nietzsche's method of philosophical writing, then, can plausibly have as its aim not to convince us of some abstract truth, but of growing into our hearts, changing us bodily and from within. And, thus, this writing helps return to Germany – but more importantly to Europe – the "great period".

§248

There are two types of genius, and Nietzsche all but calls them "masculine" and "feminine": the genius of begetting, and of bearing. (Compare also §§206, 207). The latter is about bringing a certain mode of expression, style, form or whole culture to its proper "fulfilment" or perfection. The former is the cause of new orders of life and is thus domineering and "lusting after foreign races". This is yet another in a series of masculine/feminine distinctions, which began in the first sentence of the Preface, and was greatly elaborated at the end of Part 7. There, we discovered Nietzsche distinguishing between a feminine will (the elemental will to life and thus also the will to falsification as the condition of life) and a masculine will (a will to break open this falsification, discover grounds, conquer itself). There is an obvious parallel between the two wills and these two types of genius. This parallel becomes still clearer when we add in Nietzsche's analysis of the distinction between the beautiful and the sublime that we analysed under §224. There we referenced *Zarathustra*, Part 2, "On Those Who Are

Sublime"; it would now appear that the necessity of the "hero" becoming beautiful in order to complete himself means: not to *neutralize* the struggle of masculine and feminine will but to *encompass it in its struggle*. We have already analysed the implications of all these ideas under §§231–9.

Certain peoples of Europe have a tendency towards one or the other of these types of genius: the Greeks (the ancient Greeks, at any rate) and the French towards the feminine genius; the Jews, Romans and Germans towards the masculine. Thus Nietzsche explicitly ties together a key problem of Part 7 (the relation between, and misunderstanding of, women and men), and of Part 8 (Europe and the relations among its peoples). In both cases, the issues were of different but complementary functions. Both equally valued, both equally damaged by a misunderstanding or a reduction of differences.

§249

Every people must be insincere concerning its peculiar virtues. What is best in us we do not and cannot know. Here we hear an echo of the perpetual and unaswerable question "what is German?" (from §244) and the German deceptiveness. Moreover, there should also be heard an echo of the self-misunderstandings of women and men (in the closing sections of Part 7), and of that third gender, the scholar (in Part 6). To these sets of isomorphic misunderstandings we must add the accounts of the English and French that, likewise, find virtue in what is misunderstood or misrepresented. Only a supra-national ear, a good European, would be able to hear the genuine characters and differences of these peoples.

§250

Having just spoken of the "Tartuffery" of peoples, Nietzsche then proceeds to discuss the Jewish people. But, interestingly, there is no hint here of such insincerity, deliberate or otherwise. By shunting these two sections next to one another, Nietzsche wants us to hear this contrast. The Jews are the only truly sincere people. Notice that if this implication deliberately runs against anti-Semitic prejudice, Nietzsche reverses again with "*verfänglichsten*", "most insidious". As we saw near the beginning of the book, in discussing Socrates and Plato, Nietzsche characteristically builds complex analyses by running together simple, unequivocal but differently valued statements (see the discussion under §10 above). That is why what Europe owes to the Jews is both "the best and the worst": namely, the grand style in morality, infinite and sublime demands and meanings. This is a reference both to the problem of style from earlier in this Part, and in particular Luther's translation of the bible into German; but above all also to the "masculine" characterization of genius in §248. This grand style is the most attractive among the play of colours in the sunset that is now glowing, and fading out.

On the other hand, what Nietzsche has called the "slave revolt" in morality originated with the Jewish people, although it carried on under the banners of Christianity, socialism or democracy. So, what is best is also worst: a force that tends to the diminishing of humans and the weakening of will. Those of us who are artists among the spectators and philosophers are "grateful" to the Jewish people. This means three interconnected things: first, grateful simply for the *example* of a revolution in morality – an example that the free spirits and philosophers of the future wish to repeat. Secondly, this history of the weakening of the spirit may be in a number of complex ways (see for example §242) the condition of the emergence of an unprecedented strength. Thirdly and finally, of course, it takes us back to the *amor fati*, a gratitude for everything that has been and will be in its connection with what is.

§251

Within the general insanity that is nationalism, there will be particular fits of "*Verdummung*", a "becoming-stupid" or "stultification". Nietzsche's examples are either of a particular antipathy (against Jews or Poles), or a particularly narrow nationalism (Wagnerian, Teutonic, Prussian). Nietzsche too has become infected by this stultification (like the first section of this Part) and is "worrying about things that are none of my business", and thus again he turns to the Jewish people. However, of course, he is not turning, because the previous section was about the Jews. So, does Nietzsche mean that the comments of §250 are *not* part of this stultification? Or perhaps his whole disclaimer is ironic and Nietzsche is not "infected". In any case, the distinction is between a merely national point of view (even if not a nationalism strictly speaking), which as we saw must misunderstand its virtues, and a supranational or European view. Section 250 is straightforwardly supranational, or at least Nietzsche clearly intends it to be. But this current section is not so clear; what seems most likely is that Nietzsche is wearing the mask of nationalism (that is, using its language, taking up its themes and concerns) in order to intervene within that discourse (and that of "modern ideas"), and change it from within.

Anti-Semitism is universal among Germans, Nietzsche claims, even if many disavow its most immoderate forms. There is likewise a demand to close the border to the East and even to Austria (whose connections with the "East" have always been strong). Why? Nietzsche claims that this betrays an instinct to protect a weak and still indistinct people (a people who have no today) from the outside. To describe this, Nietzsche uses the metaphor – although as we have seen on several occasions, it is much more than a metaphor – of digestion. The Germans have weak stomachs (compared to the English, for example). Anti-Semitism is fear of the neighbour (see §201). The Jews are the strongest and purest people, who know how to prevail under adverse conditions (we should hear in this an echo of Nietzsche's oft-repeated claim that genuine advances and acts of creativity occur under conditions of duress and under the thumb of arbitrary laws). Although previously named as among the "begetting" geniuses, the Jewish people nevertheless have a "today", and change very slowly. What they lack is a home, a region in space as well as a distinct type of life and thus an era in time. Playing to a particularly acute and infamous paranoia of anti-Semitism, Nietzsche argues that the Jews could achieve "mastery over Europe", but that they do not want this. Instead, they want assimilation, to come home and stop wandering. The pure masculine drive or genius *wants and needs the feminine*. This, Nietzsche argues, should be accommodated (as the English aristocracy has done), even to the extent of throwing the anti-Semites into exile. Nietzsche even proposes that the most clearly defined among the Germans (e.g. the officer class from the Berlin region) would benefit from "getting involved" [*sich einlassen*] with the Jewish people, in order to bring together a more comprehensive range of virtues. (Again, deliberate provocations of anti-Semitic beliefs and fears.) These virtues include, above all, spirituality – which should remind us by contrast of the "spiritual flattening" discussed in §241. Only with the help of the Jews might the Germans recover what was previously a position of spiritual leadership, and indeed greatness, in Europe.

Nietzsche breaks off his fit of nationalism (which was a nationalism only as a mask). He was starting to betray his real purpose and goal; that is, the mask was starting to slip. The real purpose is the cultivation of a new European ruling "caste". Note that this brief and partly ironic discussion of the "assimilation" of the Jews is one of the few times that Nietzsche speaks specifically about what this cultivation or breeding would involve.

§§252–3

These two sections concern the English, and the one following is devoted to the French. Nietzsche's characterization, taken in isolation at least, is virtually a lampoon; there are few new ideas here. The English are not a philosophical race, he decides quickly. The English are described as more primitive than other peoples: stronger in will, to be sure, but also sensual, brutal and vulgar. Thus, there is a need for the discipline of Christianity: "a subtler poison against the coarser". Although that which Nietzsche has called "modern ideas" (e.g. of democratic politics) have spread across

Europe from France, in fact they originated in the indiginous "mediocrity" and plebeianism of England. The French were merely imitators, and victims, of these ideas.

Their apparently natural concern for empiricism leads to a certain important type of scholarship (exemplified by Darwin in §253) but is not genuinely philosophical. The empiricism of "mediocre minds" is particularly skilful at collecting and classifying small facts and drawing conclusions. This leads Nietzsche to a distinction between those who know and those who "are able". This is a very similar distinction to that which we saw in Part 6. This may be "knowing" in a relatively superficial sense, but it has its significance in so far as it is a necessary tool of philosophy; that is, necessary for that which does not just know, but can create values and act "in the grand style" (notice the repetition of this phrase from §250). Nietzsche uses the language of scholarship to describe this creation: to "mean" or "signify" [*bedeuten*] or "exhibit" [*darstellen*] not just something that already exists (a fact) but something new. That this language is being used is more than a convenience. It shows first that, for Nietzsche, this creative philosophy must sometimes work through (in the mode of intervention or mask) the scholarly. It also reminds us that the means of expression (Nietzsche has been writing about music and style), the means by which that which is new is "exhibited", is not a separable or incidental part of creation, but is integral to it.

What is lacking in the English is any real power and profundity of spirituality (and thus, again, the wisdom of the English welcoming of the Jews). This is related to a lack of music, rhythm or dance. English women are beautiful "doves" and "swans", Nietzsche says, but like those birds, just watch them try to walk! For Nietzsche, as we have seen, the (metaphorical but, as he says, much more than metaphorical) capacity for rhythmic dance is a prime characteristic of that which is noble, spiritual, free and strong (see §§188, 213, 216), and thus a characteristic of the philosopher of the future, or at least of that type of people capable of providing raw material, so to speak, for the cultivation of higher types. Dance represents a perfected integration of the spiritual and the body (a form of the spiritual that does not abhor the body, as in many forms of Christianity; a form of the body that does not prohibit spirituality). A form of life that has been raised to fullness or perfection, celebrates its well-being, and justifies independently its own existence – such a form of life will *dance*. Recall from §244, the "inner and agile tightrope dance". Put together with the characterization of the north in the next section, the connotations seem to be a cold, grey, abstract, conceptual dance – quiet and inward, disconnected from the body and deaf to the rhythms of life and speech – that involves peril and makes even the gods afraid (see also §14). What is lacking in both the English and the German, but for importantly different reasons, is the *integration* suggested above. Not surprising, this problem of integration or synthesis is taken up in the next section.

§254

The last sentences of §253 form the transition to this discussion of the national characteristics of the French. There we had a France infected and diminished by "modern ideas" from England. The "noble inventiveness" [*erfinderische Vornehmheit*] it displayed in the sixteenth and seventeenth centuries, and which was the source of the invention [*Erfindung*] of all European "noblesse", now seems impossible. (The repetition of "*Erfindung*", "invention", signals that Nietzsche wants us, at least in this context if not necessarily more generally, to identify his particular conception of nobility [*Vornehmheit*] with "noblesse". The phrase frequently translated as "English nobility" in §251 is, not surprisingly, "*englische Adel*". That is, it uses the other, more general, word translated as "nobility".)

France, then, is Europe's foremost school of taste; although the "foreground" today is coarse because the primary figures of this taste tend to keep themselves hidden from bourgeois stupidity. However, as a people they seem singularly vulnerable to the "invasion" of other ideas – first, in the eighteenth century, English ideas; then, in the nineteenth, Germans such as Hegel, Schopenhauer and even Wagner found a foothold there despite overt resistance to "Germanization". The French have, Nietzsche says, three particular virtues: (i) an artistic passion for small or intimate form; Nietzsche is not clear with which, if any, of the two senses of beauty we should identify this artistry; (ii) an old, manifold "moralistic" culture, which provides considerable psychological insight, perhaps in part by providing the raw material and the experiences for something like Nietzsche's "natural history" of morality announced in §186; (iii) a partly successful synthesis of northern and southern cultures, with the south providing protection against the grey, anaemic, concept-spectres [*Begriffs-Gespensterei*] of the north. This is a particularly German bad taste. The blood and iron of Bismarck's nationalism is another "prescription" against this anaemia, but one in which Nietzsche invests no hope. This synthesis means that the French already seem to anticipate those "wide-ranging" beings, the good Europeans and thus also the future ruling caste of Europe. The last sentence involves an ambiguity: "For them, *Bizet* made music . . ." Is the "them" the French, or the wide-ranging beings? Nietzsche's account of Bizet's music elsewhere suggests the latter. He writes "Yesterday I heard *Bizet*'s masterpiece for – would you believe it – the twentieth time" (*The Case of Wagner*, §1). Compare the phrasing with the first sentence of *Beyond* §240 and the notion we discussed there of a culture not having a "today". The rest of the account of Bizet in *The Case of Wagner* verifies this: the work is light, it has the refinement of a race not an individual, it "makes you perfect". Indeed, "Bizet makes me fertile [*fruchtbar* – literally 'fruitful']", and this ties the passage back into our analysis of the *encompassing* of masculine and feminine wills and geniuses.

In any case, however, the synthesis is only "half-way" successful. In *The Case of Wagner*, Bizet is not considered typically French, but *more* southern, even African, "scorched" (*ibid.*). In the construction of a pan-European identity, we have seen the south as protection from the excesses of north, but have not yet seen what the north could contribute. The last two sections of this Part will give us a hint.

§255

The metaphors of protection and prescriptions are carried over into this section from the previous one. Nietzsche recommends "precautions" against German music. The south is seen as a place of mental and physical rehabilitation – and this is indeed autobiographical, since Nietzsche spent much of his last dozen or so working years in Italy. German music will risk both taste and health. These two risks are, of course, linked for Nietzsche: the noble spirit is identified with the health of the will, and *for just this reason*, with a higher taste. As we saw in the first section of this Part, Nietzsche identifies the south with dance, grace, and clarity – including even logic; a spiritualized sense of clarity or order. This is contrasted with the damp, blurred, mistiness of the German type; it is also contrasted with the "concept-spectres" of the previous section, by which Nietzsche is presumably describing German philosophy, or most of it, anyway. In this section, to this characterization of the south, he adds health and "a self-satisfied existence that believes in itself [*selbstherrliches, an sich glaubendes Dasein*]".

What would a convert to the south imagine the future of European music to be (naturally, for reasons we have already rehearsed, this is not a thought about merely a specific art form – but a thought of the essential characteristics of a future pan-European culture that would *have* to express itself in such a way)? Certainly, it would be supra-German. But because pan-European it must also be supra-European – the desert and beast of prey images are surely meant to suggest Africa; see the references to Bizet in the previous section. Such music would be profound, powerful and evil. Perhaps there would be an occasional "sailor's homesickness" – a nostalgia for what was now past – and such music would be profound and hospitable enough to welcome refugee colours from the sunset of the moral world. This last idea is a direct echo of the discussion of Europe's gratitude to the Jews in §250. This new music, and the world it sings of and to, could not be further from a wider but still closed-down version of nationalism. Such a nationalism would repeat, on a larger scale, the same fear of the neighbour; it would resist the outside out of fear rather than out of self-sufficiency. Instead, as supra-European it feels at home in Africa, recognizes its debt to Asia, and welcomes even those from the past it opposes and supersedes.

The music would be "evil", to be sure, in the sense that, from our current moral perspective, anything beyond good and evil would have to be accounted evil. In *The Case of Wagner*, Nietzsche gives an example: the account of love in Bizet's *Carmen* as anything but a romantic, naive, selflessness (§2). But such love could be accounted "evil" only within a perspective that remains tied to the latter conception. Nevertheless, the reference to the title of the whole book is important: this is not just a musical problem, nor a problem that can be solved merely by bringing south and north together. Rather, this future music will be one manifestation of the new supra-European philosophical being, who is achieved partly by way of the revaluation of values. This imaginary future music provides a metaphor for the much broader political and cultural question of the European future. It is "more than a metaphor" in the sense that, for Nietzsche, music and literature are fundamental forms of cultural life, part of the manner in which that life "lives". Nevertheless, it remains only a metaphor here because Nietzsche does not draw the *specifically* political implications.

§256, and discussion of politics

The insanity of nationalism does not allow one to see that Europe wants to become one. All the "more profound and wide-ranging [*umfänglicheren*]" minds of the century tended towards this, preparing for this synthesis, experimenting in the "European of the future". (Recall that the notion of "wide-ranging" appeared in a very similar way just above, in §254. These profound and wide-ranging minds, then, would appear to be those anticipated by the French virtues.) Their "multiple and impetuous [*ungestüm*] art" was the longing of the one soul of Europe for . . . for what? Nietzsche refuses a simple answer to this question, which was also the question we were left with at the end of §§254 and 255. Instead, he continues the description of these profound people. Several of his generalizations should be drawn out of this long and breathless description. First, the "wide range" shows itself in their being steeped in world literature, and in the mixture of genres and forms. But is this wide range to be understood as the comprehensiveness of the noble type (the whole in the multiple, §212), which is related to the new metaphysical idea of wholeness that was seen, for example, in §56 on eternal recurrence; or of the plebeian type (indiscriminate mixture, broad tastes, and lack of selectivity, cf. §224)? Secondly, the wide-ranging minds make their discoveries in the realm of the sublime as well as the ugly – but, in any case, not the *beautiful*. We must compare the very similar discussion in §224: a taste for the sublime, and likewise for the disgusting, is a characteristic of the mixed races and classes of contemporary Europe. There, Nietzsche contrasts this with the taste of those who are noble for bringing things (including themselves) to measured perfection. Thirdly, those of whom Nietzsche speaks are characterized by a longing for the exotic (compare this longing with §248) and thus enemies of logic and straight lines. This is the second mention of "logic" in this Part; it was initially employed to indicate the specific spiritual clarity of the noble south. Here, though, we have its enemies. Fourthly, Nietzsche confirms what we suspected above: these humans are plebeians on the up, fully aware of their incapacity for nobility. These are the higher humans, or those who envisage the higher humans, but whose almost universal crumbling in the end before the Christian cross is an inevitability. Why?

This Part began with a brief nationalistic episode on Wagner, and so it will end. But this is entirely appropriate since of all the examples of profound artists and leaders, it is to Wagner that Nietzsche kept returning. The similarity of the discussion here to that in §240 makes this still clearer. Wagner, Nietzsche suggests, derives from "supra-German" sources (Nietzsche here and elsewhere makes much of the fact that Wagner's first successes were in Paris). But he remains a German, northern, artist – more barbarian, stronger and higher. The figure of Siegfried (the principle hero of the "Ring Cycle" of operas) is too free for the understanding of mature, Latin races. In the end, though, Wagner's music (Nietzsche is thinking of the opera *Parsifal*) turned to "Rome" – that is, to Christianity. This was not an *individual* failing on Wagner's part, but rather integral to the mode of life and music that he *represented*.

Despite their accomplishments, vision and gifts, then, something was missing from the figures Nietzsche is discussing. In fact, it is *two* somethings. First of all, these ignoble talents but *not quite geniuses*, are what the north (most of the examples are German) can offer the south, thus answering the problem of the end of §254. To be sure, one must protect oneself against German music (§255), but this is done not by silencing it but by *listening from the south*. Secondly, however, none of these figures was sufficiently profound or original for a "philosophy of the *Antichrist*". Thus, they all kneel before the cross, in the end. One of Nietzsche's last books was called *The Antichrist*. The idea of the antichrist is, of course, the discussion of an ideal for humanity that necessarily and centrally involves a revaluation of the values inherited from the Christian tradition. Nietzsche, then, is thinking of another revolution akin to the slave revolution. But, significantly, it is not a *reversal* of the slave revolution, neither in the sense of going *back* to some earlier form of life, nor a simple inversion of Christian morality (for that would be *reactive*). So, "antichrist" – a word chosen for rhetorical effect – may not be the best description. The "originality" Nietzsche stresses must prohibit thinking the new ideal simply as an "anti-". At best, the negative, critical "anti-" is a moment in this revaluation, a mask of destruction worn by the truly creative.

In §254, Nietzsche said the French were only half-successful in the synthesis of south and north. At the time it seemed this was because of the absence of the north's "gift". However, Nietzsche has already told us that the French are incapable of resisting the influx of German ideas, including many of the very same figures mentioned in this section, even Wagner. So, the absence of the *materials* or *elements* of the synthesis is not the problem. Perhaps the problem is nationalism itself, thinking in terms of, or from the point of view of, discrete nations and peoples – or even from the point of view of some characterization of the "soul" of Europe – rather than *from the beginning* in terms of the possibilities of the human. North and south are not to be merely mixed or arbitrarily integrated, they are to be made whole. So, the problem is not just German or French nationalisms, but also a pan-European nationalism. Although it might serve as a first step, a European-nationalism would be simply a displacement of the problem of the advancement both of Europe and of the human more generally. Only, Nietzsche suggests, a philosopher (of the future) could achieve this holistic view of the development of the human, as part and parcel of the realignment of will and the revaluation of all values.

Nietzsche's political thinking tends to divide into two halves, negative and positive. First, and most of the time, it is a damning critique of the politics of his day (especially the German nationalism of Bismarck, and democracy, but socialism and anarchism too). Throughout this Part we have seen this critique of nationalism, as based upon a narrow conception of national virtue and thus a circumscribed notion of virtue as such. It is a failure to think in terms of the advantages to the "mixing" of types, manifested as an absurd concern for purity or the closure of borders. This previous failure is thus also a failure in the capacity or vision for Europe or, indeed, the human; and an increased, if unintentional, vulnerability to "modern ideas" (parliamentary democracy, equal rights). To such ideas a shut border remains open. Similar ideas are expressed concisely in *Zarathustra*, Part 1, "On the New Idol". That section ends "Where the state *ends* – look there, my brothers! Do you not see it, the rainbow and the bridges of the overman?" That passage is typical of Nietzsche's less often and less specifically articulated *positive* politics – that is, the politics he expects or hopes will pertain among the "new ruling caste" of Europe. There has been a great deal of work on Nietzsche's political thought in recent years (see Bibliography).

What is important here is a single basic principle: political organization must grow out of the nature of the noble philosopher of the future. By "nature" here I mean from out of the health and strength of the will to power, of the underlying form of life. Here, briefly, we will explore several important implications of this principle. First of all, as we know, this "nature" involves social relations characterized above all by "distance" (indeed, the very next section will speak famously of a "pathos of distance"). Nietzsche writes, "the strong strive just as naturally and necessarily *away* from each other as the weak strive *towards* each other" (*Genealogy*, Third Treatise, §18). This is particularly true in the era of the individual. That is to say, political organization is a kind of irritation, something unnatural, an oligarchy of opportunity. Therefore, it is thought of as a provisional and temporary arrangement, something that is *in itself* historically contingent. Accordingly, Nietzsche speaks of we good Europeans who are "homeless" (*The Gay Science*, §377). This is one reason, then, why Nietzsche's political thought must seem relatively vague, certainly compared to his political *critique*.

Previous forms of political organization or exercises of political power (the Church, for example, or the newspaper industry, the state, or just the self-identifying of a people), Nietzsche believes, took as their basic purpose the *moral* moulding of the human, the impressing upon them of the values that were made concrete in political institutions. To be sure, Nietzsche more or less accepts his own variation on social contract theory: he argues that the state exists to protect itself, and its subjects, from themselves (see, for example, *Genealogy*, Second Treatise, §16; *Twilight of the Idols*, "What I Owe to the Greeks", §3). But with the exception perhaps of fully aristocratic states, this aim is subsumed in the former one, the moral moulding. "A tablet of the good hangs over every people" (*Zarathustra*, Part 1, "On the Thousand and One Gods"). Such organizations were, that is, indispensable instruments of moral imposition. In terms of European history, this amounts to "a truly *great* politics of revenge" (*Genealogy*, First Treatise, §8). It is not surprising, then, that a subject or citizen confused himself, merged himself, with a social, political or economic role. A modern state, which encourages belief in equality and thus in the availability of any role to anybody, also encourages one to think of *oneself* as precisely "any role" – that is, as an *actor*. (That analysis comes from *The Gay Science*, §356.) It is this that Nietzsche's future politics must avoid. Let us think of this in terms of the theme of masks, as an analogy of the theme of political and social roles. An *actor* exists only in order to wear masks; an actor is a series of masks. On the other hand, one can imagine a bad actor who wears a mask too deliberately, too seriously; or an "anthrophobe", an urban hermit, who wears a mask *simply* as a defence mechanism. The noble mask, as we have seen, is worn as a direct expression of the spiritualized will to power of the dominant drive, but *laughingly*. In that sense, at least, this future political organization will be more free than any supposedly free, democratic state.

The provisional nature of the future aristocratic politics will, in part, borrow its basic structure from that of the friend. The structure will also be related to that of the lover, of course. However, for our purposes here the latter is much complicated by three factors: sex, which preoccupies Nietzsche's discussion of it in Part 4; by the complex trope of man and woman in Nietzsche, as we discussed in §231–9; and by its use in "love of God" and "love of man", which take us in slightly different directions. We will return at least briefly to the conception of love under §260. Here, though, we will focus on the notion of friendship. Now, the traditional notion of friendship is based upon union or merging. Nietzsche carries on this tradition in only one respect: the friend must be one's peer on the order of rank, sharing a common interpretation and thus language of affects. (The reasoning is given in §268, but was already hinted at in the ironic "good friends" and their misunderstandings in §27.) In other important ways, however, Nietzsche's notion of friendship, or of love as a *passion* (see §260 below), is based upon the *agon*, a "union" based only upon reverence for *self*-overcoming. This is made particularly clear in *The Gay Science*, §338, where Nietzsche addresses those who in *Beyond* he names "free spirits": "You will also want to help – but only those whose distress you properly *understand* because they share with you one suffering and one hope – [namely:] your *friends* – and only in the way you help yourself: I want to make them braver, more persevering, simpler, more full of gaity!" That passage, significantly, is in the context of a treatment of pity (compassion) – another form of supposedly desirable "merger" of feeling. A very similar analysis is made of friendship (although in the mirror of the *ancient* concept of nobility) in *Beyond*, §260. There, Nietzsche also interestingly describes how the noble vent their simply destructive emotions on enemies, leaving the positive side of adversity – the mutual enhancement – for their friends. Politically, the necessity of enemies is the role presumably assigned to Russia in Nietzsche's description of the genesis of a new European ruling class (§208). What is clear, then, is that the agon of friendship or love serves the purpose of overcoming. This is akin to the "wide-ranging responsibility" for the advancement of the human, the overriding duty of the philosophy of the future. Accordingly, in *this* sense, the political organization envisaged by Nietzsche will be less free (because bound to this purpose; although freedom is now understood in a metaphysically empty sense) than any tyranny. (On friendship and its political or social implications, please also see the next Part, and the poem with which Nietzsche ends the book.)

This leads us to our last comment about Nietzsche's future aristocratic politics. It will be, on the analogy of the Greek *polis* or Renaissance Venice, an arrangement for breeding (see §262), one which functions almost like an organism seeking to grow (§258). However, as we shall see in our discussion in the next Part, an arrangement on those specific historical lines is no longer possible. Types and classes are too mixed, and there is no urgent external danger to organize and compel. (This is why Nietzsche is so fascinated by the *possible future* threat of Russia in §208.) We are instead in the era of the individual, not the society (§262, and see again *The Gay Science*, §356). It is unclear whether Nietzsche envisages that the advancement of the human type might eventually return to an aristocratic social order; in a sense, that is unimportant. The important problem is rather to understand how this advancement is made possible. Under these conditions political organization becomes the provisional and shifting entity we described above; almost not a politics in any recognizable sense at all, more like a supranational but subterranean leadership in the field of values – "good Europeans", who are friends though they may never meet and may not even be aware of one another's existence. Yet, they must still feel their duty to the overall advancement of the human. This is not like the model of the state discussed above as an instrument of moral typing. Its purpose is not to impose values, but to impose or create the *conditions of* value creation; that is to say, the conditions under which those capable of value creation can arise. This is exactly what Nietzsche is describing in §203. A very similar discussion is resumed in *Twilight of the Idols*, "What the Germans Lack", §§4–7. There Nietzsche sees "culture" [*Kultur*] and "state" in basic opposition. Only where the state declines is culture possible, because the function of any state (even the most liberal) is to impose values, not make them possible. Nietzsche there continues with an extended treatment of education, which, in its contemporary German form, he criticizes as, first, education for all and secondly, education for a vocation. By contrast, a genuine education is *"Bildung"* (education in the sense of *forming* or *shaping* something), akin to ripening, and Nietzsche describes this in terms of the strength and agility of will and spirit. (See also §201.)

10 What is Noble? Past and Future Aristocracies (Part 9 §§257–96)

The title of this last part is "What is Noble?" which uses the word "*Vornehm*". This reinforces our sense of that concept as particularly significant for Nietzsche's thought. This Part pursues the question of nobility from at least two directions: first, historically, in terms of the broad origins and development of aristocratic societies; secondly, in terms of nobility as it is encountered, or not encountered, *today* and particularly in philosophy. Part 9, as one might expect of the concluding chapter, is a drawing together of themes. So, we find some of Nietzsche's clearest (and least tempered) statements of, for example, the nature of plebeian morality and of what is noble. However, as the Part continues, it becomes gradually more cryptic and playful. Here, we will discuss fairly briefly the passages that recapitulate known ideas, paying most attention to the way in which they further develop the analyses. Then, we will spend more time understanding what Nietzsche is up to at the end of the Part, and how it relates to the overall philosophical strategy of the book.

§257

We have previously discussed the subtle (and not always consistent) distinction between "*Adel*" and "*Vornehm*", which are both often translated as "noble". Here, Nietzsche begins with the phrase "*aristokratischen Gesellschaft*": every enhancement [*Erhöhung*] of the human type has occurred through an "aristocratic society". Although appearing in a Part titled "What is Noble?", it is not immediately clear how Nietzsche wants us to take this idea of the "aristocratic". This is because a historical story is being told, beginning here and carrying on at least through §262, the story of an important change in the nature of the society and the individuals that make up the higher rungs on the order of rank. By the end of the section, we will be told "the noble caste always began as the barbarian caste". It follows from this that to associate what is noble *today* with what is barbarian might be a mistake. Accordingly, a distinction emerges, at least historically, between aristocracy and nobility.

Back, then, to the beginning of the section: enhancement is the work of the aristocratic. That social order that believes in the order of rank between humans thereby also believes in and requires slavery "of some sort". Nietzsche describes this as a "pathos of distance", from the Greek word meaning, broadly, "to feel" (although, given our discussion of §19 above, we should say "affect" instead). The word also has possible, more specific connotations both of passivity and of suffering. The former connotation seems confirmed by Nietzsche's talk of "ingrained differences"; the latter refers back to such affects as the loneliness of the higher human, or nausea and suffering of the new ideal at the thought of the eternal recurrence of that which is small or contemptible (see also §270). However, in §260, Nietzsche speaks of a feeling of well-being [*Wohlgefühl*] in this sense of order of rank. These propositions are not contradictory, however, for the latter refers to that sense of inner self-sufficiency of the noble that we have seen repeatedly in the book, and to which Nietzsche will indeed return shortly; the former concerns the affects of *relations* with others, and in §260 Nietzsche also speaks of despising.

We may speculate that this distance between types of humans is encountered as an instinctive or involuntary response, and one that is encountered as both delight and suffering. Nietzsche adds that this first pathos leads to a second, mysterious pathos: the "desire" [*Verlangen*] or need for the widening of distances within the "soul", for the development of higher or more wide-ranging states. This is "enhancement", the continuous "self-overcoming of the human". In so far as it is a desire or need, and a cruelty to self, this second pathos too is a suffering; and it relates back to the "longing" [*Begierde*] of §56. Nevertheless, we have also seen Nietzsche speak of this self-overcoming in terms of joy or laughter. Again, this contradiction is only apparent. The notion of "self-overcoming" [*Selbst-Überwindung*] Nietzsche calls a moral formula – because it could equally apply to, for example, the overcoming of egoism, or the overcoming of desire, in the quest to become increasingly moral – in a supramoral meaning. The moral usage of the phrase would be one that *either* belonged within an existing framework of values, and only strove to realize those values more fully, *or* which understood spiritual growth as the *transcendence* of some given human reality. Here, the notion has supramoral sense *both* because, as we have seen, at this point "tables" of values are up for grabs, they are in the process of being created, *and also* because self-overcoming does not mean transcendence but is always a move towards *immanence.*

We have noted before that the first section in each Part seems to be a methodological statement, although not obviously so in every case. Here, it is difficult to spot indeed. There are at least two possibilities. First, Nietzsche is drawing attention to the importance of resisting certain humane illusions about the origins of society and of aristocratic society in general. This resistance would, methodologically, take us all the way back to §2, and the notion of the inter-implication of apparent opposites. The methodological statement then is that, historically, we must look for development where our inherited moral instincts, our "heart", want only to see discontinuity. Secondly, though, Nietzsche is asking us to investigate a process of internalization. If aristocratic societies from the beginning are founded on an affect of distance, this state is a condition of an internal, spiritual development through that other "mysterious pathos". This latter is what Nietzsche, here as before, is calling the "noble". The methodological clue then is that the roots of this esoteric nobility are to be sought in changes in social or political climate.

There should be no illusions, then, about how aristocratic societies came to be: the domination of a peaceful group by a barbarian one. So, at its beginning, the noble was the barbarian. Such humans did not necessarily have physical strength, but rather spiritual strength; they were "more whole" [*ganzeren*] as both human and beast. What does Nietzsche mean by this "wholeness"? It is a reference both to the notion of wide-ranging or comprehensive, and to the often repeated notion that herd types (and also scholarly types) repress a part of their living being (certain drives or instincts) either out of existence, or into reactive sublations such as revenge. The next section picks up this idea of incompleteness.

§258

This section not only continues with the notion of completeness and incompleteness, from §257, but more obviously picks up again on "corruption" [here, *Corruption*; in §257, *Verderbnis*]. The two notions are linked. Corruption is defined as near-anarchy in the instincts; this happens when life, the foundation [*Grundbau*] of the affects, has been "shaken" [*erschüttert*]. This latter image is of an earthquake, for example, shaking (and thus threatening to crack up or break open) the foundation of a building. The "foundation" in life is an image of unity or wholeness; this unity is somehow lost. Accordingly, in Nietzsche's example of the French aristocracy, in the period leading up to the Revolution, one set of affects (extravagant moral feelings) eliminates another (privileges of rule).

The emphasis we have placed on the notion of unity above makes it seem as though Nietzsche's point is about some kind of balance or harmony among the instincts or affects. This is probably incorrect. The rest of the passage explains: a healthy aristocracy must see itself as the highest purpose of society. This entails that there be subordinate humans who are "incomplete", merely instruments. The distinction is thus Kantian in nature. In one of Kant's famous formulations of the moral law, a moral rule is defined as one that treats human beings always as ends-in-themselves, and never merely as means. Nietzsche's point is that this moral law has validity, but only among those who are in fact capable of being, and of recognizing themselves as, ends-in-themselves. (He picks up this "only among those . . ." in the very next section.) An instrument or means is "incomplete" in the sense that it must be used *for* something; its purpose is given it from outside. This echoes nicely the cluster of ideas such as self-contentment or self-respect (see, for example §§46, 206, 224), which is contrasted with the self-loathing and dependency characteristic of, for example, the one who pities, or the born slave (§§194–5).

Note also that the word *Grundbau* is echoed in *Unterbau*, "sub-structure". There, it is society itself that must serve as sub-structure, which exists only to make possible the noble types. The self-sufficiency is a self-sufficiency in *value*; it does not mean, for example, that the aristocratic layers of society do not need the slaves. It only means that they do not need them to *validate their sense of self*. The "slave revolt" shows that the reverse is not true: the "slaves" need the aristocratic order to rebel against, it needs their values to invert, it needs their threat to maintain the necessity of its values, it needs their "evil" in order to define for itself the "good". Life, then, is the foundation of the self-sufficiency, and thus health, of the system of affects – it is, let us say, the value foundation. The social order is the foundation of the possibility of creating or sustaining such forms of life. We can call it the material foundation.

§259

In accordance with the narrowing of the scope of validity of the Kantian moral law discussed above, refraining from violence or exploitation is "good manners" only among equals. But, as a basic principle of society, it amounts to a denial of life. That is to say, such a principle involves a meta-physical misrepresentation of the nature of life (plant and animal as well as human). It is also part and parcel of those attempts to try to repress the animal in the human. These attempts (all associated with the broad "slave revolt") damage life, turn it against itself, and weaken it. But we must think more thoroughly, and more honestly: life is essentially appropriation [*Aneignung*] (making into one's own) and incorporation [*Einverleibung*] (bringing into one's body). Nietzsche notes that these words, and others he uses here (like "exploitation") have a negative moral connotation, precisely because our language reflects the inverted values of the slave revolt. Aristocratic societies act in this way not out of morality or immorality but (beyond good and evil) because they are alive, and life is the will to power. The group that is the aristocratic component of society also functions as a body, either healthy or unhealthy. Its health lies in the fact that it acts as a single organism with respect to other levels of the society. This is more than a mere analogy for Nietzsche since, as we have seen, he claims that psychology, for example, borrows its sense of what is its unit of study from morality (e.g. §12). It focuses on *individual* psychology, as if the individual were necessarily unified, and as if groups were nothing but contingent collections of individuals. (Compare also §268.)

The last three sections have been, Nietzsche claims, an account of the "primordial fact" [*Ur-faktum*] of all history. Nietzsche is staking his claim to be operating within, and surpassing, a whole tradition of philosophical approaches to history, that is, trying to understand the basic principles by which history happens: societies and institutions form and develop, moral codes or laws emerge, disciplines and sciences take shape. The most obvious predecessors in this broadly historical task were Hobbes, Locke, Rousseau and Hegel; these philosophers all argued that the meaning and validity of the state, for example, could only be understood as a *development*. In Nietzsche's thought, the basic "fact" of history consists in this: epochal historical events consist of a healthy or diseased mode of life finding a new way to manifest its will to power. The creation of values, moral systems (such as the Christian attitudes towards the body and sex), institutions (e.g. a monastic order), practices (cultural forms, such as the popular theatre), declarations of war or peace, constitutions or tyrannies – all are expressions of underlying will to power. Again, we are brought back to "morphology of development" (§23), which we defined as the study of the forms of the development of forms. Notions like sublimation, spiritualization, internalization, inversion or revolution are all historical forms *of development*. They are the mechanisms by which a mode of life makes its will to power "visible" and in some way historically effective. On the other hand, morals, values, social organizations, cultural types, are all forms *that develop*. (In his next book, again, Nietzsche sums up this idea in the concept of "genealogy".) To be able to see this, and to be able to track developments across centuries and varying fields of enquiry, requires not only a historical sense but also the capacity not to be the slave to one's historical sense. Accordingly, the democratic mixing of classes and types (linked to "historical sense" in §224) is both the greatest diminishment of the human and also the unique opportunity for a new advancement of the human.

§260

The opening claim of this section should, by now, sound familiar: there are two basic moralities, that of master and of slave. Notice that although Nietzsche uses the word "*Wanderung*" (wandering), which suggests a haphazard approach, otherwise the data collected and the use to which he puts it (discovering types and differences) fits the methodological points made at the beginning of Part 5. Nietzsche is careful to add that there have been many more or less subtle moralities, and in all cultures beyond the most basic these two moralities have been mixed, and exist even alongside each other – or in the same soul. These last two points provide a mirror image of the analogy of the body given in the previous section: the purely healthy aristocracy, we saw, would function as a single organism. Here, though, Nietzsche is saying that this is rare and perhaps now impossible, and that even the single organism or soul is or can be (as it was expressed in §12) a complex society.

Among the ruling group, "good" refers to the noble, "bad" refers to the contemptible. In other words, these designations do not refer to actions, much less consequences or works, but to types of people. A moral philosophy (a moral naturalism, say) that tries to uncover the rationality of praising certain types of acts, for example in terms of their utility, misses this. The wholeness and self-sufficiency of the noble human means that no rational explanation for values is needed or could be given. We have seen this analysis before concerning Socrates and moral instincts in §191. Values stem from the feeling of fullness of power, consciousness of abundance that wants to give, not from pity but precisely from the feeling of power.

At this point we see an important combination of ideas. First, from just above, the notion of life is appropriation or incorporation – the movement all inward, on what would appear to be the model of consumption, growth or preservation. But, early on in §13, we saw Nietzsche talk about the will to power in terms of a "discharge" [*auslassen*] of power, the movement outwards. Here, likewise, Nietzsche describes noble valuation in terms of an outward movement of "gift" or overflowing. Significantly, though, both of these are forms of appropriation, a "making one's own". This is expressed here by "Everything he knows of himself honours him", just as, in §§207 and 211, the being that is value-creating and self-sufficient is said not merely to be accepting of the world as will to power (to get along with what is, §56), but *to complete it, and indeed, to justify it*. For such a being, to give outwards (for example, to be charitable or merciful) and to take inwards (to take ownership of or to assume responsibility) are spiritually identical acts; similarly, to be reverent and grateful to one's conditions is no different to being self-reverent.

Nietzsche's description of nobility here is lengthy, and includes several familiar ideas:

1. The noble finds alien an action from pity or selflessness or disinterest.
2. She knows how to honour and to feel an enthusiastic devotion (Nietzsche's example, at the end of the passage, is love as a *passion*), especially to peers and to the past, this is her realm of art and invention.
3. She has duties only to her peers, and only with respect to those of lower rank she may act from feeling, perhaps even pity.
4. She has no reason to disguise herself when among her peers, but believes that all lower orders lie.

All these characteristics, Nietzsche claims, are hard to understand today *as virtues*. Slave morality, on the other hand, will have mirror-image moral values:

1. Because it commences from a pessimism concerning the state of the human, or even condemnation of man (e.g. through the concept of original sin), its virtues are those that have utility for the easing of the suffering of existence.
2. Because of its pessimism concerning the *current state* of the human, it can only look to the future as the location of its redemption, it will believe in progress, and may conceive of this progress partly as liberation.
3. Because it cannot allow itself to recognize the authority of the masters, it must elevate a god over them, or else represent noble power as a threat and as evil; accordingly, all rights and all duties are equal and universal under god (or, within the class).
4. It believes that the masters lie, their happiness is not genuine, and accordingly believes in its suffering as the true state of all humans.

Nietzsche notes, finally, that this last idea of threat is so significant that the good becomes associated with the stupid. It should not surprise us that these virtues and beliefs should line up so neatly in opposition, for those of slave morality are arrived at by a "reversal" of noble morality. That is, they are not truly creative, but rather parasitic.

We should spend more time on the second of these paired virtues. As we have seen, especially in Part 1, Nietzsche's conception of freedom (as in "free spirit") is entirely different from other important metaphysical traditions. Freedom as a kind of liberation from something, he argues, is morality disguising itself as metaphysics. Here, then, in characterizing the noble morality as inventive in its devotion to or reverence for things, Nietzsche is repeating the claim frequently made before that genuine creativity only occurs under conditions of law or constraint. Reverence or devotion is thus a recognition of this condition – accordingly, Nietzsche picks out ancestors and traditions as the most natural objects of noble honouring. Similarly, love as a *passion* means love that suffers to fulfil itself, and which is experienced as *subjected*, and it is *inventive* in its love for precisely this reason. In other words, this is neither love as (i) peaceful contentment; (ii) selflessness; (iii) the simple opposite of selflessness, namely self-aggrandisement via another; (iv) the union or merging of selves; or (v) the utility of sex, reproduction and family. Love (like friendship) is agonistic, a sphere of productive and creative overcoming. The analysis of "passion" should remind us of *pathos* in §257. Love and friendship are both examples of the pathos of distance (and thus not a "union", for example). No doubt Nietzsche also intends us to hear, ironically, the notion of the passion of Christ or Christian martyrs; and we are thus reminded of "to love man for God's sake" in §60.

The third pair of virtues brings up again the theme of honesty, which we saw in Part 7, and which will become a virtually constant companion here in Part 9, starting with the idea of vanity in the very next section.

§261

The noble human finds vanity (to have and at the same time not to have a good opinion of oneself) inconceivable. Those "dependent" layers of society were what they were thought to be, their opinion of themselves comes from outside; that is, the masters had the right to value their slaves. To be vain, then, is to be delighted by *every* good external opinion of oneself, because of the internalization of this submission. Again, we should notice the idea of a "mixed" modern society. But a quite startling and new idea is found in this section too: because of this mixture, the original, rare, noble desire to give value to oneself is much more common now. (Though, to be sure, it is often outweighed by the atavism of the earlier slave mentality.) This point prepares us for the more explicit and detailed analysis of the next section.

§262

A relatively fixed and healthy type of life emerges through living under unfavourable conditions. (On the other hand, supra-rich nourishment yields unending variations and monstrosities.) Aristocratic societies can be viewed as arrangements for breeding. These societies may also exist under the unfavourable conditions of external threat; the qualities of the society are related to its survival. But these conditions are internally reinforced by "hardness" of education or justice. The qualities of this type, few in number but strongly defined, come to be called "virtues". We must notice, however, an apparent contradiction. It was precisely the utility of the aristocratic virtues, or the rationality of their origin, that Nietzsche discounted in §260. But utility is narrowly defined there in terms of a rational strategy for the easing of existence. Here, though, Nietzsche is describing a type that needs and wants itself, knows which of its properties protect it and maintain its strength. The question is what virtue X will be such as to sustain in existence a being with precisely virtue X, and also bring about an intensification of virtue X. Thus, rather than remaining rational in the sense of utilitarian decisions, or being moral codes that repress or redirect drives in order to ease the suffering of existence, these virtues become instincts (§191 – and instinct rather than rational decision is the subject of §263). This analysis accords well with the double meaning of virtue: that in which one habitually excels, and that characteristic which is good. Despite this more subtle understanding of Nietzsche's point, it remains difficult to reconcile fully the two claims: it still looks like a rational utility at work within aristocratic societies, at least in their origin.

What happens, though, when conditions change, becoming more fortunate? There is variation, and the "individual" emerges who must give only to himself the laws of his type. The corruption is precisely a new "unfavourable condition" that leads to advancement in a new direction. Instead of the image of the single vine climbing the single oak (§258) we have many, mutually entangled growths as barbarian egos turn against one another. The morality that built up energies is "outlived" and an uncanny point is reached where a greater, further-reaching, multiple life transcends this old morality. The threat which is always the "mother of morals" returns; this time it's a threat (external or internal) against the individual instead of against the group or type. What ancestors or traditions can a noble *individual* revere? To what friends or lovers can she be devoted? We are left with the individual as lonely, withdrawn, constantly wearing masks, and fragile because left without the natural "sub-structure" of the lower orders of his society. The analysis echoes that given in §209 and §242. The individual is by no means fundamental in Nietzsche (we have seen this in §56 and §259, for example). Rather, the individual is a mode of the manifestation of the will to power under certain historical conditions. We are presented with the temptation for psychology and politics to develop theories that assume the individual is the fundamental ontological characterization of human life. Moreover, we are also faced with the problem of thinking nobility (which was originally aristocracy and indeed barbarian) in terms of the individual. With the individual, the problem of nobility essentially changes from the simple and superficial situation of the barbarian (for which, admittedly, Nietzsche probably harbours some nostalgia), to something more complicated, richer, a spectacle for the gods (see *Genealogy*, Second Treatise, §16).

These new conditions do not allow a stable type to emerge, and thus also not a stable morality that can be the basis of a new social order. The *social* solution to this corruption is to strive for the men of tomorrow: the mediocre. We can define the mediocre, on Nietzsche's behalf, as an individualism of sameness, which thus removes the threat. This morality is preached, although it has to be done so ironically.

What we have here is a new version of the history of morality. It does not contradict the slave revolution story. For the revolution story was told from the point of view of the slaves; this history of the emergence of the individual is told from the point of view of the noble. This completes (at least for now) the historical account Nietzsche began in §257: we have witnessed the origin of aristocracies, their corruption under new conditions, the emergence of the individual, and of the morality of the mediocre. Such individuals might be identified with the "free spirits" that we first saw in the Preface; or likewise with the good Europeans or "profound" European spirits that Nietzsche discusses from §§254–6 and who represented the striving soul of Europe itself. Such individuals appear to be presented with a responsibility, which is somehow to prepare the way for the emergence of the philosophers of the future and ultimately for the new "ruling caste" of Europe. That is to say, to create the political and social conditions under which not just isolated individuals but a new aristocratic social structure can emerge.

This Part, "What is Noble?", will contribute to that task in so far as the social structure involving the noble will emerge from out of the characteristics of *individual* nobility. So, the question "What is Noble?" is also, indirectly, the question of a specifically noble mode of social/political organization. Thus, for example, Nietzsche often returns to ideas such as friendship and love. What this Part does not take into account or further elaborate upon, however, is the relation of political organization to the presence of an external threat (as in the earlier depiction of Russia).

§263

Following the historical narrative given just above, there will of necessity be individuals who walk unprotected by the "shudders of authority". To recognize them – to have an instinct for rank – is itself the best sign of high rank. This is different from the "historical sense" (§224), which first of all depends upon the vestiges of all types and classes within us, and thus primarily refers to the past. But second, the historical sense is defined by a lack of taste, which also means a lack of a capacity to revere. A certain discipline grows up around a "holy vessel", which teaches the masses that "they cannot touch everything" with their dirty hands, and which thus raises them to the highest humanity of which *they* are capable. Scholars and believers in modern ideas are the worst, lacking shame, and *touching everything*. The metaphor of cleanliness (we have seen it in, for example, §74) will return shortly, as will the notion of shame. For the moment we should notice an important implication. In §257, we interpreted the "pathos of distance" primarily as the distance up the order of rank. Here, we can see most clearly that it must also be a characteristic of aristocratic association, and that even friendship and love as passion are marked by an honoured distance, are not too "familiar".

§264

This section largely repeats the idea that habits and preferences are inherited. We have already said that this means three different things. First, that the *type* of being, which naturally has certain preferences in so far as these are expressions of its dominant drives, will be inherited. Secondly, that the acquired preferences of the parents will be passed *genetically* to the children; this is a largely discredited theory. Thirdly, that the social and cultural environment is both a product of a type of life, and also its cause (in the form of parenting, for example). This inheritance, Nietzsche claims, is the "problem of race". Even the best education (Nietzsche might be thinking of Socrates here) can, at most, deceive about this inheritance. It might deceive the plebs into believing they will be free, or are capable of self-knowledge, for example. Indeed, education might be helpless even before the third type of inheritance above, since any education is likely to be a *function of* the given social and cultural environment.

§265

This Part is full of sly warnings to the reader: the "but let us be honest" of §257, and here, "at the risk of displeasing innocent ears . . ." This may be because, as we have already noted, Nietzsche's claims in Part 9 are particularly intemperate; and his apologies serve to draw still *further* attention to this. The claim here is that that which is noble is egoistic, though not in a simple sense. The noble human believes that others are subordinate to him and that this is not because of some contingent factor, but of the nature of things. This is "justice" itself. Likewise, the noble soul possesses an instinct of "repayment" [*Vergeltung*]. This word also means "retaliation", i.e. "payback" – a deftly chosen word because its varying moral overtones tend to cancel one another out. This instinct serves the exchange of honours among equals (the celestial mechanism of the stars, in Nietzsche's striking metaphor, and one that again reveals a fondness for astronomical figures) that is the basis of the noble social order. The notion of "grace" – the gift of mercy from the divine to the human, essentially undeserved – is unintelligible. Such beings do not look up, that is, they *do not recognize* up as a possible direction for looking, they look out, or down.

   This not looking up has several important implications. First, and most obviously, it is a denial of a transcendent being, a God, with respect to whom all humans are *equally* sinful, dirty, weak. Secondly, there is an order of rank, but it is not open-ended; it has a very definite highest point, and that is the noble. She who is noble will strive for self-overcoming and the expansion of her spiritual horizons, but success or failure in this striving (actions and works) is no increase or detriment to her nobility. Thus we described the "new ideal" of §56 as "immanent", not represented as different from those for whom it is an ideal. This second point has important further consequences towards the end of this Part. Thirdly, this egoism is not a mere selfishness, because it *does look down*. It not only looks, but *goes* down, like Zarathustra, like the select spirit predestined for knowledge in §26, and thus takes on the comprehensive responsibility for the human race. This defining responsibility exists, although it does not take the form of progress towards equality and freedom, and has no relation to universal pity.

§266

The *knowledge of* being at a height will mean that Nietzsche agrees with the quotation from Goethe. The noble do not have to seek themselves, although their special task might well be to seek the overcoming of themselves. This section is the first of a good number in the Part that have more in common with the aphorisms of Part 4. The mixture here of sustained discussion and brief, sharp entries like this one is one of the features that make Part 9 particularly complicated and difficult to get a grip on.

§267

It is a characteristic demand of late civilizations to "make your heart small". The image of smallness should remind us of the dwarf, for example, and is in contrast to the notion of "expansiveness". This passage comments upon the "mediocrity" in §262.

§268

How is a people defined, what is it they have in "common" [*Gemeinheit*]? The word means something that is the same, but it also means "common" as in "common people" – and thus the equation of commonness and herd-like at the end of passage. Nietzsche commences from a fairly unsophistic-ated account of language: words stand for concepts, and concepts for groups of experienced characteristics. A *functioning* common language thus assumes common inner experiences. Likewise, common inner experiences betray a common table of values and position on the order of rank. Where the words are the same, and the experiences different, there will be deep and frequent misunderstandings. In situations of urgency, a common language not only allows communication, but even abbreviation; people hardly need even to speak to be understood, to reach agreement. We find here a brief but intriguing discussion of the danger of misunderstanding in love and friendship. Love could not survive such a misunderstanding not because of an issue of trust, say, but because the misunderstanding *ipso facto* betrays a difference in rank.

A variation on this account of language can be found in *The Gay Science*, §354. There, Nietzsche argues that consciousness developed in order that a *common symbolic order* (i.e. sets of concepts and the language to express them) could be established. Nietzsche further suggests that the origin of consciousness and language might be found especially in the communication between those who command and those who obey. Therefore, the gap between the experiences that ultimately found this symbolic order is vast (between noble and pleb, perhaps). Thus language involves a necessary original falsification. Section 268 begins with the notion of commonness, but Nietzsche continues by asking the question of the intelligibility of the noble *as noble*. Where a type of being exists whose experiences are not ordinary, not already similar to others, he will be at a disadvantage, isolated, prone to accidents. Thus, commonness works to the advantage of commonness – and an immense force is required to resist this becoming similar, becoming herd-like, of humans.

Nietzsche claims that where experiences are the same, they must be ordinary in nature. But this is contradicted (if only in part) by the earlier historical account of an aristocratic society, which at least shared virtues and values, and thus should share relevant experiences on the account given in this passage. Nietzsche even insists that aristocratic social groups can "name" their virtues in common (§262). However, we can argue on Nietzsche's behalf that precisely this assumption of common experiences is alien to the noble type: it is bad taste, over-familiarity, prying. Moreover, there is the oft-repeated claim that to be noble is to strive for new experiences and states. Those who are noble are not "akin" to each other in the same way as the herd. So how are we to understand Nietzsche's conception of a noble communication? First of all, we must remember that we are not dealing with a historically constant sense of nobility; for modern Europe is in the age of the individual, not in the age of Athens or Venice. Thus, the close, aristocratic societies of the past cannot be *our* model in the present. Secondly, we should also recall that even with those aristocratic societies, the virtues were consolidated into "instincts", and not as clearly defined concepts of dispositions and their utility.

This problem of language reiterates Nietzsche's general methodological problem: how to communicate about the world as will to power when ordinary and even philosophical language is saturated in moral evaluations that are ultimately falsifications of just that world? What this over-simplistic account of language (word – concept – group of experiences – values) misses is, for example, the significance of gestures and silences. Indeed, these were particularly significant just a few sections earlier (§263) where Nietzsche is speaking of the identification of noble rank by noble rank. Likewise, such non-verbal means of communication return later in §288. Moreover, the simple account of language here also misses Nietzsche's own stress on notions of style, tempo, rhythm, not to mention all the "rhetorical" strategies we have identified throughout the book, and thus the important notion of "taste".

§269

The psychologist investigating rare souls may suffer from pity, for ruination is the rule for such souls, and may indeed lead to the ruination of the psychologist. This pity becomes also a contempt for what the rare soul has become. Consequently, most psychologists will prefer to sojourn, silently, among the ordinary, as a relief. There, though, the psychologist will have to hear elevated opinions of precisely those figures he knows to have become corrupted. The reason is that, as we have seen, while nobility is a characterization of a "soul", greatness is popularly conferred upon someone for his works and deeds. Nietzsche's examples are poets known for colourful or tormented lives. The successful work "invents" the greatness of the worker. "Success", Nietzsche writes, "has always been the greatest liar".

The section then apparently veers, quite abruptly, to a discussion of love. In doing so it picks up the discussion of friendship and love from §268. These "great" poets attract the pity and love of women, who have a boundless faith that their love "makes *all things* possible", though are more likely to destroy than rescue. Nietzsche then retells the life of Jesus as a man who could not ever be sufficiently loved, and had to invent a God who was all love. Other than miscellaneous psychological observations, what is the significance of this passage? Most obviously, it gives two painful examples of the ruination of exceptional spirits, one at least in part by external agents (women who love poets) and the other by internal deficiencies. Moreover, it reiterates the notion that "common" humans receive their self-valuing from outside them, like poets falling prey to the idolatry of their admirers, or Jesus having an insatiable thirst for love from outside. However, it is also an account of social relations that have gone terribly wrong because of the assumption that love gives rights of access, so to speak, the right to *touch everything*. (Essentially the same claim was made about language in the previous section.) We contrast this with the idea of noble friendship and love that demands, in some essential way, that lovers remain strangers.

Accordingly, the section ends with the question of why the psychologist should look into such painful things. Not only, Nietzsche implies, are they painful for the observer, but also such investigations are indecent, ignoble, dirty. "Assuming you do not have to –", Nietzsche ends the section with a cryptic long dash. The free spirit, in investigating the forms of the development of forms, may have to "go down" or "into", as part of the task of preparing the ground for the philosopher of the future. However, there may be investigators who do not have to, who are not part of this task, but whose own disease makes them want to search out dirt. The next section picks up this contrast explicitly.

§§270–71

Profound suffering makes noble, provides and is perhaps equivalent to a level of insight or knowledge. It is accompanied by a type of arrogance but also nausea (again, note the double-affect of "pathos" we discussed under §257 above). Such a sufferer requires many disguises in order to protect herself from those who are not her equal in suffering. Epicurian cheerfulness is among the most refined of these disguises, as is science and, indeed, calling oneself a "free spirit" (in later editions, Nietzsche provides Hamlet as an example of someone who wears a mask to hide knowledge). It follows that a psychologist, if he is himself of refined humanity, should respect the mask and not look "in the wrong place". To look in the wrong place would be to cross the pathos of distance. What it does not mean is that a psychological investigation should not be carried out concerning, for example, states of and reactions to suffering. But its proper object are not one's peers on the order of rank. Now, in this passage "mask" here is understood simply as a distancing mechanism. Notice, however, that Nietzsche's choice of examples of noble masks is telling: all of them are more than masks in the limited sense of protection, but also tools of investigation, ways of identifying issues, of working through or solving sub-problems, discourses that must be understood in order to be inhabited ironically. The figure of Hamlet is an obvious example of this – he does not just seek to hide, but to know and to intervene by way of the mask.

Section 271 continues this theme under the (partly) metaphorical heading of "cleanliness". It is at least partly a metaphor because it so clearly stands in for broader notions like respect (in §270) or distance. On the other hand, the notion of health on the one hand and decay on the other is clearly meant, by Nietzsche, not only spiritually but physiologically as well. Good will, Nietzsche claims, is of no avail if two people cannot bear the smell of one another. This leads those with the highest instinct of cleanliness towards separation and loneliness, towards "holiness". The saint's pity is for those who are *in their being* dirty; there are "heights" where this pity is experienced as itself "dirty", that is, something of which one should cleanse, or in any case *distance*, oneself. (See the discussion of pity under

§202 above.) The analysis of holiness as a noble state is an interesting one, referring back to the earlier accounts of religious cruelty and self-tyranny. It helps us to understand the difference between a true and false saint, as discussed in §§30 and 51. Finally, this passage again reminds us that the philosopher of the future will employ religion as a tool (indeed, a mask) in his purpose of shaping the future of the human.

§272

Our duties are not for everyone; that would be to degrade them and indeed be undutiful towards them. Similarly, sharing and delegating responsibility are not noble virtues. To have certain responsibilities is an honour and privilege. Reciprocally, even noble privileges are experienced as duties, on the same reasoning.

§273

Those who strive for something great are impatient, knowing that they are condemned to the appearance of comedy and that their goal is necessarily hidden. Others are either obstacles or means. The graciousness of the noble is possible once the height has been attained. This passage can be read as a simple psychological observation. If self-overcoming is continuous, however, then we should expect both of these essential states *simultaneously*. Here it is the same noble being that is characterized *essentially* as impatient, mean-spirited, without serious purpose, *and* as gracious. Such simultaneity would pose a problem to a straightforward characterization of psychological dispositions as belonging to an atomically simple subject. Nietzsche seems to have three ideas in mind. First, he wants to indicate indirectly how naive such psychological generalizations are; secondly, that actions and works (in this case, either the great achievement or the various behaviours) are no sign of order of rank; thirdly, in this simultaneity that doesn't follow an externally intelligible order of events, we can identify the untimeliness that we have seen before, and which not surprisingly is picked up in the very next section.

§§274, 276

These sections concern broadly the vulnerability to ruination of higher humans. Not only, as we have seen, is there an accidental quality to the "breeding" of higher people and to their development, but this quality applies to their being able to do that for which they are destined. When the moment arrives it may already be too late, limbs and spirit having gone to sleep, essential self-confidence gone. The "Raphael without hands" is a reference to the idea that artistic talent (generalized to include all higher creativity) is spiritual and does not depend on actual opportunity, although bringing that talent to fruition in works obviously does. The lizard's "lost finger" in §276 repeats this idea. Genius may not be that rare, but the capacity (which is not entirely in an individual's control) to seize chance is.

Notice the metaphor of "explosion" or "eruption", triggered by some tiny event. This is a common notion in Nietzsche, and belongs with the images of "tension", "bent bows", "damming up" and so forth. Nietzsche is evidently fascinated by the idea of sudden electric discharges, delicate explosives, and other unstable and unpredictable systems. Such "sudden-ness" serves Nietzsche's analysis in several ways: clearly, one of these is that the vanishing insignificance of the trigger provides another argument both against the traditional notion of cause and effect, and against the meta-physical idea of will as sufficient. The suddenness of the discharge of energy provides a model of something like "decision" that is an alternative to the metaphysical notion of a free will. Also, the notion of "seizing chance" provides Nietzsche with a way of understanding how the philosophers of the future though few in number will be able to influence events. The accu-mulated energy or tension of our late, modern Europe only requires the smallest of triggers to explode, provided it is at the right time. Of course, in so far as it is within anyone's power, it will be a task of the new ruling caste to analyse, predict, bring about and take advantage of these "right times". (See the comments on accident and history in §203.) Finally, there remains a difference between the accumulated energy and the trigger. Among other ways, this difference manifests itself as the untimeliness of the philosopher: both in the sense of being "at odds" with his culture and its basic drives, and also in the sense of the danger of being too early or too late, the concern for which is a "problem of those who are waiting".

§275

The ignoble are betrayed by the fact that they focus on what is "low" and in the foreground. This recapitulates first of all the notion of the "dirty hands" of scholars, who do not have the instinct for reverence of rank. It is also, secondly, an echo of the bad taste of psychologists who do not respect masks. The notion of "low" and "foreground" refers both to the fact that higher persons now (in Nietzsche's Europe) will almost inevitably be of a mixed type, and not of the purity demanded by the "insanity" of national-ism; and also to the fact of mask-wearing (thus "foreground", the idea of what is presented to vision). The ignoble not only do not respect the mask but also fail to recognize it as a mask, and consequently are incapable of looking beyond it *except for* what is low. That is, masks are only understood as ways of hiding shame.

§277

This section brings to a conclusion the problem of lost opportunities and untimeliness (§§274, 276). Taking up again the metaphor of "foundations", Nietzsche makes his analogy a process of building that needs knowledge only available after its completion. Nietzsche writes of the melancholy of everything "finished" [*fertigen*], meaning something completed – and which cannot now be made better, stronger – but also something that has run out of time and is now in ruins – because of a built-in defect of which one only now is aware. It is entirely possible that Nietzsche is referring to his own book, that is nearing its end, and lamenting missed opportunities. This would anticipate the famous last section (§296) in which the "too late" is not contingent or accidental, but a necessary feature of all creative endeavours. It is also likely that this section is meant to summarize the whole problem of the ruination of higher persons, the sense of waste and the temptation of pity.

But, this section also describes a *general*, *structural* problem in the project of free spirits and future philosophers. This general problem is addressed in the next section.

§278

The section is a parable. The wanderer [*Wanderer*, and see §260] is encountered, with "inscrutable eyes" like a plumb-lead, he has returned without satisfaction from the deep. We wish to help, to offer conventional hospitality and rest. This is rebuffed as a kind of intrusion (along with the many questions: who are you? what did you find?). The wanderer does ask for "one more mask! a second mask!" The mask is to defend him from just such questions and offers of help; but it also expresses the tireless readiness to plumb other depths. The necessary distance and loneliness of the noble soul renders it impossible to offer help (at least certain forms of help) even should the occasion arise. Such help (like the example of love for poets in §269) would be a ruination. The "too late" of §277 is structural in character, it is (using again the foundation metaphor) built in. By the time the higher person might need help, he is incapable of accepting it. What, then, could it mean for the philosopher of the future to "take responsibility" for the overall advancement of the human type? It means that the job is *always preparatory*, which is exactly how Nietzsche describes it in §203. Conditions are manipulated, breeding arrangements made, tests prepared, but that the "new ideal" emerges or does not emerge is down to "small accidents", and likewise the success or failure of her endeavours. The "wanderer" should remind Nietzsche's readers of Wagner's *Siegfried* (already evoked at the end of Part 8). In the opera, the wanderer is the god Wotan in disguise. But, here the wanderer is *also* Siegfried, the hero who is free of divine influence, who cannot be helped.

§279

That happiness must run away from him is, again, not a contingent feature, but reflects the structure of the noble, philosophical soul. He is and must be continually confronted by the double pathos of §257. This section marks the beginning of a series of five (§§279–83) that are tempting to read as autobiographical.

§280

The "he" would appear to be the suffering, wandering philosopher of the previous few sections. This section is a reply to an obvious but naive inference concerning the end of §278 and reinforced by §279: if the wanderer is donning a new mask, clutching at ephemeral happiness, isn't this a sign of weakness? Only if mask-wearing is just a question of protection and isolation, and not itself (as we have been arguing) an integral part of a project. But this passage is also self-referential. Does Nietzsche seem to be "going back", retreating from something? Again, the last two sections have focused on the difficulties of the free spirit. More broadly, we have seen that the whole of Part 9 seems to be a retreat from the "serious" political problem of §251, and in particular from a description of, much less any pursuit of, the project that it is the duty of free spirits and future philosophers to undertake. Instead we get warnings, suggestions of difficulties, accidents, "too late"s. Nietzsche reassures his readers that he is going back like one about to make a great leap.

§281

"– Will anyone believe me?" The beginning of the section is a deftly constructed ambiguity. Beginning with a dash, often a mark of continuation for Nietzsche, does it refer to the claim about the great leap in §280? Or does Nietzsche demand belief that he thinks only rarely about himself, in accordance with a general dismissal of the possibility of fulfilling Socrates' injunction to "know oneself". The section is thus a riddle within a riddle. For one thing, because the referent of the belief is unclear, the section broadens itself into a discussion of self-belief in general. Moreover, the legitimacy of the demand to believe is also a riddle: by what right does someone demand to be believed who is incapable of self-knowledge? The demand, though, is not *epistemological* in character – that is, not a question of inference and evidence – but rather an ontological characteristic of the noble being who is self-assured. Self-knowledge is in fact a ruse of plebeian thinking, of a type, that is, whose instincts are muddled. The structure of the self-knowing enquiry ensures the impossibility of self-knowing (see §16) because it commences from morally motivated misunderstandings of the nature of its object. (Thus also Nietzsche's critique of Socratic and Platonic dialectics.) Thus, the attempt at, the desire for, self-knowledge does indeed betray the type of life, and just for this reason the riddle is "not for me".

§282

The Harpies are composite monsters in Greek myth that bring rottenness and contagion. Thus, the opening figure is of a sudden attack of nausea at what is presented at the dinner table. Note first of all the resumption of the theme of cleanliness; and second, the "suddenness" that is emphasized, and its connection to the complex figure of explosion or discharge discussed above. In this case, the explosion is ill-timed and ineffectual; thus the shame which is itself no less nauseating. The metaphors of food, cleanliness, digestion we have seen before; but more important is the company: the plebs. It is difficult for the most spiritual to find a table that does not offend; thus, broadly, implying the idea that the conditions of growth and health of one type are repellent for another. Thus, this section neatly combines the themes of loneliness and separation with the problem of the contingency of conditions and the associated dangers.

§283

One should praise, if at all, only where there is no agreement, otherwise praise would be self-praise, which is bad taste. But this creates misunderstandings, and attracts around one all sorts of asses (see also §§8, 239 and 284). It is necessary to live among people whose subtlety is such that even their mistakes are amusing, and not offensive (compare §27). This section appears nothing short of banal. However, the section makes sense if we understand the praise of that which disagrees, and those who disagree as the essence of mask. A mask is an engagement with a fundamentally flawed mode of thinking or living, in the mode of irony – equivalent, then, to praise where one does not agree – so as to employ it for a different purpose, or to change it from the inside, all of which are necessary because *as yet* it has no outside. This is, of course, dangerous precisely because of the inevitable misunderstandings – it "spoils half our life", but significantly *only half*.

§284

This section, with its "three hundred foregrounds and dark glasses" is a continuation. Again, the theme of masks and again the mask is presented as first and foremost that behind which one hides in order to maintain solitude. But again it is also a mode of engagement: this section is all about masks *in use*. When one is in control of one's affects, or riding them like a horse or ass (the figure of the ass is important, as in the previous section) for a few hours (see §241) one is thereby putting them to use; both are composure.

Nietzsche's list of virtues is interesting. It varies from other lists he gives, such as in *Daybreak*, and overlaps with Plato's famous four in the *Republic*, but these ambiguous resonances are presumably part of the point. Without being unserious, the list itself is also a kind of mask; specifically, it is an intervention into how his readers might be understanding the noble way of life and thinking. Some of the four are obvious, such as solitude, about which Nietzsche has been making noise quite often. But mixed in, without comment, is "sympathy" [*Mitgefühl*], and this is meant to catch us off guard. It is a surprise, not only because it seems to have a similar meaning to "pity" [*Mitleid*], but because the very idea of wearing a mask which involves titanic composure, and yet also having "sympathy" seems contradictory. But, once we as readers notice that, then we also notice other things – for example, that it also seems contradictory to be hiding behind a mask while having the virtue of courage; or wearing "dark glasses" and yet having "insight"? The whole passage only makes sense if we stop thinking in terms of the mask and what lies behind the mask as *two quite separate things*. The idea of a sovereign, calculating, unitary and transparent "I" behind the mask is clearly unNietzschean, and we have been reminded of this as recently as §281. Likewise, recall from §40 that the masks grow even without intention, as a natural accretion of any interaction with those not of the same order of rank. The masks could in principle be removed only in the company of one's peers; and there, that would be bad taste, for the mask should be respected *on both sides* (this point is made implicitly also in §194). Accordingly, we have been insisting throughout that the mask is both a mechanism for solitude, and a mode of engagement, and one cannot separate these two functions. The noble being exists, at least in part, *as mask*; her very virtues are masks, without thereby ceasing to be essential virtues. What lies behind the mask is perhaps *another mask* (§§278 and 289), though not exactly in the sense of the old trope of peeling the layers of an onion. A mask is a mode of relation; the noble being is a totality of relations. Her integrity does not subsist in what lies behind the mask, but in the fact that all thoughts and affects, and whether they are expressed or not, are manifestations of the health of the underlying form of life.

Section 284 introduces the last phase of the prose part of this book, an intense and often cryptic set of reflections specifically on the nobility of the philosopher. This phase seems to culminate in the passage about Dionysus (§295), leaving §296 as a mere epilogue. We shall investigate at the time if and how §296 belongs to this "last phase".

§285

The greatest thoughts are the greatest events and they are always "untimely"; they come to be recognized and understood much later, generations later. A similar notion is discussed in §263 – and there too the issue is of the etiquette or discipline of not grasping too soon. The passage makes a nice contrast with the vulnerability of all noble beings, that they might be too late; so here the inherent danger of being understood too early. The solitude of the noble being is complete: not just distant and lonely, but "out of time" also.

§286

Another quotation from Goethe, this time from Faust, about ascending, looking up. Nietzsche contrasts this vision of *transcendence* with the noble idea of being at a height and looking down, which is the immanent study of, involvement with, and responsibility for the advancement of the human. (Compare the Prologue in Heaven to *Faust* I.) Let us say that the higher human is "higher" within a dimension that does not exceed the possibilities of the human (e.g. §45). It is not that the higher human is not still ascending, but rather than the mode of ascent is not to look up and long for the transcendent, but rather to look (and indeed *go*) down in order to overcome. This whole passage should be compared with the very similar passage at §265, and also the Goethe quotation on the "eternal feminine" at §236.

§287

Again, that which is noble does not emerge from actions or works. These are products of specific relations of someone to their wider world; they can be misinterpreted or, rather, are always already misinterpreted by those incapable of understanding. Moreover, the need for nobility (Nietzsche might be thinking of the successful plebs *and their works* discussed at the end of Part 8) is something quite different from the needs of nobility. The former are exposed thereby as lacking self-certainty and self-reverence, as *seeking* for themselves (§266) or seeking *into* themselves (§281). Instead it is that old religious word "faith", used in a new sense, that is decisive. We should compare the use of "faith" in §191, where it is clear that Nietzsche cannot here mean by "fundamental certainty" any self-knowledge in a Socratic sense. Nietzsche has been busy redeeming old religious words such as "reverence" [*Ehrfurcht*] in §260, or "holiness" in §271, or indeed "redemption". What has been creeping subtly back into Part 9 is the problem of a new sense of the religious in general that we saw in Part 3, a religion without a transcendent God, centred on the vision of the immanent "new ideal" who joyfully affirms eternal return. In general, Nietzsche is rethinking "faith" in terms of the *health* of the instincts and thus the idea at the end of the passage of self-reverence.

§§288–90

An interesting question would be: are there people whose spirit is *not* inevitable? Presumably Nietzsche means to note that high spirituality saturates every part of a soul, even in highly mixed beings, and is therefore impossible to avoid or fully hide. Enthusiasm, with its trappings, is one good disguise; virtue is one of the trappings. Other than a further adumbration on the theme of masks, why is this section here? One reason is because it introduces the next. Enthusiasms, virtuous and stupid at the same time, describe the philosopher, "in his strongest words, even in his cries". Assuming all philosophers were "hermits" – by which Nietzsche insinuates that he means all philosophers in a genuine, noble sense – then behind these words and cries will lie the silence of desolate regions and caves. Philosophers, then, do not write their actual and final thoughts in books. One's books (or enthusiasms) serve rather to hide one's final thought. Or, perhaps, we should doubt the possibility of "final" thoughts altogether. Every cave has a deeper cave behind it; and Nietzsche adds, for the benefit of Platonists, there is a strange and richer world "above every surface [*Oberfläche*]". There is something arbitrary and indeed suspicious about a philosopher stopping just *here*, and not digging further. This not revealing itself reveals something. Involuntarily or not, every philosophy is the mask of a philosophy.

One reason for stopping might be "sympathy" (one of the virtues above, and this is stated explicitly in §290). The philosopher is more afraid of being understood than being misunderstood, for the former would mean that her reader must suffer too. Some thoughts are not for others. But why should we assume that a philosophical text lays its philosophy out at a single level of the cave or surface? If a text is a concealing or a mask then must it always conceal or mask in the same way, for the same purposes and, most importantly, *for each type of reader*. In other words, why do we assume that although the philosopher can find no one true, final interpretation of world or self, there is nevertheless a true, final interpretation of her book? Nietzsche himself has claimed the opposite (§30 is among the most obvious places); indeed, he did so by talking of "echoes" and "odours" in the opening sentences of §289. In short, here as in the naive conception of language in §268, Nietzsche is being deliberately simplistic, and acting out exactly what he is talking about. What is a mask that conceals for some readers will be a "hand" that reveals (§288) for other readers. A philosophical text will find a way to communicate – perhaps despite its author – if only we have the ears (the taste) for it, that is, only if the reader too is enough of a philosopher in Nietzsche's sense. The answer to the sympathetic question "why do *you* also want to have it so hard?" – notice the emphasis is on the pronoun, not the "why", "also" or "hard" – is "*because I am your peer*".

§291

This section addresses the theme of the possibilities of the human, which we mentioned above. Humans are multiple, cunning, "artificial" [*künstlich*]; they invented good conscience and the "falsification" of morality in order to enjoy the soul as "simple" [*einfach*]. The word means unitary – and thus is in opposition to Nietzsche's description of the soul as multiple and a society of drives and affects. It can also mean naive, which is also appropriate here. Notice the self-deception this must involve. We have seen this self-deception most recently in the notion of vanity above, but more generally lying (as opposed to mask-wearing) has been a constant theme of this Part. However, the creative falsification is also how Nietzsche understands the art of superficiality, from the fundamentals of the account of perspective in Part 1 to the notion of redemptive beauty in §59. This deception is part of the condition of life, part of the justification of existence that makes continuance possible.

One consequence of there being a simple soul, of course, is that it (and its products: namely, morality) would have no hidden depths. Thus we see that this section is carrying one step further forward the discussion of a nominally one-levelled philosophy (just communication, or just mask as concealment) as in fact a mask of philosophy. Not only does philosophy – let us say, for example, *moral* philosophy – mask something "deeper" and more "dangerous", but even the concept of morality itself (by virtue of the notion of a simple soul) serves as a mask *of the mask*, concealing the fact that it conceals.

§292

This section gives two contrasting descriptions of the philosopher. First, the *human* who constantly experiences extraordinary things, and is the centre of – even pregnant with – violent storms, and the inciter of uncanny actions. He is struck by his own thoughts as if by lightning bolts from outside – see the discussion of the inward and outward movements of "appropriation" in §§259, 260. The language is mythic in tone. Secondly, alas, the *being* who frequently runs from himself in fear, though, in curiosity, always comes back to himself. (Notice the subtle move from "frequently" to "always".) This second description shifts to an entirely different rhetorical register, much more akin to the sections above on ruination, accident and pity. The two tones are like those of the Old and New Testaments. The contrast between "human" and "being" may prove instructive below. For now, can we raise the question: which type of philosopher is Nietzsche, assuming he is not somehow *both*? The next three sections are troubled by this question.

§293

This section describes a figure closely akin to the barbarian with which this Part began. When such a natural "master" has the affect of pity, then that means something. But the pity of the sufferer, or those who preach pity to sufferers, has no value (because it is nothing more than an attempt to escape suffering). (See the discussion of pity under §202 above.) The barbarian-like figure is chosen for his relative simplicity, and because he has a historical relation to the beginnings of human nobility. This creates the starkest possible contrast with the "unmanly" sensitivity to pain of contemporary Europeans, although they may use philosophy and religion to try to present it as something "higher". The notion of "gay science" [*fröhliche Wissenschaft*] should serve to exorcise this latest bad taste. This refers to a title of an earlier book of Nietzsche's, which he would shortly issue in a new, expanded edition. (See our discussion of "gaity" and "seriousness" under §§24–5 above.) What Nietzsche calls "gay science" – the joy that comes from the realignment of will to the nature of life, and the serious non-seriousness with which scientific masks (broadly speaking) are employed – is the only possible avenue towards a heightening of the spirit today. It is not equivalent to a return to barbarism.

§294

In a continuation of the theme of "gay science" in §293, this section discusses laughter. The quotation from Hobbes appears to be from Nietzsche's imagination; he is making Hobbes the vehicle for a general dismissal of English philosophy (and likewise the English people). It is likely that, among other things, this is meant to identify the English with the "unmanly" sensitivity above, and connect this sensitivity also with an incapacity for noble laughter. The order of rank of philosophers is determined by the capacity for laughter, up to "golden laughter". This laughter is both *from* joy, and *at* absurdity, suffering, pettiness, cruelty and waste.

"Even the gods philosophize". If it is the case that a genuine philosophy is not theology, depending upon something transcendent to which it looks up – and, again, if philosophy is continual self-overcoming as an immanent ideal – then there is no reason why gods *should not* philosophize. Nietzsche continues the discussion of what this might mean in the next section. However, here we need to note a particular puzzle posed by this passage. This whole book, of course, has been in part an attempt to show what genuine and noble philosophizing must mean, including characterizations of method and of the nature of the philosopher herself. The most recent explicit contribution to this attempt was §292. So, even the gods, that is, are to be characterized in the double way of that section. In §292, however, the first definition of "philosopher" – the one that seems more godlike, involving lightning bolts and such paraphernalia – is explicitly called a "human" [*Mensch*]. Whereas the second definition – the one that seems more human, involving fear and curiosity – is called just "being" [*Wesen*] (with the philosophical overtone of "a being with such an essence . . ."). In philosophizing, human beings can be nearly godlike, but philosophizing gods? Where do they fit in this characterization of philosophers; perhaps those who run away? Nietzsche is playing an elaborate prank, ensuring that the reader is unsure how to employ and value the distinctions he has been making. This game serves to delicately undercut precisely the crescendo Nietzsche is building. There is a similar game being played with the notion of "laughter". Philosophizing gods have a supra-human [*übermenschlich* – an adjective formed from the infamous *Übermensch* (overman) of *Thus Spoke Zarathustra*] way of laughing, at the expense of everything serious; they laugh even through holy rites. This is the "Olympian vice" [*Laster*]. One is initially tempted to take this word "vice" ironically. Surely the gods, for Nietzsche, are beyond good and evil? But the joke we have just elaborated makes us unsure. And in the very next section the god Dionysus will use the word "evil".

§295

Dionysus is the "genius of the heart" and "pied piper of consciences", the "tempter god" (*Versucher* is the name Nietzsche gives to the new philosophers in §42; it also means "attempter" or "experimenter"). Dioynsus is the god who knows how to lure away, who knows how to be exactly that which would lure away. This temptation or seduction is, in part, another way of naming the object of longing and faith. (On *faith* in Dionysus see *Twilight of the Idols*, "Skirmishes of an Untimely Man", §49 – significantly a section on Goethe.) Notice, importantly, that Dionysus does not, or per-haps cannot, present himself as he is, but rather in the mask of that which is most tempting. This is of course how we have been understanding the philosophical mask: something which cannot be removed as such. But, the description is still more akin to the description of the great actor, the alternate response of one who has lost self-respect, in §205. (Not incid-entally, Nietzsche is also thereby evoking his discussion of the relation between Dionysus and the advent of Greek tragic drama, in *The Birth of Tragedy*.) So, before Dionysus is properly *praised*, before he is even *named*, Nietzsche ironically undermines the praise. As the rest of the passage makes clear: above all, one should not take one's gods too seriously, forgetting one's own nobility, humanity and happiness. Dionysus is an invention and project of nobility (e.g. *Genealogy*, Second Treatise, §23), and even in the act of worship *this is known*. One is enriched by Dionysus, not with some kind of external riches (see the notion of "grace" above) but with the feel-ing of being new to oneself, broken open, full of new "wills and currents and full of new unwillings and reverse-currents [*Willens und Strömens . . . Unwillens under Zurückströmens*]". (We will return just below to the significance of this often overlooked last phrase.) Dionysus is, in short, the philosophical lure, the name of that which experiments with humans by tempting philosophers to ever further attempts.

Dionysus is not actually named until later, after Nietzsche "realizes" that he has failed to be courteous (§284) and introduce Dionysus to the reader. Nietzsche calls himself the *last* disciple and initiate of Dionysus, although the prophetic tenor of his book suggests that he also thinks of himself as the first of a *new* set of disciples. Nietzsche would like to praise this god with ceremonial names: the explorer, daring honesty, truthfulness and love of wisdom (this last being the most common literal translation of "philo-sophy"). But Dionysus has no need of such beautiful names to hide his nakedness. The reference to hiding nakedness is to the expulsion from the Garden of Eden. The god is lacking in shame; that is, any sense that what is hidden in him should remain hidden. Recall, however, that Nietzsche inter-prets shame in terms of the order of rank (see §40 and the first sections of Part 4, which also use Eden and the Fall as a metaphor). Knowledge is encountered as shameful because it is *not for everyone*. The overcoming of shame is the overcoming of a lower-order way of evaluating knowledge; for example, as a knowledge that is somehow forbidden. Dionysus has no shame because he has no overcoming left to achieve; he is fully liberated or distanced from human ways of evaluating. (See *The Gay Science*, §352.) Interestingly, however, this evidently does not mean "beyond good and evil", since Dionysus uses the concept of evil himself just below (just as the previous section had used the word "vice"). The distinction of good and evil arrives, Nietzsche has claimed (§260), because of the slaves' reactive revolution against the values of their noble masters. Dionysus *could* be using the term ironically, thinking from the point of view of the herd. Or, he is acknowledging that the pathway beyond good and evil must at first appear evil (cf. §23). Or, perhaps the very godliness of Dionysus makes of what he wants, *and what he is*, in some way evil with respect to any possible human perspective.

Recall that in breaking us open, we discover in ourselves new wills but also, at the same time and equally, new "unwillings" and "reverse-currents". I suggest that this might refer to two things. First, to the always *synthetic* nature of the philosopher of the future, who is not only wide-ranging but manages to consolidate this range, make it her own, to make it her *measure*. Secondly, to the idea of reaction or revenge, born of fear or jealousy, and characteristic of the ignoble. Both "fear" and "jealousy" have cropped up prominently in recent sections, and not in connection with the ignoble but precisely in connection with higher philosophers. Faced with Dionysus, we are faced with a temptation to what – no matter how far our type has advanced – must still be encountered as evil. Dionysus may be beyond good and evil, but human beings (even in their utmost development) are so only intermittently, in part, or in glimpses.

Nietzsche asks permission to give a little taste of what he has learned from Dionysus. The claim that the gods philosophize is repeated, and Nietzsche says this will be difficult for philosophers to hear. This is for two reasons: first, philosophers have, since Plato and especially since the Christian take-up of Platonic thought, conceived of God as all-knowing, and in no need therefore of the human philosophical activity of coming to knowledge or wisdom. Nietzsche is suggesting that we *misunderstand* philosophy if we conceive it as such an inquiry; we become like the bumbling dogmatists at the beginning of the Preface. Dionysus is a philosopher literally: a lover of wisdom (see the reference to Ariadne below). Secondly, certain philosophers and "friends" have claimed themselves atheists, and therefore do not like to believe in gods at all. Indeed, atheism is often associated with Nietzsche, although it is not commonly encountered in his work. For these "friends", the philosophy of Dionysus will come at the wrong time – notice the theme of the untimely again. The implication seems to be that once one is *committed* to atheism, it is already too late for philosophy. But Dionysus' philosophy goes further, much further, than merely the suggestion that the gods philosophize.

Dionysus loves the human, under certain circumstances, and Nietzsche tells us this is an allusion to Ariadne. Ariadne was the daughter of King Minos of Crete. She fell in love with the hero Thesesus and helped him to kill the Minotaur by teaching him how to find his way out of the labyrinth. Thesesus took Ariadne to Naxos, where he abandoned her; there, the god Dionysus found her and married her. Ariadne is thus a figure of wisdom or truth (recall "truth is a woman" from the Preface) who is abandoned by the human only to be taken up by the god. The myth thus summarizes Nietzsche's theme of the historical diminishment of the human following the slave revolution in morality – the falling away from the noble and thus from noble ways of knowing – and now the lure of Dionysus to once again make it great. (There are many alternative or supplementary ways of reading Nietzsche's reference here to Ariadne, including speculatively thinking of her as the ideal feminine counterpart to the ideal "manliness" represented by Dionysus.) Significantly, also, notice that the god philosophizing includes even the looking and going down.

Dionysus would make the human stronger, more evil and more profound; and he adds, after Nietzsche's "startled" question, "more beautiful". Nietzsche makes two more points. First, that this addition of "beautiful" indicates that the god lacks more than just shame, although he does not tell us what this other divine lack is. Again, like the assertion that the gods philosophize, the idea of a divine "lack" runs against traditional conceptions of the divine. Secondly, we can suppose the gods could learn something from humans – namely, to be more human [menschlicher], which can also mean "humane". The tone of the passage is difficult to judge. Is talk of lack and learning ironic? In which case, it is an expression of how difficult it is for even Dionysus' disciples to follow him, how easy to fall back on old ways of thinking. The passage is more difficult to understand, but also more rewarding, if we assume Nietzsche is not being wholly ironic.

What, then, might Dionysus "lack"? Which is to say: what merely human feature of philosophizing is he able to dispense with? We have seen Nietzsche use the beautiful in two distinct ways. First, and most obviously, as the superficial illusion that protects one from dangerous knowledge and justifies the suffering of existence (e.g. §59). Secondly, as the beauty of measure and composure associated with the noble (see our discussion of §224) that does not abandon itself to the dangerous ecstasy of infinity. This second beauty would be possible only for a being who has overcome her fear of the cruelty of nature, of the implications of thinking to its end the world as will to power, and who has indeed somehow learned to live, if only briefly, at moments, in a "realigned" way. That is, to live in such a way that the thorough falsification of nature (beauty in the first sense) is no longer a condition of its continuing to live; or rather, that one's beautiful mode of existence is also the beauty that redeems and justifies. It is, in short, the beauty of *he who finds joyful* the total faith in eternal recurrence. (Earlier in the section, with the "again and again" crossing my "path", Nietzsche seems to have made oblique reference to eternal recurrence using the language he had employed in *Zarathustra*, "The Vision and the Riddle".)

It is immediately obvious that Dionysus lacks something like *sympathy*, for the way of making humanity more beautiful is to expose it to great suffering, danger and perhaps even extinction. Thus, the "charming compliment" is the faith of Dionysus that human beings *can* become more beautiful, without thereby ceasing to exist. That is, there are indeed further "possibilities" of the human, as Nietzsche put it in §45. Still, a god who does not understand the relationship between the order of rank and the conditions of possibility of life (and thus the cruelty, suffering and danger of overcoming) will therefore also have no recognition that suffering is the condition of advancement. Nietzsche, as we have seen, claims that falsification of nature is a condition of *all* life. This might also explain why Dionysus blithely uses the term "evil". Such a god's perspective will also not be able to include the idea that the project of overcoming oneself repeatedly towards the Dionysian ideal must be understood as a going "beyond good and evil". To call it "evil" is to lock the ideal *either* within the framework of Christian and democratic morality, or to assume that *man can become a god*.

The complex strategy of the previous few sections is becoming clear. The distinction between two types of philosopher in §292 is not exclusive, but rather a characterization of the philosophizing human being with his new wills and new unwills too. A philosophizing god is a different being altogether, an impossible ideal. Similarly in §294, the "golden laughter" of the highest human rank is never identified with the "superhuman" laughter of the gods. The god tempts us forward, to be sure, but Dionysus is not the new ideal of which Nietzsche spoke in §56 in connection with eternal recurrence. If he were, we would be back in a theism. Thus, there, the new ideal is explicitly a human being. In the *Ecce Homo* passage we have already discussed, Nietzsche very carefully writes *both* "I am a disciple of the philosopher Dionysus" *and* "I won't be setting up any new idols" (*Ecce Homo*, Preface, §2). To be a god is not among the possibilities of the human; and to strive to be a god is not an appropriate ideal of the human. Accordingly, one does not look up to a transcendent ideal, rather one looks inward (the esoteric, §30) or, still more fundamentally, down (e.g. §§286 and 26 – and of course the famous opening of *Thus Spoke Zarathustra*). In §73, Nietzsche writes "Whoever reaches his ideal by that very fact goes beyond it". That is why in §211 we had to speak of the ideal as a different way of relating to the future. The ideal is not the end of the journey – for that is a religious idea of reward in heaven – it *is* the journey. The human, philosophical ideal is to be engaged in, and to understand the meaning of, development on the order of rank. The philosophers of the future are still only and always involved in the "preparation" for the new ideal.

The observation by Nietzsche that ends the passage now is made clear. The gods can learn to be more human. That is to say, they can learn that the beautiful being of eternal recurrence is a "new ideal" (§56) – a *project* undertaken by philosophy precisely in so far as it is noble, but not an end that is necessarily, or perhaps ever, achieved. To be human is to be a being that can expand itself, becoming deeper and more "wide-ranging". The human can expand itself continuously, even altering the basic structure of its living being. We are tempted in these attempts by the tempter-god. Again, then, the contrasting descriptions of the philosopher in §292 are not a *choice*, but are a characterization of the essential human condition. The human philosopher can penetrate cave after cave, labyrinth after labyrinth but we still live, with all that that entails, and are not immortal – that is, *we do not thereby become gods.*

§296, and discussion of style

This last section, which might have seemed an afterthought or kind of elegiac epilogue, therefore fits well with the message of the climactic appearance of Dionysus in the previous section. Sections 295 and 296, so apparently mismatched, are in fact elegantly paired. The former section concerned the *finitude* of the philosophy of, and ultimately the living being of, the human, which nevertheless contains the temptation of ever-expanding but still synthetic nobility. This section concerns the finitude of philosophical *writing*, which can only communicate what is already old or fading, despite the provocation of *wicked* thoughts. The thought was anticipated earlier, for example in §160.

The double reference to "immortal" in this section is Nietzsche giving notice of the symmetry between the two sections. In the first, immortality (in the sense of Dionysus as god) is the impossible ideal of a philosophy unwaveringly realigned to the will to power; in the second, immortality (as the frozen or dead word) signifies the impossibility of capturing the perpetual youth and newness symbolized by Dionysus. Ironically, but perfectly intelligibly, our being is human, all too human, when it longs not to be; while our writing purports to be godlike (the view from eternity), although it may long to be *new*. In addition to these metaphysical parallels, we should also note that simply by shoving these two sections into proximity, Nietzsche is forcing us to consider the possibility of a *repetition* in the personal of the global themes. This idea of a microcosm (the world reflected in miniature) is common enough in Nietzsche; we've analysed it before in §§31–2. Thus also, for example, the idea of the soul as a society of drives, in which the "inside" of soul is structured just as the "outside". (See also "our organism is set up oligarchically" in *Genealogy*, Second Treatise, §1.) And, finally, the self-overcoming of every free spirit is a microcosm of (not just an *instance* of) the struggle between modes of life. Note that through the introduction of this personal theme, just here, Nietzsche is also preparing the reader for the first person narration of the poem that ends the book.

One reason for this finitude of writing relates back to the account of language in §268: words signify concepts, but concepts are *synthetic* and consequently can only grasp that which has been repeated, or, as Nietzsche says, that which has become true, and thus dull. The concept comes too late to grasp the newness of the new. Accordingly, although Nietzsche is explicitly lamenting only the capacity of language, what is also at stake is the *capacity of thought* in so far as it is conceptual in nature. (There is an echo of the first section of Hegel's *Phenomenology of Spirit*, "Consciousness". However, the two philosophers draw opposite conclusions.) That is why, throughout our discussion of this book, we have come up against the basic problem of methodology. This methodology was obsessed with language (e.g. the "new language" of §4), and with style. Language and style, as Nietzsche has argued over and over, are not *secondary* problems with respect to knowledge or truth, but are fundamental. This is because the structure of language (in turn based upon physiology) constitutes the structure of conscious thought. Before even the problem of communicability (although related to it), philosophical thought itself is *by virtue of its basic constitution* unable to penetrate the depths of existence. That means, among other things, to penetrate to its singularity and interconnectedness (e.g. §§21, 192 and "precisely this spectacle" in §56), and to the principal feature of noble becoming which is the striving for ever new experiences and states (e.g. §257). "Wicked thoughts" are wicked, at least in part, because they emerge from deeper than philosophical thoughts; deeper in the body, deeper in the "submersion in reality" (*Genealogy*, Second Treatise, §24). To be sure, we can try to rid this thought of metaphysical (and ultimately moral) prejudices, which infest it, and cause certain important misunderstandings. However, this *project* of the making genuinely philosophical all our philosophical thought is, like the above project of becoming like Dionysus, essentially not capable of *absolute* completion.

Broadly, this project is a project of style. We have encountered the notion of style often enough in the book. Let us recapitulate some of these earlier occasions:

1. The strategies of writing that we discussed in the Preface: for example, the double-takes, puns, or uncompleted statements. These strategies do not just point to multiple interpretations, but make a virtue of the ambiguity among these meanings. Similarly, we encountered in the Preface unanswered questions, irony and statements in the hypothetical mode. These we identified, broadly, with the double function of the mask: to hide or be silent about something, but also to assert or engage.
2. The notion of tempo in §28, wherein the dominant style of an age or a people was characterized in terms of physiology and even

metabolism. This raised a problem of translation or, ultimately, of communication.

3. In our introduction to Part 4 we discussed the aphorism as a stylistic strategy which is meant to suggest spontaneity of thought, and pose an interpretative challenge.

4. Part 8, "Peoples and Fatherlands", is crowded with references to national types and their characteristic styles. Several examples: §246 and the regret that modern Germans have no "ear" for style and its meaning; §250 and again in §253, the "grand style" of moralizing or value creating; §247, a discussion of the possibilities of style in terms of lung capacity and the modern shortness of breath.

Important throughout all these were three basic claims. First, a style is not superficial with respect to the meaning of communication, but integral. Secondly, a style is a symptom of, and thus a means of access for the careful observer, into the order of rank of the stylist and the basic configuration of their drives. Consequently, style is a *direct* manifestation in language use of underlying physiology. Thirdly, style is an important part of Nietzsche's sense of the method proper to his sense of the task or responsibility of philosophy. Let us look more closely at the third of these.

Frequently above, we have described Nietzsche's method in terms of "masks" or "interventions". By "mask" is meant a form of ironic detachment that is, at the same time, a form of engagement with others. "Intervention" (my word, not Nietzsche's) is more general still: it refers to the employment of particular types of discourse (for example, the discourse that belongs to the physical sciences, to traditional metaphysics, to philology, nationalism, or scholarly enquiry), although with the intent to change that discourse from within, to release it in some manner, and thus also to put it to work in the service of something quite different. (See the discussion in Chapter 3 of my *Kant's Philosophies of Judgement*, Edinburgh University Press, 2005.) This notion has a long history, under the heading of "dialectic". In Plato's dialogues, the figure of Socrates often takes up the language and basic conceptual apparatus of one of his interlocutors, in order eventually to show its limits or defects. However, he does not only show this, but rather *through* those limits or defects moves the discussion forward to a quite different language or conceptual scheme. (A good example would be the way that Socrates deals with Simmias' and Cebes' objections in the *Phaedo*, beginning at 91d.) This "dialectic" in Plato is one of the reasons that Kant terms the second major section of his *Critique of Pure Reason* "The Dialectic of Pure Reason". In it, traditional metaphysical positions are shown to lead, inevitably and on their own terms, to self-contradictions of various kinds. Again, though, these contradictions are such as to render entirely plausible and indeed necessary Kant's resolution of the self-contradictions by a fundamental change of concepts (i.e. the change to the distinction between appearance and thing-in-itself). Still more clearly, and still called "dialectic", Hegel's whole philosophical method relies upon describing how a certain way of understanding something (e.g. consciousness and its immediate objects) *in and of itself* – that is, in its own terms – comes both to recognize the limits of its understanding and then to overcome those limits *in itself* through a modification.

In Nietzsche, something directly analogous seems to be happening, although here perhaps best understood as a strategy, involving irony. For example, in Part 8, Nietzsche takes up *as if they were his own* some of the key themes of nationalism. He does this in order to show that nationalism itself leads to a violation of its own ideals (e.g. closing borders leads to an increased vulnerability to influence from outside), and thus to suggest, while still in the frame of the discourse of nationalism, the ideal of Europe. There are three aspects to this strategy of intervention that we need to observe. First of all, it is in part a straightforward argument form (*reductio ad absurdum*): something that can be shown to lead to impossible consequences must itself be impossible. Secondly, though, the analysis of one discourse is designed to lead to a new, quite distinct, realization. In this sense, the method is also a rhetorical strategy: it seduces from within (just as Dionysus was said to in the previous section) and like the pied-piper, leads one to danger. Thirdly, this strategy is not merely a *conceptual* movement from one understanding or discourse to another, but is historical (as it is for Hegel, too). In order that she may see with "many eyes", the education of the philosopher of the future must pass through prior stages and she thus runs the risk of never emerging, or doing so too late, too tired. Likewise, historical periods might, in their culture or mode of life, reach a self-contradiction and overcome it through a creative evolution to a new mode. The slave revolution in morality is the most obvious example of this, but Nietzsche sees another such event coming as Christianity discovers an unsustainable nihilism as *its* ultimate conclusion. The structure of thought, individual development and history are all linked, for Nietzsche. This is another version of the macrocosm/microcosm relation that we have seen here in the juxtaposition of §§295 and 296. This microcosm idea is not just a useful analogy, for Nietzsche. Rather, it reflects the fact that it is the same natural forces and structures at work inside as well as outside the individual. Indeed, the affirmation of eternal recurrence would require an explicit affirmation of the seamlessness of this inside and outside.

One thought that Nietzsche pursues for unpicking many of the problems of style and method is "taste". Taste appears to be a kind of touchstone of the nobility or otherwise of one's experience, a touchstone that is prior to both language and thought. Subtlety of taste is indeed sometimes used as a kind of substitute for philosophical rationality. As we saw in §188,

Nietzsche is influenced by Kant's *Critique of Judgement* on this point (or perhaps influenced by those who were in their turn influenced by Kant, such as Schiller or Schelling). To be sure, he rejects as morally inspired nonsense the notion of disinterestedness so important to Kant. But, Kant argues that a judgement of taste proceeds independently of our "determinate concepts" – that is, for Nietzsche, the concepts that organize and ultimately falsify experience – and that nevertheless taste is "communicable". Of course, for Kant (and this is related to the notion of disinterestedness), taste is or should be *pure*; not of the body, and thus not related to the "race" of the human being who judges. For Nietzsche, taste is a direct expression of physiological type. This is exactly what Nietzsche needs if he is to find a way of leaping over the built-in limitations of language and thought; communicating from body to body.

Thus style, the "how" of the use of language in its appeal to the *prior* taste of one's equals, becomes a project, which may actually be impossible to complete but not impossible to *push forward*. The project is not only to bring to expression something of the newness, immediacy and singularity of an experience, but also thereby to form part of the conditions for the advent of the philosophers of the future. Style itself is also a temptation, a seducer. In an important sense, moreover, this project might be capable of overcoming an element of its own structural impossibility. Zarathustra says, "Companions the creator once sought, and children of his hope; and behold, it turned out that he could not find them, unless he first created them himself" (*Zarathustra*, Part 3, "On Involuntary Bliss"). Those capable of reading Nietzsche will not simply *show up*, but must be *developed*; and style – the demands it places upon us – is an important mechanism of this development. Style develops taste; that means it also develops the underlying conditions of taste. The mutual relationship of style and taste is a forceful phenomenon that can change a reader from *within* (see §247). If philosophy is properly concerned with the task of bringing about this future, then *philosophy is style*. With that thought, Nietzsche turns from prose to poetry, as a new stage in this project.

11 From High Mountains: Aftersong

The poem with which Nietzsche concludes his book should be seen as its culmination, as the foremost of Nietzsche's attempts to push forward the above project of writing. As he notes in §3 of the "Attempt at Self-Criticism" in *The Birth of Tragedy* (written a few months after the completion of *Beyond*), that early book should not have been written as it was, it should have been *sung*: "What a shame I did not say what I had to say then as a poet". "Aftersong" is a literal translations of "Nach-gesang", which is in turn a literal translation of the Greek "epode". Nietzsche does not follow the characteristic two-line structure and rhythm of a classical epode; he is more concerned with it as the *last, completing* part of an ode.

We will reference the poem by the stanza number, one to fifteen. Broadly, the poem is a very simple narrative. The narrator awaits friends who, when they arrive, do not recognize him. He doubts himself, wonders whether he has destroyed any sense of himself. He realizes that he has changed to something more suitable or aligned to the world as it is (the hunter), and they have not, and that therefore this place has grown dangerous for them. They leave at his bidding, and he contemplates their memory and the nature of their friendship. He awaits new friends; it is Zarathustra who arrives. The poem thus clearly replays one of the central dramas of the book as a whole, namely, the drama of the loneliness of both the free spirit and philosopher of the future. As we saw in Part 9, the aristocratic society of barbarians is no longer possible, for any number of reasons: because we are all mixed types now, because of the slave revolt and the accompanying destruction of noble attributes, because of the relative abundance of conditions that led to the rise of the individual, and because the barbarian could never tolerate wearing the range of masks that the philosopher today must. If a kind of honourable distance was a noble characteristic even during the historical periods of aristocratic societies, this distance is exacerbated today. In short, what is at stake is not just the presence or absence of friendship, but a new conception of what friendship means.

In order to read the poem we need to ask, first, in what way it belongs with the book it ends. The poem ties itself into the book by virtue of a number of themes. These themes may be direct references to philosophical ideas, or images linked to these ideas. In the poem, both direct and indirect references are treated as images or metaphors. (Again, the poem is not just philosophy put into rhyme and metre; it is meant to be a new way of thinking and employing language.) Friendship is one of these ideas, obviously; the necessity of leaving one's friends behind or at a distance. In the first line of the first stanza, we get "Oh life's midday!", and four lines later "It's time! It's time!". Then, in stanza 14, "Friend at the right hour, the midday friend". This is a reference to the repeated problem of timeliness in the book. Particularly in Part 9, we had examples of events being too soon or too late, and often not accidentally so, but as part of such events' cruel structure. Midday is a common image in Nietzsche; it is not a place in time, but a join, an instantaneous transition, between morning and afternoon, when shadows are shortest. The idea is of the opportune moment, the chance that has to be grabbed or is lost (see §274). It is also the idea of *continuous* change, in line with Nietzsche's critique of a metaphysics of substance and identity; thus, a change that has no place in time to rest, stand still. Notice that, accordingly, the poem skips over the arrival of the true friend; it is before, then it is after. Finally, the shadows that are shortest at noon represent one's own inherited self-doubt, the spirit of gravity, and one's consuming, *serious* desires. Noon, then, is the time when one can "jump over" one's shadow (*Zarathustra*, Part 2, "On Those Who are Sublime"). There is another reference to midday to which we shall return later.

Likewise, the image of the tensed bow and the arrow in stanza eight comes straight from the end of the Preface. Here, the idea is of a transformation in the self that has resulted in a gain in strength – the strength, for example, to hunt a different level of philosophical prey; indeed, to hunt *oneself* in the sense of continuing self-tyranny and self-overcoming (see also the image of the self-subduing wrestler in stanza five). Begging his old friends to leave, for their own safety or to spare them suffering, reflects the idea of sympathy we have seen frequently enough (§290 is a good example), and which Dionysus appeared to lack.

After noticing the most obvious ways in which the poem reiterates the themes and problems of the book, let us turn to a handful of passages and read them in detail, gradually building up an interpretation of the poem as a whole. Stanzas four to six depict the self-doubt of the narrator when he sees the hesitation and stares of his old friends. Why would he prefer their anger? Possibly because the stare is one of pity (cf. §29 for an illuminating comparison). That would indicate that he has sunk, no longer capable of the collective hope that made them all friends, too often wounded, a ghost. Or, possibly, because the stare signifies growing terror and out of sympathy he asks them: don't be afraid of what I am, better (for you) to be angry at what I am not. He doubts himself, accordingly: have I lost my sense of who I am? In other words, have I become something that even I would not recognize? Then, in stanza seven he retracts the "better to be angry", now realizing that it is not he who has turned out badly but they who have failed to keep up. Don't be angry, for it is proper that I inspire fear.

Stanzas ten to twelve depict the narrator tormented by the memory of his old friends. He struggles to let the memories go. Wherever in the book Nietzsche discusses memory, it is always a preserving into the present of something we want to leave behind; either a sign of our past weakness, or a record of a weakness we have overcome. (Noble forgetfulness is expressed nicely at *Genealogy*, First Treatise, §10. *Genealogy* also contains a much more sustained treatment of memory and its relation to responsibility, in the Second Treatise.) Similarly, he struggles with pity for the friend, the higher men; this temptation and trial of pity is a principal theme of the last book of *Zarathustra*. The ghost he thought he was in stanza six returns as the ghosts his friends now are, in stanza eleven.

What they all shared, those old friends, was a hope; it is now pale, browned, faded (these similar images occurs three times). This links obviously enough to the theme of youth that has been present in the book since Part 1. To change is to be perpetually young; to fail to change is to age; to advance is to be "better young" [*besser jung* – or perhaps this should be rendered "younger still"]. The suggestion of burning or scorching is prominent in §59, and it is significant that the image there relates to those who wisely cover over a dangerous insight. Moreover, the hope and love *written down* is, like the discussion of writing in §296, "immortalized" and thus already dead or dying. The parchment also should remind us of the withered, brown, autumnal colours of that section. Youth misunderstands itself, for it looks for those who are like it, kindred to it; one can then grow up or grow old together. However, if it is genuinely youth, it should look for those who will grow young with it. "*Nur wer sich wandelt, bleibt mit mir verwandt*", "only those who change themselves remain kindred to me". Notice that the ghosts of old friends knock nightly "on heart and window". A nice image of palpitations, certainly; but to knock is to try to wake. These ghosts wish to reawaken the old hope that made them all united, and perhaps also awaken pity. The narrator's hope remains constant and strong, only in so far as it too changes accordingly; advancement is its constancy.

So what is different about this new hope for new friends? First of all, presumably, the narrator is no longer vulnerable to self-doubt about the nature
and value of his self-overcoming. A comparison of stanzas one and thirteen
is instructive. For example, obviously, we have a "second time of youth" in
the latter, returning us to the above theme of youth. Equally importantly,
instead of "Where are you, Friends? [*Wo bleibt ihr Freunde?*]" we have
"The *new* Friends! [*Der* neuen *Freunde!*]". The first version contains the
verb "*bleiben*", to remain; so, literally, it reads "Where do you remain,
Friends?" Instead of awaiting the return of the past that has remained, he
now anticipates that which is fully new.

So, the poem comes full circle, friends are again awaited. Then there is a
break. Notice that the *moment* of arrival is not represented; even poetic
language cannot "capture" it. The poem resumes with "*This* song is over –
the longing's sweet cry died in my mouth". The "friend at the right hour"
has arrived. "It was at midday that one became two", the stanza finishes,
the two united not by a fixed hope that because fixed is already dying "in
my mouth", but a project of constant responsibility for advancement.
Significantly, then, it is not two become one – the friends united, as if
joined. Something like this joining might be expected at midday, when it is
possible to "leap over" one's exoteric burdens, what previously we called
the sedimentation of moral consciousness. But here the one becomes two
means that the internal struggle of self-overcoming and realignment of the
narrator – manifested in ideals, laughter, taste – is matched by the friend,
who is defined as a friend only because he too embodies this struggle, and
who is therefore *also capable of being at the same time an enemy*. Nietzsche
writes, "In a friend one should still honour the enemy. Can you go close to
your friend without going over to him? In a friend one should have one's
best enemy" (*Zarathustra*, Part 1, "On the Friend"). Similarly, the "marriage" of the last line, while also having other symbolic functions, refers us
to a conception of love that parallels that of friendship.

But do not ask who the new friend is. There is a similarity in this structure to the delayed naming of Dionysus in §295. That is, in part at least,
because the name – the *is* – doesn't matter, it's the *function* that counts –
recall the arbitrary "embrace" of §172 – the functions of tempter-god in
§295 (who incites philosophers to new advances), and "midday friend"
here. The function of the latter is not to complete something (again, if completion is possible at all it must be a moment beyond capture), but to open
a new social or political chapter in the history of noble human beings: "sure
of our victory". The coyness is also because Nietzsche expects to surprise
us; despite the similarity, the friend is *not* Dionysus as we might have
expected. Not, then, the impossible, inhuman god this time, but rather
Zarathustra. Notice also that Zarathustra is not the friend who simply
came, but literally the friend who was created – a fictionalized figure in

Nietzsche's previous book – and who then serves as a poetic instrument for the further advancement of the human (see above, §296).

In the last two stanzas the symbolic narrative of the poem has finally produced fruit: it has produced a stunningly compressed entanglement of symbols out of which one can unravel virtually every theme in *Beyond Good and Evil*. Let us begin with the second reference to midday. At midday on the day of Jesus's death, the sky grew dark, like a joining of light and darkness. Three hours later, Jesus cried out and died, and at that moment the curtain of the Temple was ripped in half (described in both Matthew and Mark). The conjunction of a cry that dies in the mouth, midday, the marriage of light and darkness, and a ripped curtain, makes it clear beyond doubt that Nietzsche is referencing the crucifixion. But why? There are any number of possibilities, and perhaps Nietzsche intends all of them. Let us unravel some of these, for they encapsulate the whole.

1. First of all, the poem does indeed depict a kind of death and resurrection, for the narrator first believes himself a ghost, and subsequently "better young". This in turn references back to a series of metaphorical resurrections throughout the book: in the dialectic of self-overcoming and change that leads from new experience, to synthesis and advancement, to a new form of life; or, in the philosopher who, always as part of the advancement of her mode of life, runs from herself only to return; or, again, in the prospect of the rebirth of nobility after the long winter of Christian morality.

2. The reference to the final moment of the death of Jesus may also signal, ironically, that unlike some apparently "good Europeans" (notably Wagner), Nietzsche at the end will not fall down before the cross, and is original enough for a philosophy of the "antichrist" (§256). That is, *not* to fall down before the cross would be to depict the death of Jesus as the *beginning of something quite other* than Christianity.

3. It is, for example, the beginning of a new revolution in values that repeats the creative event that is Judeo-Christian religion but does so in a manner that does not oppose itself to life. That is, the reference to the crucifixion refers to the way in which the aristocracy of the future, the new caste of the rulers of Europe, will finally execute a revolution in values that will end the slave revolution of Christianity, whose master symbol is the cross, and whose dominant hope is triumph and release from suffering through resurrection. Christ's death though, for Nietzsche, is just death; for to wish to triumph over death is to despise life. Nietzsche clearly admires the slave revolt of historical Judaism and the advent of Christianity for the titanic and extraordinary reversal of values it represents. Indeed, he is grateful to

it for creating the conditions for its own overcoming. The last lines of the poem then pose a historical repetition *in mirror image* – a mirror image not only in valuing opposite values, but in oppositely achieving values: creatively rather than reactively. The death of Jesus finds its ironic echo in the birth of Zarathustra.

4. It may tell us that Jesus's God had apparently forsaken him. ("My God, My God, why hast thou forsaken me?" cries Jesus at Matthew 27.46 and Mark 15.34. Intriguingly, some early "witnesses" of Mark have "why hast thou shamed me?".) God is thus represented as the kind of "friend" or "love" (cf. §269) who – because unchanging, or in any case because conceived of in terms of a morality of fear – *always presents the dangerous possibility of forsaking*. On the other hand, Nietzsche's newly arrived friend has not, *could not*, forsake him – because there is nothing in Nietzsche's conception of friendship as reverence for the will to power to forsake. The friend is *already* the best enemy. One could forsake a friend only by first forsaking oneself: degenerating, or deviating from the ideal.

5. Again, the curtain in the temple of Jerusalem represented a division of the temple into zones of sacredness; for Nietzsche, its tearing must have represented the throwing open of the temple, the beginning of the possibility of holiness and salvation *for all*. That in turn means the beginning of the Christian (and thus proto-democratic) conception of human value. However, the tearing of *that* curtain is achieved only by drawing shut *another*: namely, the "veil" that divides appearance from reality, and thus the denigration of appearance; similarly, the barrier that hides from human consideration life as the will to power. In Nietzsche's *repetition* of this event, it is this other curtain that is torn down (the famous "veil of Maya" taken from Schopenhauer, see *The Birth of Tragedy*, §1). Life does not have to turn away from itself. The death of Christ, then, inaugurates two simultaneous histories: the one that leads to contemporary Europe; the other that leads beyond it.

6. The death of Jesus is the sacrifice by which the human is redeemed from the sins of this world. Nietzsche is by no means frightened of using the concept of redemption (two key examples: *Genealogy*, Second Treatise, §24; *Twilight of the Idols*, "Skirmishes of an Untimely Man", §49). In this mirror image repetition of the crucifixion, though, it is reality that is redeemed from the human and, indeed, from God. That is, reality is released from the metaphysics inherent in the perspective of the slave, the vengeful, the sick. For example, Nietzsche is no longer driven by metaphysics to look *behind or beyond* appearance to the enduring substance, or the thing-in-itself, or the creator or author of its being, or its utility for happiness.

7. The "marriage" symbol serves several roles. Among them are the meeting of good and evil and their surpassing, and Nietzsche's conception of noble love and marriage as an agonistic and as the basis of any possible aristocratic politics. Also, marriage refers us to the phrase "wedding ring of rings, the ring of recurrence" (*Zarathustra*, Part 3, "The Seven Seals"). This last is particularly significant: Jesus's death as a consummation symbolized the triumph over death, but only in so far (Nietzsche argues) as it was also a paradoxical attempt to triumph *over life*. However, the arrival of Zarathustra, as the teacher of eternal recurrence, is the beginning of the triumph *of life* itself.

Although to more modern ears, the poem might appear sometimes crude and even pompous, the last two stanzas do provide a richly satisfying end to the book. The above was a list of the meanings of the all-important last stanza, and how they encapsulate the poem (and indeed book) as a whole. However, we should keep in mind that we are *misunderstanding* the poem by trying to *understand* it in this way. The poem is an aesthetic object appreciated by noble taste and not just philosophical thought – although proceeding *towards* taste and the synthetic mode of life *by way of* the discrete or scholarly employment of philosophical concepts may be necessary. Nevertheless, only as a uniquely poetic entanglement of symbols – rather than as simply paraphrased into philosophical concepts – is the poem the fitting conclusion to Nietzsche's masterwork.

Glossary

The following glossary consists of a handful of the key terms that Nietzsche uses in a more specific or "technical" sense. The words are given in English with the German in brackets. Many other terms could have been included but (i) those where an "ordinary English" definition will not lead the reader too far astray have generally been left out; (ii) likewise, some of those to which this book dedicates a particular discussion, or for which providing a brief definition would have been hopelessly misleading. The briefest of definitions are provided; the purpose is to orient the reader, and not to be scholarly or subtle. For full cross-referencing to passages for these terms, please see the index.

affect [*Affekt*] the immediate awareness of a relation of power between wills as an evaluation.

amor fati **(love of fate)** the feeling of profound and comprehensive gratitude to the "fate" that has led to one's identity.

appearance [*Schein, Scheinbarkeit,* etc.] like Kant, appearance does not mean illusion; rather, reality appears. Unlike Kant, appearance does not entail a thing-in-itself as that which appears understood separately from the conditions of appearance.

attempter/experimenter [*Versucher*] one of Nietzsche's names for the philosopher of the future. The word also means "tempter". The pun indicates that this figure functions partly by seducing (rather than entirely by convincing using argumentation or evidence), and this figure will exist as an experiment in existing in a new manner.

beauty [*Schön, Schönheit*] used in two ways: either the superficial, protective beauty that hides existence, or the noble beauty of a mode of life that is able to affirm existence.

breed [*Gattung*] one of a set of terms for different types of human that point to an underlying biological or specifically physiological difference. **Race [*Geschlecht, Rasse*]** is used in a similar way.

breeding, see "discipline".

discipline [*Zucht*] "discipline" in a sense specifically related to training something. Also means "breeding" or "cultivation". Nietzsche's point is that the emergence of a higher type, or anything of value, is the result of constraint, discipline or hardship.

drive [*Trieb*] the will to power understood as a basic compulsion to express power in a specific manner.

evaluation [*Wertschätzung*] a particular way of understanding objects or events that expresses power relations as values. All perceptions and cognitive propositions involve evaluations.

free spirit [*freie Geist*] one of several names Nietzsche uses to designate those who, like him, are engaged in the revaluation of all values.

friend [*Freund*] one who wishes self-overcoming for both herself and her friend. Friendship becomes an important political model for Nietzsche.

grammar [*Grammatik*] the structure of a language, or set of related languages, in its use, that at least in part determines how the structure of reality is expressed and thought.

gratitude, see "*amor fati*".

health [*Gesundheit*] a condition of life in which the mode of life is able to affirm both itself and (at least implicitly) the nature of life. An unhealthy form of life is one able to value and perpetuate itself only through a distortion or denial of the nature of life.

height [*Höhe*] a metaphor to express an evaluation of something from the perspective of health or nobility.

herd [*Herde*] the type of human beings who are essentially ignoble and who identify themselves by way of opposition to the noble. The metaphor stems from the ideas of flock and shepherd in Christianity. "Slaves", "plebs" or "rabble" are used in similar ways.

interpretation [*Interpretation*] that which appears is evaluated and interpreted; the former tends to identify the role of values in the constitution of appearance; the latter draws attention to the role of cognitive or conceptual prejudices.

justify [*rechtfertigen*] to justify something means to give it value as a whole. Something justifies existence in so far as it permits the evaluation of existence as worthwhile, that it is better for it to be than not to be.

morality [*Moral*] a system of evaluations employing "good" and "evil", and thus founded in the perspective of the herd, or at least the ignoble.

nihilism [*Nihilismus*] the rejection as basically invalid of any or all non-scientific claims about morality or justice; consistently associated by Nietzsche with the essential exhaustion of European ideals.

noble [*vornehm*] characteristic of that which is of high rank, because of health or its implicit affirmation of the will to power.

perspective [*Perspektive*] a term borrowed generally from optics, and particularly from paintings that give the illusion of depth. The idea is that value and truth are related to the "position" of the viewer, where "position" means physiology, psychology, and metaphysical or moral beliefs.

pessimism [*Pessimismus*] the claim that "goodness" or "happiness" are impossible in the ordinary course of events, and must if at all be sought elsewhere. Schopenhauer is the principal example of pessimism for Nietzsche.

physiology the structure of the human being and its basic organic functions, understood as determining "higher" cognitive functions, and as characterizing the type of human.

pity/compassion [*Mitleid*] a particular affect that Nietzsche believes is simultaneously (i) symptomatic of the extent of the decay of European humanity; (ii) at the basis of contemporary moral beliefs, what he calls the "religion of compassion". Pity is also a test for the free spirit, though pity for the higher possibilities of the human may have value.

order of rank [*Rangordnung*] a way of identifying and valuing the basic similarities and differences among humans not according to moral values but according to nobility.

scepticism [*Skepsis*] either the ancient school of Scepticism, or more generally the systematic doubting of the possibility of a particular type of knowledge.

science [*Wissenschaft*] a term of broader usage than the English word. It refers to any discipline which makes claims to method, objectivity and truth; e.g. history, physics or indeed a science of morals.

slave [*Sklave*] a mode of human being that may or may not be a slave in a literal (political or legal) sense, but is a slave in so far as it subjects itself to a moral authority presented as exterior to it (e.g. God or the church).

spiritualization [*Vergeistigung*] the process by which primitive or violent emotions are refined and abstracted so as to appear as, for example, moral principles. "High spirituality" is not equivalent to "the most spiritualization", however, but is rather a spirituality characterized by "height".

taste [*Geschmack*] the "taste" of a particular mode of life are those objects and properties that it is capable of understanding and enjoying. The concept comes from aesthetics, but Nietzsche's reference is broader than the traditional objects of aesthetics (art or natural beauty, say).

value [*Wert*] ultimately, the relation of a phenomenon to the underlying conditions of a mode of life. More generally, the significance (especially moral) assigned a phenomenon within a perspective.

will [*Wille*] the spiritualized psychological or physiological drive which is equivalent to an individual – or a group or type – valuing and having the capacity to pursue something (e.g. truth). Will is distinguished from valuing (and also from unspiritualized phenomena such as drives or instincts) only in so far as the former is represented as, quite illegitimately, free or subject to choice. "Will to power", on the other hand, refers to the relationally constituted structure of all under-lying drives.

Selected Further Reading

Beyond Good and Evil has been translated many times. I have chosen two of these as "reference" translations. Unless I have good reason to translate a passage myself, I will defer to one of these. The two are Kaufman's venerable translation (Vintage), which is still very often sold and read; and Judith Norman's translation for Cambridge University Press, because it is part of the very scholarly and extensive set of translations from that publisher. (Hackett and Oxford University Press also publish a wide selection of Nietzsche's works in modern and accurate translations.) For the German reader, there are likewise many choices, but there is no good reason not to buy the Colli and Montinari edition (de Gruyter), straight out of the standard collected works.

The literature on Nietzsche is vast and varied; probably no one philosopher in the past 200 years has been more often discussed. So, the following has to be a brief and selective list of secondary materials on Nietzsche. I have included both general overviews and books on particular ideas that are of importance in *Beyond Good and Evil*. In accordance with the aims of this book, I have tried to avoid biasing the selection towards any particular way of reading Nietzsche; similarly, I have tried to represent most of the range of interpretative traditions. For the convenience of the reader, I have also tried to include books that will be readily available in university libraries around the world. Also included below are collections of Nietzsche's letters and unpublished writings.

Allison, D. 2001. *Reading the New Nietzsche*. Lanham, MD: Rowman & Littlefield.

Ansell-Pearson, K. 1994. *An Introduction to Nietzsche as a Political Thinker*. Cambridge: Cambridge University Press.

Babich, B. and R. Cohen (eds) 1999. *Nietzsche, Theories of Knowledge and Critical Theory: Nietzsche and the Sciences* [2 vols]. Dordrecht: Kluwer.

Clark, M. 1990. *Nietzsche on Truth and Philosophy*. Cambridge: Cambridge University Press.

Conway, D. 1997. *Nietzsche and the Political*. London: Routledge.

Deleuze, G. 1983. *Nietzsche and Philosophy*. H. Tomlinson (trans.). New York: Columbia University Press.

Derrida, J. 1979. *Spurs: Nietzsche's Styles*. B. Harlow (trans.). Chicago, IL: University of Chicago Press.

Detwiler, B. 1990. *Nietzsche and the Politics of Aristocratic Radicalism*. Chicago, IL: University of Chicago Press.

Fink, E. 2003. *Nietzsche's Philosophy*. G. Richter (trans.). London: Continuum.

Gillespie, M. and T. Strong (eds) 1988. *Nietzsche's New Seas*. Chicago, IL: University of Chicago Press.

Haar, M. 1996. *Nietzsche and Metaphysics*. M. Gendre (trans.). New York: SUNY Press.

Heidegger, M. 1991. *Nietzsche* [2 vols. 4 vols in first publication]. D. Krell, J. Stambaugh and F. Capuzzi (ed. and trans.). London: HarperCollins.

Houlgate, S. 1986. *Hegel, Nietzsche and the Criticism of Metaphysics*. Cambridge: Cambridge University Press.

Kaufman, W. 1968. *Nietzsche: Philosophy, Psychologist, Antichrist*. Princeton, NJ: Princeton University Press.

Klossowski, P. 1993. *Nietzsche and the Vicious Circle*. D. Smith (trans.). London: Athlone.

Kofman, S. 1993. *Nietzsche and Metaphor*. London: Athlone.

Lampert, L. 2001. *Nietzsche's Task: An Interpretation of* Beyond Good and Evil. New Haven, CT: Yale University Press.

Leiter, B. 2002. *Nietzsche on Morality*. London: Routledge.

Magnus, B. and K. Higgins (eds) 1996. *The Cambridge Companion to Nietzsche*. Cambridge: Cambridge University Press.

Nehemas, A. 1985. *Nietzsche: Life as Literature*. Cambridge, MA: Harvard University Press.

Nietzsche, F. 1996. *Selected Letters of Friedrich Nietzsche*. C. Middleton (ed. and trans.). Indianapolis, IN: Hackett.

Nietzsche, F. 2003. *Writings from the Late Notebooks*. R. Bittner (ed.), K. Sturge (trans.). Cambridge: Cambridge University Press.

Oliver, K. and M. Pearsall 1998. *Feminist Interpretations of Friedrich Nietzsche*. University Park, PA: Penn State University Press.

Poellner, P. 1995. *Nietzsche and Metaphysics*. Oxford: Oxford University Press.

Richardson, J. and B. Leiter (eds) 2001. *Nietzsche*. Oxford: Oxford University Press.

Safranski, R. 2003. *Nietzsche: A Philosophical Biography*. S. Frisch (trans.). New York: Norton.

Schacht, R. 1983. *Nietzsche*. London: Routledge.

Schacht, R. (ed.) 1994. *Nietzsche, Genealogy, Morality*. Berkeley, CA: University of California Press.

Schacht, R. 1995. *Making Sense of Nietzsche*. Champaign, IL: University of Illinois Press.

Schrift, A. 1995. *Nietzsche's French Legacy*. London: Routledge.

Schrift, A. 2000. *Why Nietzsche Still? Reflections on Drama, Culture and Politics*. Berkeley, CA: University of California Press.

Small, R. 2001. *Nietzsche in Context*. Aldershot: Ashgate.

Soloman, R. and K. Higgins 1988. *Reading Nietzsche*. Oxford: Oxford University Press.

Vattimo, G. 2006. *Dialogue with Nietzsche*. W. McCuaig (trans.). New York: Columbia University Press.

Index